Oracle 23AI & ADBS in Action

Exploring New Features with Hands-On Case Studies

Asim Chowdhury

Foreword by Greg Pavlik, Executive Vice President, Oracle

Apress®

Oracle 23AI & ADBS in Action: Exploring New Features with Hands-On Case Studies

Asim Chowdhury
Bangalore, Karnataka, India

ISBN-13 (pbk): 979-8-8688-2067-0 ISBN-13 (electronic): 979-8-8688-2068-7
https://doi.org/10.1007/979-8-8688-2068-7

Copyright © 2025 by Asim Chowdhury

This work is subject to copyright. All rights are reserved by the Publisher, whether the whole or part of the material is concerned, specifically the rights of translation, reprinting, reuse of illustrations, recitation, broadcasting, reproduction on microfilms or in any other physical way, and transmission or information storage and retrieval, electronic adaptation, computer software, or by similar or dissimilar methodology now known or hereafter developed.

Trademarked names, logos, and images may appear in this book. Rather than use a trademark symbol with every occurrence of a trademarked name, logo, or image we use the names, logos, and images only in an editorial fashion and to the benefit of the trademark owner, with no intention of infringement of the trademark.

The use in this publication of trade names, trademarks, service marks, and similar terms, even if they are not identified as such, is not to be taken as an expression of opinion as to whether or not they are subject to proprietary rights.

While the advice and information in this book are believed to be true and accurate at the date of publication, neither the authors nor the editors nor the publisher can accept any legal responsibility for any errors or omissions that may be made. The publisher makes no warranty, express or implied, with respect to the material contained herein.

>Managing Director, Apress Media LLC: Welmoed Spahr
>Acquisitions Editor: Shaul Elson
>Coordinating Editor: Gryffin Winkler

Cover Photo by Bhautik Patel on Unsplash

Distributed to the book trade worldwide by Springer Science+Business Media New York, 1 New York Plaza, New York, NY 10004. Phone 1-800-SPRINGER, fax (201) 348-4505, e-mail orders-ny@springer-sbm.com, or visit www.springeronline.com. Apress Media, LLC is a Delaware LLC and the sole member (owner) is Springer Science + Business Media Finance Inc (SSBM Finance Inc). SSBM Finance Inc is a **Delaware** corporation.

For information on translations, please e-mail booktranslations@springernature.com; for reprint, paperback, or audio rights, please e-mail bookpermissions@springernature.com.

Apress titles may be purchased in bulk for academic, corporate, or promotional use. eBook versions and licenses are also available for most titles. For more information, reference our Print and eBook Bulk Sales web page at http://www.apress.com/bulk-sales.

Any source code or other supplementary material referenced by the author in this book is available to readers on GitHub (https://github.com/Apress). For more detailed information, please visit https://www.apress.com/gp/services/source-code.

If disposing of this product, please recycle the paper

*This book is dedicated to **Larry Ellison**, Founder of Oracle—a legend, a creator, an innovator, and one of the world's most distinguished visionaries.*

A pioneer who forever redefined technology and enterprise. Your genius continues to inspire millions, and I am profoundly humbled to call you my greatest idol.

Table of Contents

About the Author ....**xix**

About the Technical Reviewer ....**xxi**

Acknowledgments ....**xxiii**

Foreword ....**xxv**

Chapter 1: Introduction to Oracle Database 23AI and ADB-S: AI-Driven Innovations and Use Cases 1
   Introduction 1
   Oracle 23AI and ADB-S: A New Era of Intelligent Databases 2
   Who Should Use Oracle 23AI and ADB-S? 3
      Real-World Impact 4
   Getting Started with Oracle 23AI 4
      Log In to Oracle Cloud: 5
   Summary 8

Chapter 2: Performance Optimizations and Concurrency Control 9
   Introduction 9
   Unlocking High-Performance Updates with Lock-Free Reservations in 23AI 9
      Demonstrating the Traditional Locking Model 10
      Introducing Lock-Free Reservations 11
      Simulating Concurrent Sales with Reservation Logic 11
      Testing the Performance Impact of Lock-Free Reservations 12
      How Lock-Free Reservations Work in Practice 13
      Key Considerations and Limitations 13
      Internal Mechanism of Lock-Free Reservations in Oracle 23AI 14
      Real-World Use Cases and Business Benefits 14
      Common Questions About Lock-Free Reservations in Oracle 23AI 15

TABLE OF CONTENTS

Optimizing Transaction Concurrency with Priority Transactions and TRUE CACHE in Oracle 23AI 17
- The Need for Prioritizing Transactions 17
- Implementing the Inventory Schema 18
- Configuring Priority Transaction Parameters 18
- Simulating Transaction Conflicts with Priority Levels 19
- Observing Transaction Behavior 20
- Managing Business Risk: Automatic Rollbacks 20
- Business Impact of Priority Transactions at QuickMart 21
- Internal Mechanism of Transaction Concurrency with Priority Transactions in Oracle 23AI 21
- Real-World Use Cases of Priority Transactions 22
- Common Questions About Priority Transactions in Oracle 23AI 23
- JDBC-Based Read Routing 26

Automated Bigfile Tablespace Shrinking in 23AI 26
- Modernizing Storage with Shrink Modes 27
- Operational and Business Impacts 29
- Internal Mechanism of Automated Bigfile Tablespace Shrinking in Oracle 23AI 30
- Benefits Over Pre-23AI Approach 30
- Sample Real-Time Business Use Cases for the Automated Bigfile Tablespace Shrinking Feature in Oracle 23AI 31
- Common Questions About Automated Bigfile Tablespace Shrinking in Oracle 23AI 32

Chapter 3: JSON and XML Enhancements 35
Introduction 35
JSON Enhancements in Oracle 23AI 35
- Enhanced JSON Querying and Transformation 36
- Efficient and Flexible Storage for JSON Data 36
- Leveraging JSON_VALUE for Object Instantiation 39
- Bulk Collecting JSON Data into Collections 39
- Internal Mechanism of JSON Enhancements in Oracle 23AI 40
- Difference Between Oracle 23AI with Json and Pre-23AI Databases 41
- Sample Business Use Cases for JSON Enhancements in Oracle 23AI 42
- Common Questions About JSON Enhancements in Oracle 23AI 43

TABLE OF CONTENTS

JSON_TRANSFORM Enhancements in 23AI 44
- Creating the Product Catalog Table 45
- Modifying and Adding Inventory Elements 46
- Backing Up and Removing Entries 48
- Merging and Filtering Product Data... 49
- Sorting and Enriching Product Attributes 51
- Performing Nested Transformations and Arithmetic Calculations 53
- Conditional Logic and Advanced Aggregations.. 55
- Internal Mechanism of JSON_TRANSFORM in Oracle 23AI 57
- Sample Real-Time Business Use Cases for JSON_TRANSFORM Enhancements in Oracle 23AI 58
- Common Questions About JSON_TRANSFORM in Oracle 23AI 59

New JSON-Based Indexes in ADB-S 60
- Internal Mechanism of JSON-Based Indexes in ADB-S 63
- Comparison of How JSON-Based Indexes in ADB-S Differ from Pre-ADB-S Versions 64
- Real-Time Business Use Cases for JSON-Based Indexes in ADB-S 65
- Common Questions About JSON-Based Indexes in ADB-S....................................... 65

JSON, XML, and Oracle Text Search Index Enhancements in 23AI............................ 67
- Indexing JSON for Product Specifications 68
- Accelerating Logistics Queries with XML Indexing.. 69
- Enabling Full-Text Review Analysis 70
- Internal Mechanism of Unified Search Index in Oracle 23AI 71
- Real-Time Business Use Cases for JSON, XML, and Oracle Text Search Index Enhancements in Oracle 23AI.. 72
- Common Questions About JSON, XML, and Oracle Text Search Index Enhancements in Oracle 23AI 73

JSON-Relational Duality Views in Oracle Database 23AI 74
- Defining the Relational Model 75
- Creating the JSON-Relational Duality View 76
- Querying and Manipulating Data Through the JSON View.. 77
- Benefits Realized by QuickMart Solutions 78
- Internal Mechanism of JSON-Relational Duality Views in Oracle 23AI..................... 79

TABLE OF CONTENTS

- Pre-23AI and 23AI Features Related to JSON-Relational Duality Views 80
- Real-Time Business Use Cases for JSON-Relational Duality Views in Oracle 23AI 81
- Common Questions About JSON-Relational Duality Views in Oracle 23AI........................... 81
- Oracle Native JSON Data Type for Efficient Storage and Querying in 23AI 83
  - Core Capabilities of Native JSON Storage 84
  - Creating Tables and Inserting JSON Data 84
- Querying Native JSON for Insight... 85
  - Enhancing Performance with JSON Indexing... 85
  - High-Volume Efficiency and Scalability 86
  - Broad Benefits for Enterprise Workloads... 87
  - Internal Mechanism of Native JSON Storage in Oracle 23c 87
  - Real-Time Business Use Cases for Oracle 23c Native JSON Storage.................................. 88
  - Common Questions About Oracle 23c's Native JSON Storage 89
- Ensuring Data Integrity with JSON Schema Validation in 23AI 90
  - Internal Mechanism of JSON Schema Validation in Oracle 23AI 95
  - Real-Time Business Use Cases for JSON Schema Validation in Oracle 23AI 96
  - Common Questions About JSON Schema Validation in Oracle 23AI.................................. 97

Chapter 4: AI and Machine Learning in ADB-S 99
- Introduction 99
- AI/ML-Based Customer Retention Prediction in Oracle ADB-S 99
  - Internal Mechanism of AI/ML-Based Customer Retention Prediction in Oracle ADB-S 104
  - Sample Real-Time Business Use Cases for AI/ML in Oracle ADB-S 104
  - Common Questions About AI/ML-Based Customer Retention Prediction
    in Oracle ADB-S 106
- AI/ML-Based Query Elapsed Time Prediction... 107
  - Preparing the Environment for Machine Learning... 107
  - Collecting SQL Performance Metrics 108
  - Preparing Training and Validation Datasets 109
  - Training the Predictive Regression Model 109
  - Generating Predictions and Identifying Bottlenecks.. 110
  - Driving Proactive Database Management 110
  - Internal Mechanism of AI/ML-Based Query Elapsed Time Prediction in Oracle ADB-S 111

Practical Use Cases for Query Elapsed Time Prediction in Oracle ADB-S........................... 111

Common Questions About AI/ML-Based Query Elapsed Time Prediction
in Oracle ADB-S 112

Auto-Tuned Query Execution in Oracle ADB-S 113

    Creating and Populating the Sample Dataset.. 114

    Identifying the Performance Bottleneck 115

    Activating AI-Driven Auto-Tuning.. 116

    Reviewing Optimization Recommendations 116

    Ensuring Query Stability with SQL Performance Analyzer... 117

    AI/ML-Driven Optimization in Practice.. 117

    Internal Mechanism of Auto-Tuned Query Execution in Oracle ADB-S 118

    Sample Real-Time Business Use Cases for Oracle ADB-S's Auto-Tuned Query
    Execution Feature... 119

    Common Questions About Auto-Tuned Query Execution in Oracle ADB-S...................... 119

AI-Powered Optimizations in ADB-S 121

    Internal Mechanism of AI-Powered Optimizations in Oracle ADB-S 125

    Differences Between Oracle ADB-S and Pre-ADB-S Databases Based on AI-Powered
    Optimizations... 126

    Sample Real-Time Business Use Cases for AI-Powered Optimizations in Oracle ADB-S 127

    Common Questions About AI-Powered Optimizations in Oracle ADB-S.......................... 128

Chapter 5: Cloud and Blockchain Innovations 131

Introduction... 131

Managing Using DBMS_CLOUD in ADB-S 131

    Creating the Table to Store BLOB Data 134

    Internal Mechanism of DBMS_CLOUD in Oracle ADB-S.. 138

    Potential Real-Time Business Use Cases for the Oracle DBMS_CLOUD Feature.................. 139

    Common Questions About DBMS_CLOUD and File Management in Oracle 140

Blockchain Tables in Oracle 23AI 142

    Inspecting Blockchain Table Metadata 143

    Inserting and Verifying Order Records 144

    Tamper Resistance in Action 145

    Internal Mechanism of Blockchain Tables in Oracle 23AI... 146

TABLE OF CONTENTS

    Sample Real-Time Business Use Cases for Blockchain Tables in Oracle 23AI 147

    Common Questions About Blockchain Tables in Oracle 23AI 148

Chapter 6: Vector Data and AI Innovations 151

  Introduction 151

  Vector Data Types in ORACLE 23AI 152

    Defining a Table with VECTOR Column 152

    Querying Similar Images Based on Vector Similarity 154

    Behind the Scenes: How It Works 154

    Internal Mechanism of the VECTOR Data Type in Oracle 23AI 155

    Difference Between Pre-Oracle 23AI Databases and Oracle 23AI with Native
    VECTOR Data Type 156

    Potential Real-Time Business Use Cases for the Oracle 23AI with Vector Data Type 157

    Common Questions About Vector Data Types in Oracle 23AI 158

  AI Vector Search and In-Memory Vector Operations in Oracle 23AI 159

    Designing the Transactional Vector Schema 163

    Inserting Sample Transaction Embeddings 164

    Detecting Anomalies with VECTOR_DISTANCE 165

    Interpreting the Results and Investigating Anomalies 166

Chapter 7: SQL, PLSQL Enhancements and New Functions 167

  Introduction 167

  Boolean Datatype Enhancements in 23AI 168

    Creating the Availability Table 168

    Populating Sample Data 169

    Querying and Updating Boolean States 170

    Using Boolean in PL/SQL Context 172

    Internal Mechanism of Boolean Data Type in Oracle 23AI 173

    Key Differences: Pre-23AI vs. 23AI 174

    Real-Time Business Use Cases for Boolean Data Type in Oracle 23AI 175

    Common Questions About Boolean Data Type in Oracle 23AI 176

  CHECKSUM Analytic Function in 23AI 177

- Designing the Inventory Table 178
- Populating Sample Inventory Data 178
- Calculating Initial Checksums 179
- Detecting Changes After a Sale 180
- Restocking Inventory and Rechecking 181
- Internal Mechanism of CHECKSUM Analytic Function in Oracle 23AI 182
- Real-Time Business Use Cases for the CHECKSUM Analytic Function in Oracle 23AI 183
- Common Questions About CHECKSUM in Oracle 23AI 184

Enhancing SQL Readability with Column Aliases in GROUP BY and HAVING in 23AI 185
- Creating and Populating the EMP23AI Table 186
- Querying with Column Aliases in GROUP BY and HAVING 187
- Using Column Position for Grouping 187
- Practical Benefits for Business and Development 188
- Internal Mechanism of Column Aliases in GROUP BY and HAVING in Oracle 23AI 188
- Real-Time Business Use Cases for Column Aliases in GROUP BY and HAVING Clauses in Oracle 23AI 189
- Common Questions About Using Column Aliases in GROUP BY and HAVING in Oracle 23AI 190

Aggregation over INTERVAL Datatypes in 23AI 191
- Internal Mechanism of INTERVAL Aggregation in Oracle 23AI 195
- Aggregation over INTERVAL Data Types Differs Between Pre-23AI Versions and 23AI 196
- Real-Time Business Use Cases for INTERVAL Aggregation in Oracle 23AI 196
- Common Questions About Aggregation over INTERVAL Datatypes in Oracle 23AI 197

Boosting SQL Performance with Automatic PL/SQL to SQL Transpiler in 23AI 199
- Understanding the Internal Optimization Flow 199
- Creating the Sales Dataset 200
- Encapsulating Revenue Logic in PL/SQL 201
- Measuring Baseline Performance Without Transpilation 201
- Enabling SQL Transpiler and Optimizing the Query 201
- Key Business Benefits 202
- Internal Mechanism of Automatic SQL Transpiler in Oracle 23AI 202
- Comparison of the Automatic SQL Transpiler in Oracle 23AI with Previous Versions 203

TABLE OF CONTENTS

    Sample Real-Time Business Use Cases for the Automatic PL/SQL to SQL Transpiler in Oracle 23AI 204

    Common Questions About Automatic PL/SQL to SQL Transpiler in Oracle 23AI 205

Chapter 8: Database Annotations and Auditing Enhancements 207

    Introduction 207

    Annotations in Oracle Database 23AI 207

        Creating Annotated Database Objects 208

        Managing and Modifying Annotations Dynamically 209

        Querying Annotations for Governance and Reporting 210

        Business Impact of Annotations 211

        Internal Mechanism of Annotations in Oracle 23AI 211

        Difference Between Annotation and Comments 212

        Sample Real-Time Business Use Cases for Oracle 23AI Annotations 213

        Common Questions About Annotations in Oracle Database 23AI 214

    Auditing Enhancements in Oracle 23AI 215

        Creating the Audit-Enabled Table 216

        Defining the Audit Policy 217

        Executing Operations to Trigger Auditing 217

        Reviewing the Audit Results 218

        Business Implications and Takeaways 219

        Internal Mechanism of Column-Level Auditing in Oracle 23AI 220

        Oracle Database 23c (23AI) Auditing Features Differ from Previous Versions 221

        Business Use Cases for Oracle 23AI Column-Level Auditing 222

        Common Questions About Auditing Enhancements in Oracle 23c 223

Chapter 9: Security, Data Masking and Privilege Management 225

    Introduction 225

    Simplifying Privilege Management with Schema Privileges in 23AI 225

        Monitoring and Managing Schema Privileges 227

        Internal Mechanism of Schema Privileges in Oracle 23AI 227

        Real-Time Business Use Cases for Schema Privileges in Oracle 23AI 228

        Common Questions About Schema Privileges in Oracle 23AI 229

Streamlining Application Development with DB_DEVELOPER_ROLE in 23AI 230
Granting the DB_DEVELOPER_ROLE to Developers 231
Revoking and Verifying Developer Privileges 231
Real-World Impact and Operational Gains 232
Internal Mechanism of DB_DEVELOPER_ROLE in Oracle 23AI 232
Real-Time Business Use Cases for the DB_DEVELOPER_ROLE Feature in Oracle 23AI 233
Common Questions About DB_DEVELOPER_ROLE in Oracle 23AI 234

Securing Data Access with SQL Firewall in 23AI 235
Internal Mechanism of SQL Firewall in Oracle 23AI 238
Differences Between Pre-23AI and Oracle 23AI SQL Firewall 239
Real-Time Business Use Cases for the SQL Firewall Feature in Oracle Database 23AI 240
Common Questions About SQL Firewall in Oracle 23AI 241

Enhanced Redaction/Data Masking in Oracle 23AI 242
Implementing Redaction Policies with Seamless Compatibility 243
Expanding Redaction to Views and Aggregations 244
Grouping and Expression Support with Redacted Data 245
DISTINCT and ORDER BY Support for Redacted Columns 245
Using Set Operators on Redacted Columns 246
Performance Boost via Function-Based Indexes 246
Differences in Data Redaction Features Between Oracle Database Pre-23AI (e.g., 19c) and 23AI 247
Internal Mechanism of Enhanced Redaction in Oracle 23AI 248
Real-Time Business Use Cases for Oracle 23AI Enhanced Data Redaction 249
Common Questions About Oracle 23AI Redaction Enhancements 250
Read-Only User in 23AI 251
Provisioning a Read-Only User 252
Querying vs. Modifying Data 252
Upgrading Read-Only Access for Development Stages 253
Strategic Use and Best Practices 253
Strategic Implications 253
Internal Mechanism of Read-Only User in Oracle 23c 254
How Oracle 23AI Differs from Earlier Versions 254

Sample Real-Time Business Use Cases for the Read-Only User Feature in Oracle 23c...... 255
Common Questions About Read-Only Users in Oracle 23c.. 256

Chapter 10: Advanced Data Processing and Integrity Features 259

Introduction.. 259

Unlocking Advanced Data Insights with SQL Property Graphs in 23AI............................. 260
    Setting Up User and Relationship Data... 260
    Modeling the Property Graph.. 262
    Querying for Mutual Friends... 263
    Evolving the Social Network Graph 264
    Internal Mechanism of SQL Property Graphs in Oracle 23AI 266
    Real-Time Business Use Cases for Oracle Database 23AI's SQL Property Graphs.............. 266
    Common Questions About SQL Property Graph in Oracle Database 23AI.................... 267

Enhanced Data Integrity with Domain-Based Constraints in 23AI 269
    Defining Reusable Domains for Business Rules... 269
    Creating the Orders Table with Domain Constraints 270
    Inserting Data and Validating Constraints 271
    Retrieving Validated Order Data 271
    Internal Mechanism of Domains in Oracle 23AI 272
    Top Differences Between the Current Solution and the Pre-23AI Version 273
    Real-time Business Use Cases for the Oracle Database 23AI Domains Feature 274
    Common Questions About Domains in Oracle 23AI 275

Rename LOBSEGMENT in 23AI.. 276
    Creating the Table and Viewing the Original Segment... 277
    Renaming the LOB Segment in a Regular Table 278
    Working with Partitioned LOB Tables... 278
    Business Impact and Operational Benefits... 280
    Internal Mechanism of LOB Segment Rename in Oracle 23AI............................... 280
    Real-Time Business Use Cases for the LOB Segment Rename Feature in Oracle 23AI....... 281
    Common Questions About LOB Segment Rename in Oracle 23AI 282

Materialized View Concurrent Refreshes in 23AI 283

Creating and Populating the Base Tables 284
Enabling Fast Refresh Support with Materialized View Logs 285
Creating the Concurrently Refreshable Materialized View 286
Verifying Concurrent Refresh Configuration 286
Business Impact of Concurrent Refreshes at QuickMart... 287
Internal Mechanism of Concurrent Refresh in Oracle 23AI 287
Real-Time Business Use Cases for Materialized View Concurrent Refreshes
in Oracle 23AI 288
Common Questions About Concurrent Refreshes of Materialized Views in Oracle 23AI 289

Logical Partition Change Tracking (LPCT) in 23AI 290
Initial Setup and Table Creation 291
Enabling Logical Partition Change Tracking 292
Creating a Materialized View with LPCT Awareness 293
Tracking Partition Freshness 293
Simulating Data Changes and Stale Partitions 295
Querying Fresh Data During Staleness.. 295
Performing Targeted Partition Refreshes... 295
Internal Mechanism of Logical Partition Change Tracking (LPCT) in Oracle 23AI 296
Real-Time Business Use Cases for Logical Partition Change Tracking (LPCT) in 23AI 297
Common Questions About Logical Partition Change Tracking (LPCT) in Oracle 23AI........... 298

Chapter 11: Partitioning and Storage Optimization 301

Introduction.. 301
Enhanced Partitioning in 23AI... 301
Populating the Table with Sample Data.. 303
Run a Query to Check the Total Sales for Each Year and Region 304
Monitoring Partitions and Subpartitions... 304
Modern Boundary Representation with CLOB and JSON... 305
Internal Mechanism of Enhanced Partitioning in Oracle 23AI 306
Differences in Enhanced Partitioning between Pre-23c (Pre-23 AI) and
Oracle 23c (23 AI) 307
Real-Time Business Use Cases for Enhanced Partitioning in Oracle 23c........................... 308
Common Questions About Enhanced Partitioning in Oracle 23c 309

xv

TABLE OF CONTENTS

Optimizing Data Management and Efficiency with Oracle 23c Enhancements 310

    Tracking Product Updates with Enhanced DML RETURNING Clause 311

    Bulk Inserting Orders with Multirow VALUES Clause.. 313

    Internal Mechanism of Enhanced DML and Multirow Insert in Oracle 23c........................ 314

    Real-Time Business Use Cases for Optimizing Data Management in Oracle 23c 315

    Common Questions About Oracle 23c DML RETURNING and Multirow Insert Enhancements... 316

Chapter 12: Developer Enhancements and Troubleshooting 319

Introduction.. 319

Enhancing Database Efficiency with JavaScript Stored Procedures in 23AI 319

    Challenges with Java Stored Procedures Before Oracle 23AI.. 321

    Migrating to JavaScript Stored Procedures in Oracle 23AI 322

    Internal Mechanism of JavaScript Stored Procedures in Oracle 23AI................................ 324

    Performance and Maintainability Comparison with Pre-23AI... 325

    Real-Time Business Use Cases: Boosting Database Efficiency with JavaScript Stored Procedures in Oracle 23c... 326

    Common Questions About JavaScript Stored Procedures in Oracle 23AI.......................... 327

Enhancing Troubleshooting with Improved Error Messages in 23AI 328

    Creating the Customer Orders Table.. 329

    Identifying Group By Mistakes with Enhanced Syntax Suggestions................................... 329

    Before Oracle 23AI.. 330

    After Oracle 23AI 330

    Understanding System Limits with Clarity on Resource Exhaustion 330

    Before Oracle 23AI.. 330

    After Oracle 23AI 331

    Securing SQL Execution with Improved Identifier Validation... 331

Before Oracle 23AI 331

    After Oracle 23AI 331

    Internal Mechanism of Enhanced Error Messages in Oracle 23AI..................................... 332

    Real-Time Business Use Cases for Oracle 23AI's Enhanced Error Messages 332

    Common Questions About Oracle 23AI Enhanced Error Messages 333

Chapter 13: High-Speed Data Ingestion and In-Memory Processing 335

Introduction 335
Enhanced Fast Ingest for High-Speed Data Processing in 23AI 336
    Configuring Fast Ingest in Oracle 23AI 337
    Creating an Optimized Partitioned Table 337
    Ingesting High-Volume Sensor Data 338
    Flushing Buffered Data and Monitoring Usage 338
    Observing Memory Allocation 339
    Internal Mechanism of Enhanced Fast Ingest in Oracle 23AI 340
    How Oracle 23AI Enhances Fast Ingest Compared to Oracle 19c 340
    Real-Time Business Use Cases for Oracle 23AI's Enhanced Fast Ingest Feature 341
    Common Questions About Oracle 23AI Features for High-Volume Data Ingestion and Performance 342
Accelerating Real-Time Data Ingestion with Staging Tables in 23AI 343
    Creating the Shipment Staging and Final Tables 344
    High-Speed Ingestion Using the Staging Table 345
    Transforming and Moving Data to the Final Table 345
    Converting a Staging Table to a Regular Table 346
    Verifying Compression and Statistics Behavior 346
    Lifecycle Management and Cleanup 347
    Business Benefits of Using Staging Tables 347
    Internal Mechanism of Staging Tables in Oracle 23AI 348
    Differences: Staging Tables vs. Fast Ingest (MEMOPTIMIZE FOR WRITE) 349
    Real-World Use Cases of Staging Tables and Fast Ingest in Oracle 23AI 349
    Common Questions About Oracle 23AI Staging Tables and Fast Ingest 350
Revolutionizing In-Memory Performance in Oracle 23AI 352
    Automatic Enablement of In-Memory Features 353
    Automatic In-Memory Column Store Sizing 353
    Multilevel Joins and Aggregations 354
    In-Memory Optimized Dates 355
    Hybrid Exadata Scans 355
    In-Memory Columnar JSON 356

TABLE OF CONTENTS

Native In-Memory Advisor 356
Internal Mechanism of In-Memory Performance in Oracle 23AI 357
Real-Time Business Use Cases for Oracle 23AI In-Memory Enhancements 358
Common Questions About Oracle 23AI In-Memory Enhancements 358
Final Thoughts 360

Index 361

About the Author

Asim Chowdhury is a distinguished authority in Oracle database technologies, with nearly two decades of proven excellence in Oracle Database Management, Exadata, and Oracle Cloud at Customer (OCC). Renowned for his deep technical expertise and strategic acumen, Asim has successfully led high-performing teams and delivered transformative solutions for global organizations including Fidelity, NASA, HP, and Citibank.

A Senior Principal Consultant at Oracle India, Asim is also a celebrated thought leader and the acclaimed author of five widely respected technical books, including *Oracle SQL & PL/SQL Golden Diary*, *Oracle Performance Tuning Advice*, and *Oracle 12c New Features for SQL, PL/SQL & Administration*. His writings blend deep internals with practical application, earning recognition from both industry veterans and enterprise architects.

Asim's recent presentation at Oracle's Technical Insights Session—attended by senior leadership including Vice Presidents—was lauded for its clarity, depth, and actionable insights, further cementing his role as a strategic influencer within Oracle and across the wider tech ecosystem. His upcoming contributions continue to shape the future of Oracle strategy and innovation.

About the Technical Reviewer

Kirby McCord is a database leader from Chicago, Illinois. He has been using Oracle databases since 7.2.3 in the 1990s. Since then Kirby has used most Engineered Solutions and related database technologies such as Exadata and GoldenGate. Kirby has had several leadership positions for IOUG's (now Quest) Collaborate Conference including Track Lead and Conference Chair.

Acknowledgments

Writing this book has been an immensely fulfilling journey, made possible only through the encouragement, guidance, and support of many individuals.

I bow in gratitude to the Divine and my spiritual master, whose blessings have been my source of strength and inspiration. My deepest thanks go to my family—my wife Sutapa, my daughter Aditi, and my son Prathamesh—for their patience, love, and sacrifices. I also cherish the eternal guidance of my late father, Chitta Ranjan Chowdhury, and the inspiration of my mother, Sephali Chowdhury. My heartfelt gratitude extends to my brother, sisters, in-laws, and extended family for their constant encouragement.

I am profoundly grateful to Oracle's Executive Vice President, Greg Pavlik, who, despite his demanding schedule and executive responsibilities, graciously took the time to review this work and pen an inspiring foreword. His words not only capture the essence of this book but also elevate its purpose with clarity and vision.

I am indebted to Lisa Goldstein from Oracle Publishing for her pivotal support and to Tarun Mittal, Vice President at Oracle, whose guidance—along with the approvals facilitated by Rob Boucher, HR, and the Legal team—was invaluable. I extend sincere thanks to my manager and colleagues for their encouragement throughout this journey.

My appreciation goes to Shaul from Apress for his editorial direction and to Nirmal and Gryffin from the Apress team for their support in refining the manuscript. I am especially grateful to my technical reviewer, Kirby McCord, for his meticulous review of every line of code.

To my colleagues, mentors, and peers in the Oracle community: your insights, challenges, and collaboration have enriched this book and strengthened its practical value.

Although dedicated to Larry Ellison, this book is equally for the global community of database professionals, students, and leaders who continuously strive for innovation and excellence. My hope is that the features, use cases, and case studies presented here empower readers to embrace Oracle 23AI and Autonomous Database with confidence, curiosity, and vision.

With gratitude,

—Asim Chowdhury

Foreword

Oracle Database 23AI represents a transformative leap in enterprise data management, introducing more than 300 innovative features that converge the proven strengths of traditional databases with the intelligence and agility of modern artificial intelligence. As organizations worldwide grapple with increasingly complex data challenges, 23AI establishes a path for the convergence of the latest generative AI capabilities with the most reliable data management platform available. It includes advanced capabilities such as AI Vector Search for semantic data retrieval, native support for vector embeddings, and JSON Relational Duality Views that seamlessly bridge relational and JSON data models. Rather than having to bring your data to AI, 23AI brings AI to your data. This is a paradigm shift and will change the way you think about what you can do with data and how you build your applications.

The other major innovation this book discusses is Oracle Autonomous Database serverless (ADB-S). There's really nothing else like it in the industry. Rather than rely on humans to install, manage, and tune databases, ADB-S does it for you, using—what else—AI. ADB-S automates patching, scaling, and security—freeing data professionals to focus on innovation rather than administration. The cohesive integration of 23AI and ADB-S makes it easy to get AI to your data. It also helps organizations not only modernize their data environments, but also adapt rapidly to evolving business demands and emerging threats in the era of cloud computing.

This book is crafted to make the vast, sophisticated capabilities of Oracle Database 23AI and ADB-S accessible to a broad audience of data professionals, developers, and business leaders. Through clear explanations, real-world case studies, and step-by-step guidance, it illustrates both how to implement these features and why they are pivotal for staying competitive in today's data-driven landscape. Whether seeking to enhance scalability, fortify security, or infuse intelligence directly into business workflows, readers will find actionable insights and proven strategies for leveraging 23AI and ADB-S to deliver tangible value.

As you embark on this journey, I encourage you to use this book not merely as a technical guide, but as a blueprint for innovation. Oracle Database 23AI and ADB-S unlock unprecedented possibilities for redefining data management, embedding AI at

FOREWORD

the core of your operations, and preparing your organization for the future of distributed, intelligent cloud platforms. Approach each chapter with curiosity and a willingness to experiment, and you will be well-positioned to master these technologies and lead transformative change.

I am especially pleased to see Asim Chowdhury took on the challenge of presenting this material. Asim has nearly two decades of experience in Oracle database technologies and leadership in enterprise data solutions, which are reflected in this work. Asim's unique ability to make advanced database concepts accessible, combined with his hands-on expertise across industries such as banking, energy, and public sector, brings practical insight to every page. His successful collaborations on projects for real-world users—including NASA, HP, Citibank, and HSBC—demonstrate not only his technical skill but also his commitment to driving results for organizations of every scale. As a respected author of several books on PL/SQL and Oracle performance, Asim has earned the trust of teams worldwide by translating complexity into clear, actionable guidance.

I hope the knowledge shared in these pages inspires you to explore, innovate, and realize the powerful potential of Oracle Database 23AI and ADB-S within your own organization. This is the guide for transformation your business needs today.

Greg Pavlik
Executive Vice President, Oracle

CHAPTER 1

Introduction to Oracle Database 23AI and ADB-S: AI-Driven Innovations and Use Cases

Introduction

Databases today are rapidly evolving from passive data storage systems into intelligent, autonomous platforms. At the forefront of this transformation is **Oracle Database 23AI**, which seamlessly embeds Artificial Intelligence (AI) and Machine Learning (ML) into the very fabric of database operations. With these innovations, Oracle 23AI is capable of learning from past behavior, adapting to changing workloads, and making real-time decisions to optimize performance, security, and scalability—all while significantly reducing manual oversight.

Paired with **Autonomous Database Serverless (ADB-S)**, organizations are offered a robust, cloud-native environment that is not only fully managed but also dynamically adjusts computing resources based on the system's demands. ADB-S takes care of essential tasks such as performance tuning, backups, patching, and security updates, enabling teams to focus on innovation rather than administration.

To help readers fully grasp and apply these new capabilities, this book follows a consistent and intuitive format throughout. Each feature is introduced through a well-structured narrative that begins with a detailed explanation of its purpose and functionality. Real-world case studies contextualize these features by presenting common challenges and their AI-powered solutions. Readers are guided through implementation with step-by-step instructions, followed by insights into how the feature compares to previous Oracle versions. A brief dive into the internal workings of the feature helps demystify its underlying architecture, while practical business scenarios illustrate its broader industry relevance. Each feature also addresses common queries that may arise and ends with a concise summary to reinforce the key points. This structured approach ensures that readers not only understand the technology but can also confidently apply it in real-world environments.

With this foundation in place, let us delve deeper into what Oracle 23AI and ADB-S offer, starting with a high-level overview of their capabilities and significance.

Oracle 23AI and ADB-S: A New Era of Intelligent Databases

Oracle Database 23AI introduces a new standard in database technology, embedding native AI capabilities that revolutionize performance tuning, query optimization, and security. Through machine learning algorithms, the system evolves into a self-aware platform—capable of analyzing workloads, adapting strategies in real time, and delivering consistently high performance even for complex enterprise workloads.

A standout set of features revolves around AI-powered enhancements such as intelligent indexing and vector search. These capabilities allow the system to perform fast, similarity-based lookups across diverse data types like images, audio, and text—enabling advanced use cases such as recommendation engines and semantic search applications.

On the security front, Oracle 23AI introduces features such as the **SQL Firewall** and **Database Vault integration**, which proactively block unauthorized SQL statements and enforce strict separation-of-duties. Coupled with anomaly detection powered by machine learning, these capabilities provide a layered defense that mitigates threats with minimal manual intervention.

Further improving developer experience and workload versatility, Oracle 23AI strengthens support for semi-structured data formats like JSON and XML, enhancing both performance and scalability for modern applications.

Autonomous Database Serverless (ADB-S) complements Oracle 23AI by delivering these innovations through a fully managed, cloud-native deployment model. ADB-S leverages the underlying capabilities of Oracle 23AI but packages them within an autonomous service that dynamically adjusts compute and storage, handles tuning and patching, and maintains compliance—all with minimal user involvement.

Together, Oracle 23AI and ADB-S form a cohesive, intelligent platform that drives operational agility and transforms data management into a self-optimizing, secure, and highly adaptive process.

Who Should Use Oracle 23AI and ADB-S?

The powerful capabilities of Oracle 23AI and ADB-S make them highly relevant to a broad spectrum of professionals involved in data management, application development, and strategic planning.

Database Administrators (DBAs) stand to benefit immensely from AI-driven workload optimization and automated indexing. Routine tasks such as tuning and performance monitoring are handled autonomously, allowing DBAs to focus on higher-level planning and system architecture.

Developers can take advantage of advanced SQL functions, rich JSON/XML support, and cutting-edge vector search features to build intelligent applications that are both scalable and efficient. These tools open new doors for innovation in AI-powered development.

Data Scientists and AI Engineers will appreciate the ability to handle vector embeddings natively within the database. This capability simplifies tasks like image classification, sentiment analysis, and recommendation generation, as well as managing ML models within Oracle's infrastructure.

Enterprise IT and Security Teams benefit from the platform's autonomous scaling, built-in governance, and **AI-powered security features** like anomaly detection and SQL firewalls. These capabilities reduce operational burden while enhancing data protection and compliance.

Senior Management and Decision-Makers gain real-time analytics and actionable insights from system-generated intelligence, helping align IT strategy with business goals and drive innovation.

Real-World Impact

Oracle 23AI and ADB-S are not just continuing Oracle's proven track record, but **extending it with new AI-driven capabilities** that redefine existing use cases:

- **Customer analytics** now leverages *vector search and intelligent indexing* to deliver hyper-personalized recommendations in real time.

- **Transactional systems** benefit from *lock-free reservations* and *priority transactions*, achieving ultra-low latency even under peak loads.

- **Security and compliance monitoring** are reinforced with *SQL Firewall* and *ML-driven anomaly detection*, providing proactive defense beyond traditional auditing.

- **IoT and real-time streaming** are enhanced with *adaptive ingestion pipelines* that self-optimize for changing data volumes and formats.

- In **healthcare**, *AI-powered similarity search and GPU-accelerated analytics* are transforming genomic research and imaging-based diagnostics.

These advancements illustrate how Oracle 23AI and ADB-S are **not only supporting traditional enterprise workloads** but also enabling **next-generation innovations** that were previously difficult to achieve at scale.

Getting Started with Oracle 23AI

Connecting to Oracle 23AI is straightforward, whether you're exploring it in a local setup or via the cloud. Oracle provides an official installation guide for deploying the database on local environments, accessible at

```
https://docs.oracle.com/en/database/oracle/oracle-database/23/install.html
```

For those looking to harness Oracle's AI-powered database in the cloud, the **Oracle Free Tier** offers a no-cost way to get started. Simply visit

```
Oracle Cloud Free Tier https://www.oracle.com/in/cloud/free/
```

CHAPTER 1   INTRODUCTION TO ORACLE DATABASE 23AI AND ADB-S: AI-DRIVEN INNOVATIONS AND USE CASES

and then click on sign up now.

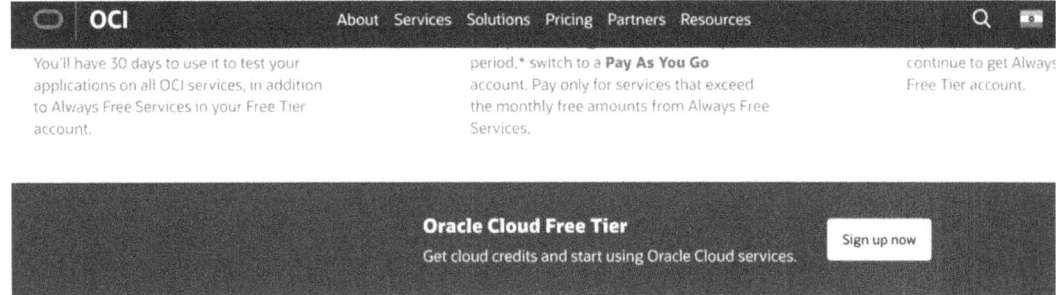

Figure 1-1. Signing up option

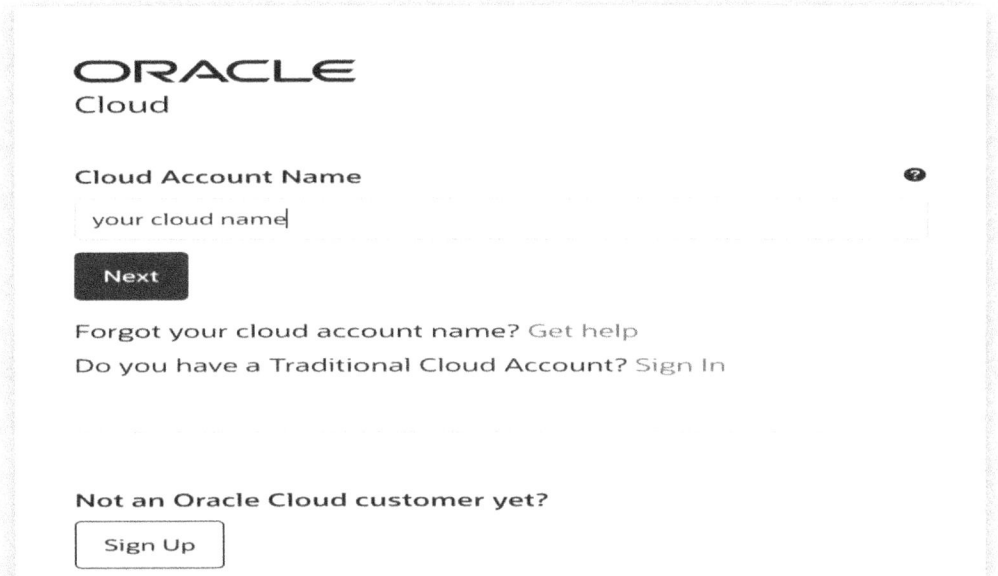

Figure 1-2. Signing up for Oracle Cloud Free Tier

Select **Oracle Database** and click **Sign Up Now** to create your account.

Log In to Oracle Cloud:

- Access the Oracle Cloud Console using your credentials.
- Upon successful login (click `Sign in to Oracle Cloud`), the main dashboard will be displayed.

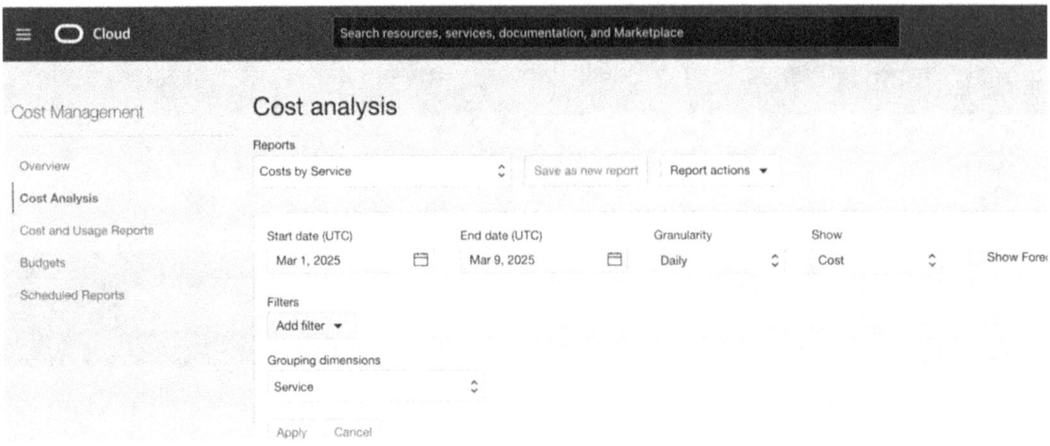

CHAPTER 1   INTRODUCTION TO ORACLE DATABASE 23AI AND ADB-S: AI-DRIVEN INNOVATIONS AND USE CASES

Figure 1-3. Oracle Cloud Console dashboard after sign-in

Once you've registered, log in to the Oracle Cloud Console using your credentials. From the main dashboard, open the navigation menu (☰) in the top-left corner and navigate to the **Autonomous Database** section under the **Oracle Database** category. Click **Create Autonomous Database**, then configure your desired settings such as database name, password, and database version. After submitting the configuration, your Autonomous Database instance will be provisioned, as illustrated in the figures below.

Figure 1-4. Oracle Cloud Console showing autonomous database option

Once you clicked on autonomous database, it shows **Create Autonomous Database** option as shown in Figure 1-5.

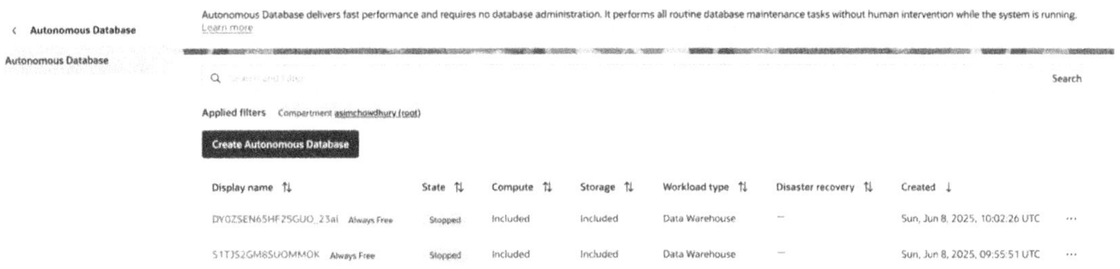

CHAPTER 1   INTRODUCTION TO ORACLE DATABASE 23AI AND ADB-S: AI-DRIVEN INNOVATIONS AND USE CASES

Figure 1-5. Oracle Cloud Console dashboard showing Create Autonomous Database option

Once you click on **Create Autonomous Database**, you can select **Oracle 23AI** as the database version, set a new admin password, and then click **Create** to proceed with provisioning the instance.

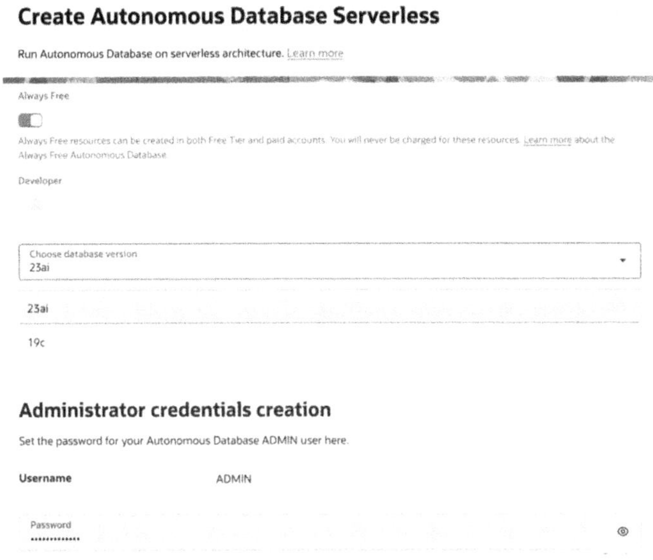

Figure 1-6. Oracle Cloud Console choose 23AI and create database

After creation, you can locate your database by its display name. Clicking on it allows access to the SQL interface, where you can begin exploring the capabilities of Oracle 23AI through direct queries.

CHAPTER 1 INTRODUCTION TO ORACLE DATABASE 23AI AND ADB-S: AI-DRIVEN INNOVATIONS AND USE CASES

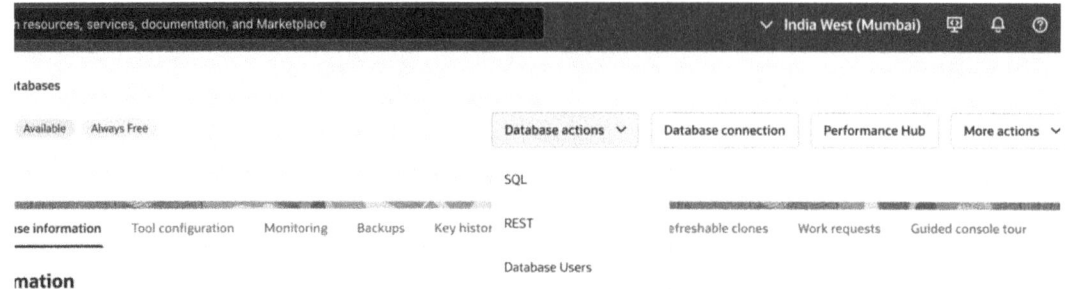

***Figure 1-7.** Accessing the Autonomous Database SQL Interface*

This intuitive onboarding process ensures that users can start leveraging the full power of Oracle 23AI and ADB-S in just a few steps.

Summary

As we've seen, Oracle Database 23AI and Autonomous Database Serverless (ADB-S) mark a pivotal shift in the way modern databases operate. By embedding AI and automation into the core engine, Oracle has created a self-managing, intelligent platform that not only handles complex workloads but actively learns and adapts to them. This chapter provided a high-level foundation for understanding what Oracle 23AI offers—from smarter query optimization to dynamic workload management, AI-powered security, and real-world business applications. We also explored the structure of this book, designed to walk you feature-by-feature through practical implementations, internal mechanisms, use cases, and comparative insights.

If you've jumped directly to this chapter, you're now grounded in the "why" and "what" of Oracle 23AI. Whether you're a developer, DBA, data scientist, or enterprise strategist, the chapters ahead will continue to build on this understanding, guiding you through targeted, real-world scenarios and hands-on applications.

In the next chapter, we turn our focus to **performance optimization and concurrency control**, diving deep into key innovations that allow for faster, conflict-free transactions and smarter resource usage. We begin with **Lock-Free Reservations**, a powerful mechanism in Oracle 23AI that enables high-performance updates without traditional locking overhead.

Whether you're reading cover to cover or navigating to a specific area of interest, the next chapter offers actionable strategies to help you unlock new levels of speed, scalability, and control in your Oracle environments.

CHAPTER 2

Performance Optimizations and Concurrency Control

Introduction

This chapter covers key new **features** in Oracle 23AI focused on performance optimizations and concurrency control. Each feature is explained clearly with real-world case studies demonstrating AI-driven solutions to common challenges. Step-by-step implementation guides help apply these features practically, while comparisons with previous versions highlight improvements. A brief look into internal mechanisms clarifies how these features work under the hood. Business scenarios show their industry relevance, and common questions are addressed for clarity. Each section ends with a summary to reinforce essential points.

Unlocking High-Performance Updates with Lock-Free Reservations in 23AI

In high-traffic environments, concurrency bottlenecks during transactional updates can severely impact application performance. Oracle 23AI addresses this challenge with a powerful new feature—Lock-Free Reservations—that redefines how concurrent numeric updates are processed. In this section, we explore how QuickMart, a fictional ecommerce company, leveraged this innovation to resolve performance issues in its order processing system.

CHAPTER 2   PERFORMANCE OPTIMIZATIONS AND CONCURRENCY CONTROL

> **CASE STUDY: QUICK MART—OVERCOMING ROW LOCK CONTENTION IN ECOMMERCE**
>
> QuickMart faced a recurring issue in its online retail platform. When multiple customers attempted to purchase the same product simultaneously, the system encountered delays caused by the wait event **"enq: TX - row lock contention"**. These delays were triggered by the conventional row-level locking approach used in updating inventory and sales counters, which serialized transactions and forced other sessions to wait. The impact was tangible—checkout lags, elevated cart abandonment, and a noticeable dip in customer satisfaction and revenue.

Demonstrating the Traditional Locking Model

To understand the limitations QuickMart faced, consider the implementation of a typical products table with numeric tracking fields, as shown in Listing 2-1.

Listing 2-1. Creating the Products Table with Stock and Sales Columns

```
drop table if exists products;

CREATE TABLE products (
    product_id NUMBER PRIMARY KEY,
    product_name VARCHAR2(100),
    quantity_in_stock NUMBER CHECK (quantity_in_stock >= 0),
    items_sold NUMBER DEFAULT 0
);
```

During flash sale events, multiple sessions might run the following update concurrently.

Listing 2-2. Traditional Update Statement Prone to Lock Contention

```
UPDATE products SET items_UPDATE produsold = items_sold + 1 WHERE product_id = 1;
```

CHAPTER 2 PERFORMANCE OPTIMIZATIONS AND CONCURRENCY CONTROL

Each of these updates attempts to acquire an exclusive lock on the same row, leading to the wait event "enq: TX - row lock contention." This causes transactions to serialize, reducing throughput and increasing latency—especially noticeable during periods of high concurrency.

Introducing Lock-Free Reservations

To overcome this challenge, QuickMart turned to **Lock-Free Reservations**, a feature introduced in Oracle 23AI. Instead of relying on exclusive row-level locks, Oracle now enables concurrent updates through **in-memory reservation slots and atomic operations**. This method eliminates contention, allowing multiple transactions to update numeric fields simultaneously.

To enable this capability, QuickMart modified the existing schema using the RESERVABLE keyword.

Listing 2-3. Enabling Lock-Free Reservations on Numeric Column

```
ALTER TABLE products MODIFY (items_sold RESERVABLE);
```

This simple schema change transforms how updates to the items_sold column are handled. Known academically as **Escrow Column Concurrency Control**, the RESERVABLE attribute allows Oracle to manage updates using a memory-based reservation system that applies changes atomically without locking rows.

Simulating Concurrent Sales with Reservation Logic

To test the system under realistic load, sample data is inserted into the table, as shown in Listing 2-4.

Listing 2-4. Inserting Sample Inventory for Simulation

```
INSERT INTO products (product_id, product_name, quantity_in_stock,
items_sold)
VALUES (1, 'Wireless Mouse', 100, 0);

INSERT INTO products (product_id, product_name, quantity_in_stock,
items_sold)
VALUES (2, 'Mechanical Keyboard', 50, 0);

commit;
```

Once enabled, concurrent transactions use a lightweight reservation mechanism that updates values in memory while still validating business constraints before committing. The following PL/SQL block demonstrates this lock-free mechanism in action.

Listing 2-5. Lock-Free Update with Constraint Validation

```
DECLARE
    v_remaining_stock NUMBER;
BEGIN
    UPDATE products SET items_sold = items_sold + 1 WHERE product_id = 1;

    SELECT quantity_in_stock - items_sold INTO v_remaining_stock FROM
    products WHERE product_id = 1;

    IF v_remaining_stock < 0 THEN
        ROLLBACK; -- Prevent overselling
        RAISE_APPLICATION_ERROR(-20001, 'Stock unavailable');
    ELSE
        COMMIT;
    END IF;
END;
/
```

This logic enables multiple sales to be processed in parallel without locking rows. Oracle checks the remaining stock before finalizing the update, ensuring data integrity while maintaining high concurrency.

Testing the Performance Impact of Lock-Free Reservations

To demonstrate the tangible benefits, QuickMart reverted the schema back to traditional behavior, as shown in Listing 2-6.

Listing 2-6. Reverting to Traditional Locking Behavior

```
ALTER TABLE products MODIFY (items_sold not RESERVABLE);
```

Upon doing so, the system once again experienced the "enq: TX - row lock contention" wait event under concurrent load. This provided a clear contrast between the two modes of operation, confirming the value of Lock-Free Reservations in high-concurrency scenarios.

How Lock-Free Reservations Work in Practice

With Lock-Free Reservations enabled, Oracle tracks updates in memory and applies them atomically during commit, while verifying any constraints like stock availability. If the remaining inventory is insufficient, the transaction is rolled back. This approach preserves transactional integrity without sacrificing speed. In QuickMart's case, the shift to this model dramatically reduced checkout latency and eliminated contention during high-demand periods.

By modernizing its backend with Oracle 23AI, QuickMart gained not only performance improvements but also a scalable foundation for future growth. This case highlights how Oracle's AI-era features can solve real-world concurrency problems with minimal code changes and maximum impact.

Key Considerations and Limitations

Lock-Free Reservations offer targeted performance improvements for specific types of operations—particularly **high-concurrency, incremental updates to numeric columns** in OLTP scenarios. However, their benefits are workload-dependent and may be limited in other contexts such as batch processing.

Scenario	Effect of Lock-Free Reservations
OLTP (High-Concurrency Incremental Updates)	Offers substantial performance gains—up to **3x higher throughput**—in scenarios where multiple users update the same numeric column concurrently (e.g., `items_sold = items_sold + 1`). Lock-Free Reservations eliminate row-level contention by allowing atomic, in-memory updates without blocking.
Batch Processing (Sequential Row Updates)	Impact is limited and highly dependent on application design. If the batch process runs in isolation or does not involve reservable columns, Lock-Free Reservations may have **minimal effect**. While contention is avoided, validation logic and commit-phase sequencing can still serialize operations. Benefit is reduced when contention is low or absent.

In summary, Lock-Free Reservations are highly effective in scenarios with intense write concurrency on numeric fields, but developers should evaluate their use case architecture carefully when applying this feature to batch-oriented workloads.

Internal Mechanism of Lock-Free Reservations in Oracle 23AI

Oracle 23AI improves concurrency by using in-memory conflict detection and deferred consistency checks instead of traditional row-level locks. With the RESERVABLE feature, numeric columns like "items_sold" are updated independently in memory, avoiding row lock contention. Updates are buffered and merged later, ensuring efficient transaction processing without blocking. Atomic fetch-and-add operations allow transactions to modify numeric values atomically, boosting throughput and reducing serialization.

This mechanism is visually represented in the flow diagram below.

Table 2-1. *Internal Flow of Lock-Free Reservations in Oracle 23AI*

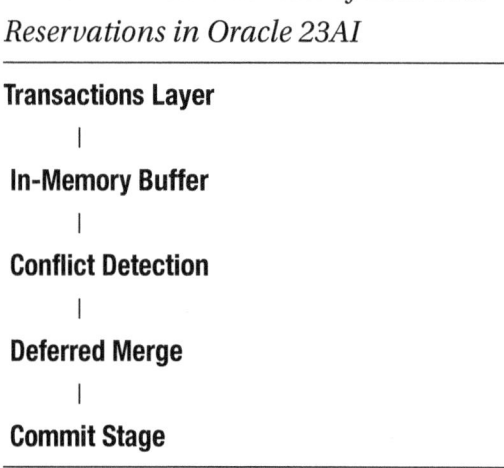

Real-World Use Cases and Business Benefits

Understanding the internal mechanism is only part of the picture. It is equally important to see how Lock-Free Reservations translate into tangible benefits across different industries. In this section, we explore several practical applications that highlight the versatility and impact of this feature.

Table 2-2. *Real-World Applications and Benefits of Lock-Free Reservations Across Industries*

Use Case	Business Scenario	Benefit
Ecommerce Order Processing	Multiple customers purchasing the same product.	Prevents checkout delays, reducing abandoned carts.
Stock Trading Systems	High-frequency trading updates.	Enables real-time, conflict-free updates.
Ride-Sharing Apps	Multiple users booking rides simultaneously.	Allows concurrent ride requests without blocking updates.
Online Ticket Booking	High-demand ticket purchases.	Eliminates contention for seamless seat allocation.
Banking and Payment Processing	Multiple simultaneous debit/credit transactions.	Improves transaction throughput by preventing row locks.
Inventory and Warehouse Management	Employees updating stock levels in real-time.	Reduces update delays, ensuring smooth logistics.

Common Questions About Lock-Free Reservations in Oracle 23AI

As with any powerful feature, Lock-Free Reservations invite questions about their practical implications, compatibility, and trade-offs. This section addresses some of the most frequently asked questions to help readers make informed decisions about adoption.

One common concern is how Oracle 23AI maintains data consistency while allowing concurrent updates. The answer lies in its in-memory buffering and deferred validation model. Updates are not written to the database immediately; instead, they're validated for constraint compliance (such as ensuring stock is not oversold) just before commit. This ensures that only valid transactions are merged into the database.

Another frequent question involves the impact on traditional wait events such as **"enq: TX - row lock contention."** Oracle's Lock-Free model addresses this by bypassing row-level locking entirely through atomic in-memory updates. As a result, this mechanism can significantly reduce contention and improve throughput in **scenarios involving high-concurrency updates to numeric columns**, such as real-time counters in OLTP applications.

It's also important to recognize the feature's limitations. Lock-Free Reservations are tailored for numeric columns in high-concurrency OLTP environments. They are not suitable for batch processing workloads, where transactions are serialized. Additionally, they don't support complex transactional logic that spans multiple rows or data types.

Lastly, in comparison to Multi-Version Concurrency Control (MVCC)—which manages concurrency by maintaining multiple versions of rows—Lock-Free Reservations update values in memory and defer their merge. This results in lower overhead and improved efficiency for high-frequency numeric updates.

Key Takeaway Lock-Free Reservations in Oracle 23AI introduce an innovative approach to handling high-concurrency updates on numeric columns. QuickMart successfully leveraged this feature to eliminate row-level locking, reduce transaction bottlenecks, and streamline the checkout process. Updates are managed in memory and finalized at commit time, enabling faster execution while preserving data integrity.

This capability proves especially beneficial in targeted OLTP scenarios such as ecommerce, stock trading, ride-sharing, and banking—where multiple users frequently update shared counters in parallel. However, the feature offers limited advantages for batch processing workloads, where contention is typically lower or behavior is governed by sequential logic.

When used in the right context, Lock-Free Reservations can deliver measurable improvements in responsiveness and throughput for specific high-concurrency operations.

Now that we've examined Lock-Free Reservations in depth, it's time to explore another groundbreaking feature in Oracle 23AI that complements concurrency optimization—
Priority Transactions.

Optimizing Transaction Concurrency with Priority Transactions and TRUE CACHE in Oracle 23AI

This section focuses on advanced concurrency optimization strategies in Oracle 23AI, beginning with a deep dive into **Priority Transactions**, followed by a brief overview of **Oracle True Cache**.

In modern enterprise systems, transaction contention is a common challenge—especially when multiple workloads with differing priorities compete for the same database resources. Oracle 23AI introduces a sophisticated feature called **Priority Transactions** that intelligently manages such conflicts by allowing critical operations to take precedence over routine or background tasks. This chapter explores how QuickMart, a fictional yet representative ecommerce platform, implemented Priority Transactions to streamline VIP order processing and eliminate delays caused by background inventory jobs.

The Need for Prioritizing Transactions

QuickMart handles millions of database transactions daily, ranging from immediate customer orders to background inventory updates. While both are essential to business continuity, they differ significantly in urgency. During peak periods, high-priority tasks—such as VIP order fulfillment or real-time fund transfers—can be blocked by long-running, low-priority batch jobs. In previous Oracle versions, this often required manual DBA intervention to identify and terminate blocking sessions, introducing administrative overhead and latency.

Oracle 23AI addresses this issue through a configurable mechanism that assigns **transaction priority levels**—HIGH, MEDIUM, or LOW—to each session. The database engine monitors transaction conflicts and enforces priority-based rules to prevent high-priority transactions from waiting indefinitely.

CASE STUDY: QUICKMART'S CONCURRENCY CHALLENGE

In QuickMart's operational model, high-value VIP customers require instant order processing to ensure a seamless premium experience. However, the platform also runs scheduled inventory reconciliation jobs that lock critical rows for extended durations. The result: VIP transactions were frequently delayed, contributing to cart abandonment and customer dissatisfaction.

Implementing the Inventory Schema

To simulate QuickMart's real-world scenario, consider a basic inventory table that tracks stock quantities, as shown in Listing 2-7.

Listing 2-7. Creating and Populating Inventory Table

```
drop table if exists inventory;

CREATE TABLE if not exists inventory (
    product_id NUMBER PRIMARY KEY,
    stock_quantity NUMBER CHECK (stock_quantity >= 0)
);
INSERT INTO inventory VALUES (1, 100);
COMMIT;
```

This setup prepares the database for concurrent transaction testing with varying priorities.

Configuring Priority Transaction Parameters

Oracle provides four initialization parameters to configure this feature. Two of them—PRIORITY_TXNS_HIGH_WAIT_TARGET and PRIORITY_TXNS_MEDIUM_WAIT_TARGET—define the maximum time a HIGH- or MEDIUM-priority transaction will wait before a blocking LOW priority transaction is forcibly rolled back.

For example, QuickMart set the high-priority threshold to 5 seconds and the medium-priority threshold to 30 seconds.

Listing 2-8. Setting Wait Thresholds for High- and Medium-Priority Transactions

```
ALTER SYSTEM SET priority_txns_high_wait_target=5 SCOPE=BOTH;   -- High priority waits 5 seconds
ALTER SYSTEM SET priority_txns_medium_wait_target=30 SCOPE=BOTH;  -- Medium priority waits 30 seconds
```

CHAPTER 2 PERFORMANCE OPTIMIZATIONS AND CONCURRENCY CONTROL

These values are modifiable at the system or PDB level and can vary across Oracle RAC instances. When combined with TXN_PRIORITY and PRIORITY_TXNS_MODE, they provide fine-grained control over transaction handling.

Simulating Transaction Conflicts with Priority Levels

In the following simulation, two sessions represent the conflicting processes running at the same time.

Session A: Low-Priority Batch Update

```
ALTER SESSION SET TXN_PRIORITY=LOW;
BEGIN
   UPDATE inventory SET stock_quantity = stock_quantity - 10 WHERE
   product_id = 1;
   DBMS_LOCK.SLEEP(20);   -- Simulating a long-running batch process
   COMMIT;
END;
/
```

This session locks the inventory row for 20 seconds. Meanwhile, a high-priority transaction attempts to access the same row.

Session B: High-Priority VIP Order

Listing 2-9. Simulating a Blocked VIP Order by a Low-Priority Transaction

```
ALTER SESSION SET TXN_PRIORITY=HIGH;
BEGIN
   UPDATE inventory SET stock_quantity = stock_quantity - 1 WHERE
   product_id = 1;
   COMMIT;
END;
/
```

If the HIGH-priority session waits more than five seconds (as defined in the parameter), Oracle will **automatically roll back the blocking LOW-priority transaction**, ensuring that the VIP order proceeds with minimal delay.

CHAPTER 2 PERFORMANCE OPTIMIZATIONS AND CONCURRENCY CONTROL

Observing Transaction Behavior

You can monitor transaction blocking with the following query:

```
select sid, event, seconds_in_wait, blocking_session from v$session where event like '%enq%';
```

Listing 2-10. Observing Wait Events and Transaction Priorities

```
sample output
SID   EVENT                              SECONDS_IN_WAIT  BLOCKING_SESSION
----  ---------------------------------  ---------------  ----------------
1093  enq: TX - row lock (HIGH priority)  4                940

SELECT TXN_PRIORITY, PRIORITY_TXNS_WAIT_TARGET FROM V$TRANSACTION;

sample output
TXN_PRI  TXN_PRIORITY_WAIT_TARGET
-------  ------------------------
HIGH     10
```

This shows the HIGH-priority session waiting for a row lock held by session 940.

Managing Business Risk: Automatic Rollbacks

While Priority Transactions improve responsiveness, they also introduce new operational considerations. For example, automatic rollback of batch transactions may disrupt long-running processes if high-priority traffic is sustained. QuickMart addressed this by

- Scheduling batch updates during low-traffic windows.
- Breaking large batch jobs into smaller, retryable units.
- Monitoring rollback frequency to fine-tune thresholds.

This approach ensured that background jobs could still complete while maintaining a fast user experience for critical workflows.

Business Impact of Priority Transactions at QuickMart

After implementing Priority Transactions, QuickMart observed a measurable improvement in customer satisfaction and system throughput. VIP orders were processed in near real-time, even during concurrent inventory updates. Manual DBA interventions dropped significantly as the system automatically handled blocking scenarios based on configured priorities. More importantly, this improvement was achieved without altering application logic—just by fine-tuning Oracle 23AI's built-in parameters.

By allowing different classes of transactions to coexist harmoniously, Oracle 23AI enables businesses to achieve higher concurrency, smarter conflict resolution, and better resource utilization. While not a one-size-fits-all solution, Priority Transactions provide a powerful lever for tuning performance in high-demand environments.

Internal Mechanism of Transaction Concurrency with Priority Transactions in Oracle 23AI

Oracle 23AI enhances transaction concurrency using Priority Transactions, which assign priority levels (HIGH, MEDIUM, LOW) to different workloads. When a low-priority transaction blocks a high-priority one, Oracle leverages a priority-based wait mechanism governed by `priority_txns_high_wait_target`. If the blocking transaction does not release the lock within the threshold, it is automatically rolled back, allowing the high-priority transaction to proceed without manual intervention. This intelligent rollback ensures smooth processing of critical tasks like VIP orders, real-time fund transfers, or stock trades.

This mechanism is visually represented in the flow diagram below.

Table 2-3. *Internal Flow of Priority Transactions in Oracle 23AI*

Transactions Layer
|
In-Memory Buffer
|
Conflict Detection
|
Priority-Based Wait Mechanism
|
Automatic Rollback (if threshold exceeded)
|
Commit Stage

Real-World Use Cases of Priority Transactions

Understanding the internal mechanism is only part of the picture. It is equally important to see how **Priority Transactions** in Oracle 23AI deliver tangible benefits across various business domains. This section highlights practical scenarios that demonstrate the value and real-world impact of this feature.

Table 2-4. *Real-World Applications and Business Benefits of Priority Transactions Across Industries*

Use Case	Business Scenario	Benefit
VIP Order Processing in Ecommerce	Prioritize VIP customer orders over batch inventory updates	Ensures fast order fulfillment without delays.
Real-Time Payment Processing in Banking	High-priority fund transfers processed before routine reconciliations.	Prevents customer dissatisfaction due to delayed transactions.
Stock Trading Execution	Prioritize high-value trade orders over batch price updates.	Ensures timely trade execution, minimizing financial losses.

(*continued*)

Table 2-4. (*continued*)

Use Case	Business Scenario	Benefit
Airline Ticket Booking System	Confirmed bookings take precedence over batch seat inventory updates.	Prevents booking failures and enhances customer experience.
Healthcare Emergency System	Critical patient record updates prioritized over routine batch reports.	Ensures doctors access crucial patient data on time.
Manufacturing and Supply Chain	Real-time order fulfillment prioritizes urgent shipments over warehouse stock adjustments.	Reduces delivery delays and improves supply chain efficiency.

Common Questions About Priority Transactions in Oracle 23AI

As with any advanced concurrency feature, **Priority Transactions** raise important questions about their behavior, configuration, and limitations. This section addresses the most frequently asked questions to help database architects and developers make informed decisions when implementing this capability.

One common question is how Oracle 23AI enforces priority-based execution and rollbacks. The answer lies in its intelligent conflict detection combined with a **priority-based wait threshold**. When a low-priority transaction blocks a high-priority one, Oracle waits for a defined period—controlled by the `priority_txns_high_wait_target` parameter. If the blocking transaction doesn't release the lock within this time, it is automatically rolled back to allow the high-priority transaction to proceed without delay.

Another frequently asked question concerns **simultaneous high-priority transactions**. Oracle continues to use its standard **row-level locking mechanisms** for concurrency control. If multiple high-priority transactions conflict, they are handled on a **first-come, first-serve (FCFS)** basis within the same priority level, ensuring fairness while maintaining transactional integrity.

The ability to **dynamically set transaction priorities** is also a notable strength of this feature. Developers or applications can use ALTER SESSION SET TXN_PRIORITY = <LEVEL> to assign a specific priority (HIGH, MEDIUM, or LOW) at runtime. In addition, system-wide defaults for wait thresholds can be configured via initialization parameters:

- priority_txns_high_wait_target – wait time before rolling back a blocker of a high-priority transaction.

- priority_txns_medium_wait_target – threshold for medium-priority transactions.

- priority_txns_low_wait_target – rollback limit for low-priority cases.

By default, transactions are assigned **medium priority**, unless explicitly changed.

- However, this feature introduces certain operational considerations. Rolling back low-priority transactions can lead to partial updates, inconsistencies in application logic, or repeated retries if not handled properly by the application. Additionally, under continuous high-priority workloads, low-priority transactions may experience starvation, delaying essential background processes such as batch inventory updates. While the mechanism avoids traditional row lock contention, it can still create resource pressure—such as increased CPU usage or redo generation—if a surge of high-priority transactions competes for access. These effects are not inherent to the feature itself but emerge from workload imbalances or poor configuration.

- In summary, Priority Transactions provide a robust framework for managing transactional urgency by enforcing clear execution precedence. While they enhance responsiveness for high-priority operations, their successful adoption depends on thoughtful workload planning, resilient application logic, and well-calibrated system parameters to ensure fairness, stability, and predictable behavior across transaction classes.

Key Takeaway Priority Transactions in Oracle 23AI introduce a structured way to manage transactional concurrency by enforcing execution precedence based on defined priority levels. This mechanism helps ensure that critical operations—such as VIP order processing or real-time fund transfers—can proceed with minimal delay when competing with lower-priority workloads in high-contention scenarios.

By reducing the likelihood of lock contention for high-priority transactions, this feature can improve responsiveness in targeted, time-sensitive use cases. It also lessens the need for manual intervention in resolving blocking issues, thereby streamlining operational oversight. While not a universal performance booster, Priority Transactions offer clear benefits in environments where responsiveness to critical events is essential, ultimately enhancing user satisfaction and system reliability when configured thoughtfully.

While Priority Transactions enhance execution efficiency under concurrency, **Oracle True Cache** in Oracle Database 23AI addresses the read-scaling challenge for latency-sensitive workloads. It provides an in-memory, read-only, fully consistent cache of the primary Autonomous Database—ideal for ecommerce, gaming, and real-time analytics scenarios.

This section offers a high-level overview of Oracle True Cache. As the feature requires a paid-tier ADB environment, it is not available for experimentation on Free Tier. However, the conceptual and implementation guidance below can help developers get started when a supported tenancy is available.

Listing 2-11. Creating a True Cache Instance via OCI CLI

```
oci db autonomous-database create \
  --compartment-id <compartment_ocid> \
  --db-name TRUECACHE1 \
  --cpu-core-count 2 \
  --data-storage-size-in-tbs 1 \
  --admin-password <YourPassword> \
  --display-name "True Cache for QuickMart Read Scaling" \
  --is-true-cache-enabled true \
  --true-cache-source-database-id <ocid_of_primary_adb> \
  --db-version "23ai"
```

This command provisions a True Cache instance linked to a source ADB, offering sub-second redo lag and consistent reads. If the CLI option is not recognized, True Cache may not be available in your tenancy or region.

JDBC-Based Read Routing

Once Oracle True Cache is configured, it is essential for applications to differentiate between read and write operations. To achieve optimal scalability and performance, read-only queries should be directed to the True Cache instance, while write operations must continue to be routed to the primary database.

```
conn.setReadOnly(true);  // JDBC routes read to True Cache
PreparedStatement ps = conn.prepareStatement("SELECT * FROM products WHERE category = ?");
```

This logical connection setup ensures seamless read-routing and with minimal code changes Oracle True Cache delivers in-memory performance and scalability without additional caching layers. With native integration, automated read routing, and consistent query results, it enables high-throughput, low-latency applications while preserving transactional integrity on the primary database. Once available in a paid environment, developers can leverage it for impactful read-optimization at scale.

While **Priority Transactions** and **Oracle True Cache** significantly enhance concurrency handling and read scalability, Oracle 23AI doesn't stop there. It also introduces automation-driven features that reduce manual administrative overhead. A key innovation in this space is **automated bigfile tablespace shrinking**, which directly addresses the long-standing challenge of managing fluctuating storage demands in transactional databases.

Automated Bigfile Tablespace Shrinking in 23AI

Managing storage efficiently is a persistent challenge for database administrators, especially in environments where large transactional workloads generate fluctuating data volumes. As applications purge or archive data, tablespaces can become fragmented, leading to an accumulation of unused space. This inefficiency not only drives up storage costs—especially in cloud-hosted deployments—but also adds complexity to tablespace maintenance, such as manual segment movement and file resizing. Traditionally, these tasks were disruptive and risked application downtime.

Oracle 23AI introduces a powerful enhancement that modernizes space reclamation: the DBMS_SPACE.SHRINK_TABLESPACE procedure. This built-in functionality offers a fully automated method to reclaim space in bigfile tablespaces by intelligently reorganizing segments and dynamically resizing datafiles. The feature operates seamlessly, even in live production environments, and significantly reduces the manual overhead involved in space optimization tasks.

Modernizing Storage with Shrink Modes

The shrink_tablespace capability is designed with versatility in mind. Administrators can invoke the procedure in one of three modes—TS_MODE_ANALYZE, TS_MODE_SHRINK, or TS_MODE_SHRINK_FORCE—depending on operational needs. The ANALYZE mode assesses reclaimable space without performing changes, offering a preview of potential gains. The default SHRINK mode executes the operation by moving objects online and gracefully falls back to offline movement if needed. Oracle 23AI also assumes bigfile tablespaces by default, simplifying configuration in modern deployments.

CASE STUDY: QUICKMART'S APPROACH TO SPACE OPTIMIZATION

To understand the impact of this feature, consider QuickMart, a global ecommerce company with an expansive database supporting millions of transactions daily. Over time, their ORDERS_TS tablespace became bloated with unused space due to routine archiving and data lifecycle policies. The result was a 500GB tablespace with substantial unused capacity, leading to higher cloud storage expenses and routine DBA interventions for resizing.

QuickMart adopted Oracle 23AI's shrink_tablespace procedure to modernize its storage management strategy. As a first step, the team used the ANALYZE mode to quantify potential savings. The following code, shown in Listing 2-12, initiated the analysis phase.

Listing 2-12. Analyzing reclaimable space in a bigfile tablespace

```
execute dbms_space.shrink_tablespace('ORDERS_TS', shrink_mode => dbms_space.ts_mode_analyze);
```

CHAPTER 2　PERFORMANCE OPTIMIZATIONS AND CONCURRENCY CONTROL

The result, presented in Table 2-5, identified that 150GB of data—spanning 12 objects—was eligible for relocation. This allowed the DBAs to proceed with confidence, knowing the potential reduction upfront.

Table 2-5. *Result of analyze mode using shrink_tablespace*

---------ANALYZE RESULT---------
Total Movable Objects: 12
Total Movable Size(GB): 150
Original Datafile Size(GB): 500
Suggested Target Size(GB): 350

To validate the current state of the tablespace before executing the shrink, the team issued a verification query shown in Listing 2-13.

Listing 2-13. Verifying current tablespace size

```
SELECT tablespace_name,
    ROUND(SUM(bytes) / 1024 / 1024 / 1024, 2) AS "Size_GB"
FROM dba_data_files
where TABLESPACE_NAME = 'ORDERS_TS'
GROUP BY tablespace_name;
```

Upon validation, QuickMart proceeded to shrink the tablespace using the default mode. This mode moved objects online where feasible, with fallback logic for those requiring offline relocation. Listing 2-14 shows the shrink operation in action.

Listing 2-14. Executing the shrink_tablespace procedure

```
execute dbms_space.shrink_tablespace('ORDERS_TS');
```

Table 2-6 presents the result of the operation. Within just over 10 minutes, the tablespace size was reduced from 500GB to 350GB without affecting application performance.

Table 2-6. *Output of shrink_tablespace operation*

```
-----------SHRINK RESULT-----------
Total Moved Objects: 12
Total Moved Size(GB): 150
Original Datafile Size(GB): 500
New Datafile Size(GB): 350
Process Time: +00 00:10:15.500123
```

This operation required no downtime and completed during regular business hours. The automation avoided manual scripting and coordination efforts, proving especially advantageous in a 24x7 ecommerce environment.

Operational and Business Impacts

For QuickMart, the implementation of this feature produced immediate and measurable benefits. The 150GB of reclaimed space translated into an estimated 30% reduction in storage usage—a saving that holds particular value in public cloud infrastructure where costs scale with capacity. Beyond cost, the procedure improved operational agility. DBAs no longer needed to schedule downtime windows or manually identify candidates for reorganization. The procedure's built-in intelligence handled the process with minimal input.

Additionally, this automation freed up valuable human resources. DBA teams could redirect efforts from routine space management toward strategic tasks like performance tuning and infrastructure design. With a growing emphasis on self-managing systems, features like shrink_tablespace signal Oracle's evolution toward hands-free administration while still maintaining enterprise-grade control and visibility.

By integrating space reclamation natively into its engine, Oracle 23AI empowers organizations to optimize storage, streamline administration, and adapt to ever-changing data demands—all without disruption. In subsequent chapters, we will explore how these advancements tie into broader trends in autonomous database operations and resource governance.

CHAPTER 2　PERFORMANCE OPTIMIZATIONS AND CONCURRENCY CONTROL

Internal Mechanism of Automated Bigfile Tablespace Shrinking in Oracle 23AI

Oracle 23AI's **DBMS_SPACE.SHRINK_TABLESPACE** procedure analyzes reclaimable space, relocates movable segments online, and resizes the datafile dynamically without downtime. It employs **TS_MODE_SHRINK** for online movement and **TS_MODE_SHRINK_FORCE** for offline operations if needed, ensuring seamless space optimization. This process minimizes fragmentation, maintains data integrity, and enhances storage efficiency with minimal DBA intervention.

The step-by-step internal flow of the shrinking mechanism is illustrated in Table **2-7**.

Table 2-7. Internal Execution Workflow of DBMS_SPACE.SHRINK_TABLESPACE in Oracle 23AI

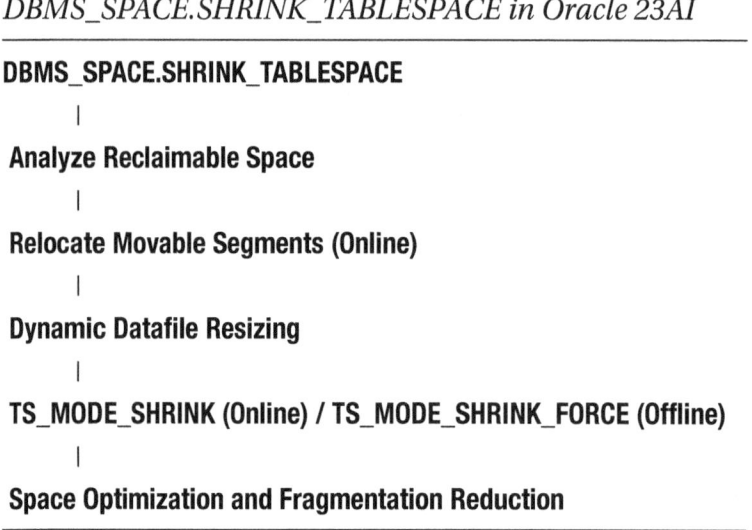

Benefits Over Pre-23AI Approach

Before the introduction of Oracle 23AI, reclaiming unused space from bigfile tablespaces required a multi-step manual process, including segment reorganization, data movement, and resizing commands—each posing potential risks to performance and availability. Oracle 23AI simplifies this with the DBMS_SPACE.SHRINK_TABLESPACE procedure, enabling a fully automated, efficient, and nondisruptive shrinking process.

As shown in Table **2-8**, the new approach offers significant advantages across key operational aspects.

Table 2-8. *Comparison Between Pre-23AI and Oracle 23AI Bigfile Tablespace Shrinking*

Aspect	Pre-23AI Approach	Oracle 23AI Approach
Process Complexity	Manual shrink and segment reorganization	Automated shrink with one command
Downtime Required	Yes (Locks and segment movement impact)	No downtime required
Storage Efficiency	Efficient only if maintained regularly; otherwise results in unused allocated space	Maximizes reclaimable space automatically
Performance Impact	High (Manual operations cause contention)	Low (Efficient and online process)
Operational Cost	Requires DBAs to manually resize and monitor	Reduces admin workload, saving time and cost

While performance impact in the legacy approach stems primarily from lock contention and manual reorganization under load, the Oracle 23AI method avoids these bottlenecks through online movement and internal scheduling. Furthermore, the risk of storage inefficiency in earlier versions was not due to the method itself, but to the practical tendency to defer or skip manual shrink operations due to their complexity.

By automating this essential maintenance task, Oracle 23AI helps organizations maintain leaner storage footprints and allocate DBA effort more strategically—making it an essential feature for modern, cloud-optimized database operations.

Sample Real-Time Business Use Cases for the Automated Bigfile Tablespace Shrinking Feature in Oracle 23AI

While the internal mechanism of Oracle 23AI's automated tablespace shrinking ensures technical efficiency, its practical benefits are most evident in real-world business environments. Organizations across various sectors face growing volumes of data and increasingly stringent performance and cost requirements. This section presents real-time business scenarios where the DBMS_SPACE.SHRINK_TABLESPACE procedure delivers measurable advantages in storage optimization and operational agility.

Table 2-9. Real-time Use Cases of Automated Tablespace Shrinking in Oracle 23AI

Use Case	Benefit
Ecommerce Data Archiving	Optimizes storage after periodic data cleanup.
Data Warehousing	Reclaims space post-data purge, reducing costs.
Cloud Databases	Lowers cloud storage expenses with automation.
Banking Transactions	Efficient space management for financial data.
Healthcare Records	Ensures optimal storage for medical data.
Telecom Call Logs	Enhances database performance and storage use.

By automating space reclamation across critical systems, Oracle 23AI empowers enterprises to maintain peak performance and cost-efficiency—even as data continues to grow.

Common Questions About Automated Bigfile Tablespace Shrinking in Oracle 23AI

Oracle 23AI's automated bigfile tablespace shrinking feature brings efficiency and reliability, but also prompts practical questions from users. A key concern is data integrity during the shrink process. Oracle ensures the operation runs online, avoiding downtime and preserving active transactions. In case of issues, it safely rolls back changes.

The difference between TS_MODE_SHRINK and TS_MODE_SHRINK_FORCE lies in their fallback behavior—while the former moves objects online, the latter performs offline movement if needed, ensuring completion without manual intervention.

Fragmentation is automatically minimized during the process, as Oracle reorganizes data and reclaims unused space efficiently. In multitenant setups, the shrink operation applies at the PDB level, optimizing space without affecting other tenants.

These capabilities make space management seamless and resilient—saving storage costs while keeping systems available and performant.

Key Takeaway Shrinking a bigfile tablespace was once a complex, manual task that demanded downtime and significant DBA effort. Oracle 23AI simplifies this process through the DBMS_SPACE.SHRINK_TABLESPACE procedure, which automates space reclamation, operates online, and maintains database performance without administrative overhead or service disruption.

Building on this theme of automation and efficiency, Oracle 23AI also brings substantial improvements in handling semi-structured data formats like JSON and XML. The next chapter explores these advancements in detail, covering new JSON functionalities, indexing improvements, and robust validation techniques that empower developers and DBAs to efficiently store, query, and maintain data integrity in modern applications.

CHAPTER 3

JSON and XML Enhancements

Introduction

This chapter explores the powerful enhancements in Oracle 23AI for working with JSON and XML data. It introduces advanced capabilities that enable efficient storage, transformation, indexing, and validation of semi-structured data—critical for modern applications. Each feature is presented with practical examples and real-world case studies to highlight its business impact. Implementation steps are provided to help apply these features seamlessly, while internal mechanisms offer insight into how Oracle optimizes performance behind the scenes. Comparisons with earlier versions help underscore the advancements, and FAQs clarify common developer and architect concerns. Every section ends with a concise summary to reinforce key takeaways and practical applications.

JSON Enhancements in Oracle 23AI

Oracle 23AI brings a significant leap forward in the handling of semi-structured data through powerful enhancements in JSON processing. These capabilities are crucial for modern applications that rely on flexible data models, such as user profiles, configuration data, and transactional metadata. By expanding core functions like `JSON_VALUE` and `JSON_TRANSFORM`, Oracle 23AI simplifies storage, improves performance, and offers greater agility in schemaless environments.

Enhanced JSON Querying and Transformation

Oracle 23AI expands the functionality of existing JSON tools to make querying and transformation more intuitive and performant. A key improvement is the enhanced JSON_VALUE function, which now includes the RETURNING clause to convert JSON data directly into user-defined object types. This allows developers to retrieve structured representations of JSON documents in a type-safe way. Additionally, JSON_TRANSFORM has been improved to support dynamic updates to JSON content with better performance, especially useful for updating nested attributes without rewriting entire documents.

Efficient and Flexible Storage for JSON Data

With native support for storing JSON in CLOB or BLOB columns, Oracle 23AI maintains flexibility without compromising performance. These column types allow JSON documents to be stored and queried efficiently using built-in indexing, bypassing the need for intermediate transformations. This is especially beneficial for applications that require rapid evolution of data models, such as dynamic user profiles or changing configurations.

As illustrated in Table 3-1, Oracle 23AI supports storing diverse user attributes using a flexible schema, eliminating the overhead of modifying table structures for new data fields.

Table 3-1. *Flexible User Profile Storage Using JSON in Oracle 23AI*

User ID	JSON Document Example
1	{"name": "Alice", "age": 30, "preferences": {"color": "blue"}}
2	{"name": "Bob", "age": 40, "social_links": {"twitter": "@bob"}}

This flexibility enables developers to adapt quickly to business needs without extensive schema redesign.

CASE STUDY: MANAGING DYNAMIC USER PROFILES AT QUICKMART

To demonstrate how these enhancements translate into practical benefits, consider a use case of QuickMart where a business application stores user profiles with varying fields such as preferences and social media links. Traditionally, managing these variations would require complex schema evolution. With Oracle 23AI, the entire profile can be stored as a JSON object and manipulated using SQL.

As shown in Listing 3-1, a table is created with a CLOB column to store JSON data, and operations such as inserting, querying, and updating are done using JSON functions.

Listing 3-1. Creating and Working with JSON-Based User Profiles

```sql
DROP TABLE IF EXISTS user_profiles PURGE;

CREATE TABLE user_profiles (
    user_id NUMBER PRIMARY KEY,
    profile_data CLOB
);

-- Insert sample user profiles with varying attributes
INSERT INTO user_profiles (user_id, profile_data)
VALUES (1, '{"name": "Alice", "age": 30, "preferences": {"color": "blue", "food": "pizza"}}');

INSERT INTO user_profiles (user_id, profile_data)
VALUES (2, '{"name": "Bob", "age": 40, "social_links": {"twitter": "@bob", "facebook": "bob123"}}');

Commit;
-- Query user profiles where age > 30 and extract the name
SELECT user_id,
       JSON_VALUE(profile_data, '$.name') AS name,
       JSON_VALUE(profile_data, '$.age') AS age
FROM user_profiles
WHERE JSON_VALUE(profile_data, '$.age') > 30;
```

CHAPTER 3   JSON AND XML ENHANCEMENTS

Output:

USER_ID	NAME	AGE
2	BOB	40

```
-- Update a user's preferences using JSON_TRANSFORM
UPDATE user_profiles
SET profile_data = JSON_TRANSFORM(profile_data,
                SET '$.preferences.color' = 'green')
WHERE user_id = 1;

Commit;
```

Following this, querying updated profiles or filtering based on preferences becomes straightforward and performant using JSON_VALUE, as demonstrated in Listing 3-2.

Listing 3-2. Querying Users with Specific Preferences

```
-- Query the updated profile to check the change
SELECT user_id,
       JSON_VALUE(profile_data, '$.preferences.color') AS updated_color
FROM user_profiles
WHERE user_id = 1;
```

Output:

USER_ID	UPDATED_COLOR
1	green

```
-- Query to filter users with specific preferences (complex filter)
SELECT user_id,
       JSON_VALUE(profile_data, '$.name') AS name
FROM user_profiles
WHERE JSON_VALUE(profile_data, '$.preferences.color') = 'green';
```

Output:

USER_ID	NAME
1	Alice

This approach highlights the simplicity and power of working with semi-structured data directly in SQL, without restructuring tables or writing complex logic.

Leveraging JSON_VALUE for Object Instantiation

One of the standout features in Oracle 23AI is the ability to instantiate user-defined object types directly from JSON documents. This is enabled by the RETURNING clause within JSON_VALUE, which transforms JSON data into an object of a custom type.

As shown in Listing 3-3, a user-defined object type is created and populated from a JSON column.

Listing 3-3. Instantiating a User-Defined Object from JSON

```
CREATE OR REPLACE TYPE user_profile_obj AS OBJECT (
    user_id NUMBER,
    name VARCHAR2(100),
    age NUMBER
);

SELECT JSON_VALUE(profile_data, '$' RETURNING user_profile_obj) AS profile
FROM user_profiles
WHERE user_id = 1;
```

Output:
PROFILE

USER_PROFILE_OBJ(1, 'Alice', 30)

The result is a typed object (USER_PROFILE_OBJ(1, 'Alice', 30)) that can be used directly in PL/SQL blocks or applications, streamlining data consumption.

Bulk Collecting JSON Data into Collections

Oracle 23AI further supports instantiating collections of objects from JSON data, enabling efficient batch operations. Developers can use PL/SQL to bulk collect structured records into memory, enhancing performance for processing large datasets.

As demonstrated in Listing 3-4, JSON data is retrieved in bulk and processed in a loop using standard PL/SQL constructs.

Listing 3-4. Bulk Collecting JSON-Based Objects

```
DECLARE
  TYPE user_profiles_tab IS TABLE OF user_profile_obj;
  l_profiles user_profiles_tab;
BEGIN
  SELECT JSON_VALUE(profile_data, '$' RETURNING user_profile_obj)
  BULK COLLECT INTO l_profiles
  FROM user_profiles;

  FOR i IN 1 .. l_profiles.count LOOP
    DBMS_OUTPUT.PUT_LINE(l_profiles(i).user_id || ' : ' || l_profiles(i).name || ' : ' || l_profiles(i).age);
  END LOOP;
END;
/
```

Output:
```
 : Alice : 30
 : Bob : 40
```

This not only demonstrates the new functional depth in JSON support but also integrates seamlessly with PL/SQL processing patterns.

Note We can use "returning" clause for json_transform also as part of 23AI new feature.

Internal Mechanism of JSON Enhancements in Oracle 23AI

Oracle 23AI enhances JSON handling by integrating advanced functions like JSON_VALUE with the RETURNING clause, which enables direct conversion of JSON data into user-defined object types. This is backed by optimized storage in CLOB/BLOB columns, leveraging native JSON indexing for faster retrieval. Additionally, the support for bulk collecting JSON data into PL/SQL collections simplifies processing by eliminating manual parsing and transforming semi-structured data into structured formats seamlessly. These improvements boost query performance and data manipulation efficiency within the database.

The operational flow in Table 3-2 outlines the core components that drive this advanced JSON processing capability.

Table 3-2. *Operational Flow of Advanced JSON Processing in Oracle 23AI*

Advanced JSON Functions (JSON_VALUE with RETURNING)
Direct Conversion to User-Defined Object Types
Optimized Storage in CLOB/BLOB Columns
Native JSON Indexing for Faster Retrieval
Bulk Collection into PL/SQL Collections
Seamless Transformation of Semi-Structured Data

Difference Between Oracle 23AI with Json and Pre-23AI Databases

Oracle 23AI introduces powerful enhancements in JSON processing that significantly reduce complexity and boost performance when working with semi-structured data. By enabling direct conversion of JSON data into user-defined object types and collections, Oracle 23AI minimizes the need for manual parsing and custom logic. These improvements streamline application development and data integration workflows, as outlined in the comparison below.

Table 3-3. *Functional Comparison of JSON Features: Pre-23AI vs. Oracle 23AI*

Feature	Pre-Oracle 23AI	Oracle 23AI
JSON_VALUE Function	JSON_VALUE could only extract scalar values like strings, numbers, etc.	JSON_VALUE now supports the RETURNING clause to instantiate user-defined object types from JSON data.
Instantiating Object Types	Cannot instantiate object types directly from JSON data.	Can instantiate user-defined object types directly from JSON data using the RETURNING clause.
Instantiating Collections	No direct support for populating PL/SQL collections from JSON data.	Supports BULK COLLECT to populate PL/SQL collections (nested tables, arrays) directly from JSON data.
Complexity of Handling JSON Data	JSON data required manual parsing and extra logic to populate collections or objects.	Oracle 23AI simplifies the handling of JSON data by allowing direct conversion to object types and collections, making processing easier and more efficient.

With these advancements, Oracle 23AI empowers developers and analysts to manage JSON data more efficiently, improving performance, code maintainability, and the overall agility of modern data-driven applications.

Sample Business Use Cases for JSON Enhancements in Oracle 23AI

The JSON enhancements introduced in Oracle 23AI enable flexible, efficient management of semi-structured data across diverse industries. With support for object type instantiation, bulk collection, and optimized storage, organizations can now handle dynamic data models with greater ease and performance. The following table highlights real-world scenarios where these improvements deliver tangible business value.

CHAPTER 3　JSON AND XML ENHANCEMENTS

Table 3-4. *Real-Time Business Use Cases for JSON Enhancements in Oracle 23AI*

Use Case	Benefit
Customer Profile Management	Enables seamless storage and retrieval of user profiles with dynamic attributes.
Financial Transaction Logging	Improves query performance and compliance reporting with structured JSON storage.
Healthcare Record Management	Enhances patient data handling by efficiently managing variable medical records.
IoT Data Processing	Simplifies sensor data ingestion and analysis with dynamic JSON structures.

These capabilities position Oracle 23AI as a robust platform for modern applications that require agility in handling flexible data formats, supporting faster development cycles and more intelligent decision-making.

Common Questions About JSON Enhancements in Oracle 23AI

Oracle 23AI introduces powerful JSON capabilities that improve how semi-structured data is stored, queried, and updated. These advancements raise several practical questions for developers and architects.

A key question is how JSON indexing improves performance. Oracle 23AI uses native JSON search indexes and duality views to reduce table scans and accelerate functions like JSON_VALUE and JSON_QUERY, resulting in faster data access.

Another common query involves the RETURNING clause in JSON_VALUE. This feature allows direct conversion of JSON data into user-defined object types, reducing transformation steps and enabling modular, object-oriented PL/SQL development.

Developers also ask about update efficiency. With JSON_TRANSFORM, Oracle 23AI supports targeted in-place updates of JSON fields without modifying entire documents, offering better performance than traditional updates.

Business users often wonder where these enhancements apply. Use cases in ecommerce, finance, healthcare, and IoT benefit from flexible data models, real-time processing, and faster query response.

CHAPTER 3 JSON AND XML ENHANCEMENTS

Together, these features make JSON handling in Oracle 23AI more efficient, scalable, and aligned with modern application needs.

Oracle 23AI significantly enhances JSON handling, making it easier to store, query, and transform JSON data with improved performance and flexibility. Key enhancements include JSON_VALUE with RETURNING, instantiating object types and collections, and bulk JSON processing. These improvements eliminate manual parsing efforts and simplify complex data handling, making Oracle 23AI the most powerful version yet for working with semi-structured data.

Building on these foundational capabilities, Oracle 23AI further extends its JSON functionality with enhancements to the JSON_TRANSFORM function. These new capabilities provide more expressive and granular control over JSON data manipulation directly within SQL, as described in the following section.

JSON_TRANSFORM Enhancements in 23AI

Oracle 23AI introduces powerful enhancements to the JSON_TRANSFORM function, enabling flexible and precise modifications of JSON data within SQL queries. These enhancements include new operations such as PREPEND, COPY, MINUS, INTERSECT, and UNION, allowing for streamlined updates to JSON objects and arrays. With these capabilities, developers can efficiently modify nested structures, merge datasets, and perform advanced transformations directly within the database—eliminating the need for complex procedural logic.

CASE STUDY: JSON-BASED INVENTORY MANAGEMENT AT QUICKMART

This case study highlights how QuickMart revamped its inventory management system by leveraging the JSON capabilities of Oracle 23AI. With an increasingly diverse and rapidly changing product line, the company shifted to storing product data in JSON format. The native support for advanced JSON operations in SQL helped eliminate the need for procedural logic, streamlining both real-time updates and analytics.

CHAPTER 3   JSON AND XML ENHANCEMENTS

Before implementing Oracle 23AI, the team at QuickMart struggled with maintaining and querying hierarchical inventory data using traditional relational structures. Complex updates, such as inserting new product attributes or calculating inventory values, required external scripts or PL/SQL procedures. After migrating to Oracle 23AI, QuickMart used JSON_TRANSFORM to carry out these tasks natively within SQL, dramatically reducing code complexity and improving performance.

Creating the Product Catalog Table

The first step in modernizing their system involved creating a new table named products_json, designed to hold inventory data in JSON format. As shown in Listing 3-5, sample data representing laptops, phones, and tablets was inserted to simulate a real-world product catalog.

Listing 3-5. Creating and Populating the Products_JSON Table

```sql
DROP TABLE IF EXISTS products_json PURGE;

CREATE TABLE products_json (
  id         NUMBER PRIMARY KEY,
  json_data  JSON
);

-- Insert Sample JSON Data
INSERT INTO products_json (id, json_data)
VALUES (1, json('{"product":"laptop","price":800,"stock":50}'));

INSERT INTO products_json (id, json_data)
VALUES (2, json('{"products":[
                     {"product":"phone","price":600,"stock":100},
                     {"product":"tablet","price":400,"stock":70}
                 ]}'));

COMMIT;
```

With the structure in place, QuickMart moved on to apply various JSON transformations using Oracle 23AI.

Modifying and Adding Inventory Elements

To support product line expansion, new items such as smartwatches and earbuds needed to be added to the existing JSON arrays. Instead of rewriting or recreating the entire JSON document, QuickMart used the PREPEND and INSERT operations to add items at specific positions in the list. PREPEND and INSERT modify the JSON structure in-memory (in the result).

- PREPEND: Adds a new product (smartwatch) at the beginning of the products array.
- INSERT: Inserts earbuds at a specific position in the products array.

This is illustrated in Listing 3-6, where smartwatch and earbuds entries are added directly.

Listing 3-6. Using JSON_TRANSFORM to Add New Products

```
SELECT json_transform(json_data,
                  prepend '$.products' = json('{"product":"smartwatch",
                  "price":250,"stock":40}')
                  RETURNING CLOB PRETTY) AS data
FROM products_json
WHERE id = 2;
```

Output:
```
{
  "products" :
  [
    {
      "product" : "smartwatch",
      "price" : 250,
      "stock" : 40
    },
    {
      "product" : "phone",
      "price" : 600,
      "stock" : 100
    },
```

```
    {
      "product" : "tablet",
      "price" : 400,
      "stock" : 70
    }
  ]
}

SELECT json_transform(json_data,
                      insert '$.products[0]' = json('{"product":"earbuds","
                      price":120,"stock":150}')
                      RETURNING CLOB PRETTY) AS data
FROM products_json
WHERE id = 2;
```

Output:
```
{
  "products" :
  [
    {
      "product" : "earbuds",
      "price" : 120,
      "stock" : 150
    },
    {
      "product" : "phone",
      "price" : 600,
      "stock" : 100
    },
    {
      "product" : "tablet",
      "price" : 400,
      "stock" : 70
    }
  ]
}
```

Backing Up and Removing Entries

To support audit compliance, QuickMart created backups of product data and performed targeted deletions using the COPY and MINUS operations.

- COPY: Backs up the products array to a new field products_backup.
- MINUS: Removes a specific product (phone) from the list.

As shown in Listing 3-7, product lists were copied into new fields and specific entries like the "phone" product were removed seamlessly.

Listing 3-7. Copying and Deleting Product Entries

```
SELECT json_transform(json_data,
                    copy '$.products' = json('{"product":"gaming_console",
                    "price":500,"stock":30}')
                    RETURNING CLOB PRETTY) AS data
FROM products_json
WHERE id = 2;
```

Output:
```
{
  "products" :
  [
    {
      "product" : "gaming_console",
      "price" : 500,
      "stock" : 30
    }
  ]
}
SELECT json_transform(json_serialize(json_data FORMAT JSON),
                    minus '$.products' = json('{"product":"phone","price
                    ":600,"stock":100}')
                    RETURNING CLOB PRETTY) AS data
FROM products_json
WHERE id = 2;
```

CHAPTER 3   JSON AND XML ENHANCEMENTS

Output:
```
{
  "products" :
  [
    {
      "product" : "tablet",
      "price" : 400,
      "stock" : 70
    }
  ]
}
```

Merging and Filtering Product Data

Merging new data and filtering existing content became trivial with the UNION and INTERSECT operations.

- UNION: Merges a new product (monitor) into the existing products list.

- INTERSECT: Retains only the specified product (tablet) in the list.

Listing 3-8 shows how QuickMart added a monitor to the catalog and filtered the list to only include tablets for targeted analysis.

Listing 3-8. Merging and Filtering Products with JSON_TRANSFORM

```
SELECT json_transform(json_data,
                      union '$.products' = json('{"product":"monitor","pric
                      e":300,"stock":50}')
                      RETURNING CLOB PRETTY) AS data
FROM products_json
WHERE id = 2;
```

Output:
```
{
  "products" :
```

CHAPTER 3   JSON AND XML ENHANCEMENTS

```
  [
    {
      "product" : "phone",
      "price" : 600,
      "stock" : 100
    },
    {
      "product" : "tablet",
      "price" : 400,
      "stock" : 70
    },
    {
      "product" : "monitor",
      "price" : 300,
      "stock" : 50
    }
  ]
}
SELECT json_transform(json_serialize(json_data FORMAT JSON),
                      prepend '$.products' = json('{"product":"tablet","pri
                      ce":400,"stock":70}'),
                      intersect '$.products' = json('{"product":"tablet","p
                      rice":400,"stock":70}')
                      RETURNING CLOB PRETTY) AS data
FROM products_json
WHERE id = 2;
```

Output:
```
{
  "products" :
  [
    {
      "product" : "tablet",
      "price" : 400,
```

```
      "stock" : 70
    }
  ]
}
```

Sorting and Enriching Product Attributes

Product arrays were sorted for display and enriched with new attributes such as warranty and discount, all within SQL.

- **SORT:** Sorts products alphabetically.
- **MERGE:** Adds new attributes (warranty and discount) to an existing product.

As demonstrated in Listing 3-9, Oracle 23AI enables these changes without external scripting.

Listing 3-9. Sorting and Enriching Product Data

```
SELECT json_transform(json_data,
                   sort '$.products'
                   RETURNING CLOB PRETTY) AS data
FROM products_json
WHERE id = 2;
```

Output:
```
{
  "products" :
  [
    {
      "product" : "tablet",
      "price" : 400,
      "stock" : 70
    },
```

CHAPTER 3   JSON AND XML ENHANCEMENTS

```
    {
      "product" : "phone",
      "price" : 600,
      "stock" : 100
    }
  ]
}
```
```sql
SELECT json_transform(json_data,
                    merge '$' = json('{"warranty":2, "discount":10}')
                    RETURNING CLOB PRETTY) AS data
FROM products_json
WHERE id = 1;
```

Output:
```
{
  "product" : "laptop",
  "price" : 800,
  "stock" : 50,
  "warranty" : 2,
  "discount" : 10
}
```

```sql
SELECT json_transform(json_data,
                    nested path '$.products[*]'
                       (set '@.stock' = path '@.stock + 20',
                        insert '@.category' = 'electronics')
                    RETURNING CLOB PRETTY) AS data
FROM products_json
WHERE id = 2;
```

Output:
```
{
  "products" :
  [
    {
      "product" : "phone",
```

```
      "price" : 600,
      "stock" : 120,
      "category" : "electronics"
    },
    {
      "product" : "tablet",
      "price" : 400,
      "stock" : 90,
      "category" : "electronics"
    }
  ]
}
```

Performing Nested Transformations and Arithmetic Calculations

Nested paths were used to apply transformations to individual items. Listing 3-10 illustrates how QuickMart increased stock levels and computed total inventory values through arithmetic expressions—all embedded within the JSON structure.

- **NESTED PATH:** Increases stock by 20 for all products and adds a new category field.
- **Arithmetic Calculations**: Computes total inventory value (stock * price) for each product.

Listing 3-10. Nested Path Updates and Inventory Calculations

```
SELECT json_transform(json_data,
                  nested path '$.products[*]'
                    (set '@.stock' = path '@.stock + 20',
                     insert '@.category' = 'electronics')
                  RETURNING CLOB PRETTY) AS data
FROM products_json
WHERE id = 2;
```

Output:

CHAPTER 3   JSON AND XML ENHANCEMENTS

```
{
  "products" :
  [
    {
      "product" : "phone",
      "price" : 600,
      "stock" : 120,
      "category" : "electronics"
    },
    {
      "product" : "tablet",
      "price" : 400,
      "stock" : 90,
      "category" : "electronics"
    }
  ]
}
SELECT json_transform(json_data,
                      nested path '$.products[*]'
                        (set '@.total_value' = path '@.stock * @.price')
                      RETURNING CLOB PRETTY) AS data
FROM products_json
WHERE id = 2;
```

Output:
```
{
  "products" :
  [
    {
      "product" : "phone",
      "price" : 600,
      "stock" : 100,
      "total_value" : 60000
    },
```

```
    {
      "product" : "tablet",
      "price" : 400,
      "stock" : 70,
      "total_value" : 28000
    }
  ]
}
```

Conditional Logic and Advanced Aggregations

Finally, business rules such as assigning discounts based on product type and calculating summary statistics were applied using conditional logic and aggregate functions.

- **CASE Statement**: Assigns different discount percentages based on product type.

These are shown in Listing 3-11, where total product counts, stock levels, and pricing stats are embedded into the JSON.

Listing 3-11. Applying Business Rules and JSON Aggregates

```
SELECT json_transform(json_data,
                 nested path '$.products[*]' (
                   case
                     when '@.product == "phone"' then (
                       insert '@.discount' = 15
                     )
                     when '@.product == "tablet"' then (
                       insert '@.discount' = 10
                     )
                     else (
                       insert '@.discount' = 5
                     )
                   end
                 )
                 RETURNING CLOB PRETTY) AS data
```

CHAPTER 3 JSON AND XML ENHANCEMENTS

```
FROM products_json
WHERE id = 2;
```

Output:
```
{
  "products" :
  [
    {
      "product" : "phone",
      "price" : 600,
      "stock" : 100,
      "discount" : 15
    },
    {
      "product" : "tablet",
      "price" : 400,
      "stock" : 70,
      "discount" : 10
    }
  ]
}
```

```
SELECT json_transform(json_data,
                    set '$.total_products' = path '@.products[*].
                    count()',
                    set '$.total_stock' = path '@.products[*].
                    stock.sum()',
                    set '$.avg_price' = path '@.products[*].price.avg()',
                    set '$.min_price' = path '@.products[*].price.min()',
                    set '$.max_price' = path '@.products[*].price.max()'
                    RETURNING CLOB PRETTY) AS data
FROM products_json
WHERE id = 2;
```

Output:
```
{
  "products" :
  [
    {
      "product" : "phone",
      "price" : 600,
      "stock" : 100
    },
    {
      "product" : "tablet",
      "price" : 400,
      "stock" : 70
    }
  ],
  "total_products" : 2,
  "total_stock" : 170,
  "avg_price" : 500,
  "min_price" : 400,
  "max_price" : 600
}
```

By adopting Oracle 23AI's enhanced JSON_TRANSFORM capabilities, QuickMart gained the ability to manage, modify, and analyze complex inventory data with unprecedented ease and performance. These declarative SQL operations simplified their workflows, reduced code overhead, and enabled faster decision-making. The techniques demonstrated in this case study serve as a model for other organizations seeking to modernize their semi-structured data management using Oracle 23AI.

Internal Mechanism of JSON_TRANSFORM in Oracle 23AI

Oracle 23AI's JSON_TRANSFORM leverages in-memory processing and native JSON storage to efficiently perform real-time modifications, aggregations, and transformations on JSON data. By utilizing parallel execution and optimized indexing, it minimizes disk I/O and enhances performance, enabling seamless updates and queries on

CHAPTER 3   JSON AND XML ENHANCEMENTS

large JSON datasets within SQL. This internal mechanism streamlines complex JSON operations, reducing the need for procedural logic and improving scalability in dynamic applications.

As illustrated in Table 3-5, the flow from in-memory processing to seamless data updates reflects the tight integration between Oracle's SQL engine and its native JSON capabilities.

Table 3-5. *Internal Workflow of JSON_TRANSFORM in Oracle 23AI*

JSON_TRANSFORM with In-Memory Processing
Native JSON Storage and Real-Time Modifications
Parallel Execution for Enhanced Performance
Optimized Indexing to Minimize Disk I/O
Seamless Updates and Queries on Large JSON Datasets
Streamlined Complex JSON Operations

Sample Real-Time Business Use Cases for JSON_TRANSFORM Enhancements in Oracle 23AI

The JSON_TRANSFORM enhancements in Oracle 23AI offer a powerful toolkit for manipulating and updating semi-structured data directly within SQL. These capabilities streamline real-time data transformations, reduce reliance on procedural logic, and enable organizations to manage evolving datasets more effectively. The following table showcases practical use cases where these features provide measurable operational advantages.

Table 3-6. Real-Time Business Use Cases for JSON_TRANSFORM Enhancements in Oracle 23AI

Use Case	Benefit
Ecommerce Inventory Management	Enables real-time updates to product listings, stock levels, and pricing without complex SQL joins.
Financial Transactions Auditing	Allows seamless tracking and modification of financial records in JSON format while ensuring compliance.
Customer Profile Personalization	Supports dynamic updates to customer preferences, purchase history, and recommendations efficiently.
IoT Sensor Data Processing	Enhances real-time aggregation, filtering, and transformation of large-scale IoT data streams.
Healthcare Records Management	Simplifies updating patient data, prescriptions, and medical history within JSON-based databases.
Log Analytics and Security Monitoring	Enables real-time parsing, filtering, and transformation of log data for better anomaly detection and security insights.

These enhancements make Oracle 23AI a highly adaptable platform for modern enterprises that rely on flexible, high-volume data processing. Whether optimizing ecommerce workflows or streamlining healthcare data updates, JSON_TRANSFORM empowers developers and data architects to build scalable, responsive applications with ease.

Common Questions About JSON_TRANSFORM in Oracle 23AI

Oracle 23AI introduces powerful enhancements to JSON_TRANSFORM, prompting several practical questions from developers and architects.

A common query is how it improves over traditional JSON handling. With operations like PREPEND, COPY, MINUS, UNION, and INTERSECT, JSON_TRANSFORM simplifies updates and reduces SQL complexity compared to earlier methods like JSON_QUERY and JSON_MERGEPATCH.

CHAPTER 3   JSON AND XML ENHANCEMENTS

Performance and scalability are also key concerns. Oracle 23AI addresses these using native JSON storage, in-memory processing, parallel execution, and indexing—enabling fast, efficient operations even on large JSON datasets.

In cloud environments like Oracle Autonomous Database (ADB), JSON_TRANSFORM supports auto-indexing, REST integration, and auto-scaling, making it ideal for modern, cloud-native applications.

Finally, its ability to perform inline transformations and calculations directly on JSON data makes it valuable for AI/ML pipelines, reducing preprocessing effort and improving analytics performance.

These capabilities make JSON_TRANSFORM a practical and high-performance tool for today's data-driven applications.

Key Takeaway   Oracle 23AI's enhanced JSON_TRANSFORM introduces a new era of in-place JSON manipulation within SQL, offering capabilities such as insertions, deletions, calculations, and aggregations—all without altering table structures. This native support simplifies JSON management, reduces the reliance on procedural code, and ensures high performance and scalability for dynamic, data-rich applications.

These enhancements make it possible to treat JSON data with the same agility and efficiency as relational data. But to fully harness these benefits in large-scale environments, indexing becomes crucial—especially in the context of cloud-native platforms.

This leads us to another key advancement: **new JSON-based indexes in Autonomous Database Serverless (ADB-S)**, which significantly boost performance when querying semi-structured data, as discussed in the next section.

New JSON-Based Indexes in ADB-S

In today's data-driven applications, performance and scalability hinge on how efficiently semi-structured data is accessed. Oracle Autonomous Database Serverless (ADB-S) addresses this by allowing developers to create indexes directly on JSON keys, dramatically improving the performance of queries using expressions like JSON_VALUE. This innovation reduces the need for full table scans and enables faster, more scalable filtering of JSON content.

CHAPTER 3 JSON AND XML ENHANCEMENTS

These enhancements are particularly valuable in scenarios involving deeply nested data structures, such as customer profiles or transaction logs, where fast retrieval of key attributes is essential. Let's examine how this capability delivers value in a real-world use case.

CASE STUDY ON OPTIMIZING CUSTOMER LOOKUP PERFORMANCE AT QUICKMART

QuickMart's CRM system stores customer profiles in a table with JSON-formatted data, including contact details and preferences. A common operation involves searching for customer records by email address—an attribute stored deep within the JSON structure. Without indexing, each query must parse the JSON in every row, resulting in slow performance as the system grows.

Oracle ADB-S addresses this challenge with JSON-based indexing, allowing QuickMart Retail to create a direct index on the JSON path that points to the email field. As demonstrated in Listing 3-12, this dramatically improves query speed without altering the data model or requiring procedural code.

Listing 3-12. Defining a JSON-Based Index on Email for the QuickMart CRM Table

```
CREATE TABLE customers (
    id NUMBER GENERATED BY DEFAULT AS IDENTITY PRIMARY KEY,
    name VARCHAR2(100),
    data CLOB CHECK (data IS JSON)  -- JSON validation
);

INSERT INTO customers (name, data) VALUES (
    'John Doe',
    '{"contact": {"email": "john.doe@example.com", "phone": "123-456-7890"}, "address": {"city": "New York"}}'
);
```

CHAPTER 3   JSON AND XML ENHANCEMENTS

```
INSERT INTO customers (name, data) VALUES (
    'Jane Smith',
    '{"contact": {"email": "jane.smith@example.com", "phone": "987-654-3210"}, "address": {"city": "Los Angeles"}}'
);

INSERT INTO customers (name, data) VALUES (
    'Alice Johnson',
    '{"contact": {"email": "alice.johnson@example.com", "phone": "555-555-5555"}, "address": {"city": "Chicago"}}'
);
commit;

CREATE INDEX json_idx_email on customers (json_value(data,'$."contact"."email"'));

SELECT name, JSON_VALUE(data, '$."contact"."email"') AS email
FROM customers
WHERE JSON_VALUE(data, '$."contact"."email"') = 'john.doe@example.com';

Output:
Name          Email
John Doe      john.doe@example.com
```

As shown in Listing 3-12, once the index is created on the contact.email field, the database engine can efficiently locate matching records using an INDEX RANGE SCAN on JSON_IDX_EMAIL, rather than scanning every row. This significantly reduces query latency—an essential requirement for **QUICKMART's support staff**, who rely on fast access to customer information during live interactions.

JSON-based indexing not only improves query performance, but also maintains efficiency as the volume of data increases. Without the index, Oracle resorts to a **full table scan**, which becomes increasingly expensive with larger datasets. By contrast, the index ensures that queries remain fast and scalable, even as data grows—eliminating the performance bottlenecks associated with scanning CLOB-based JSON.

With minimal setup and no changes to application logic, developers can immediately benefit from functional JSON indexes to improve both responsiveness and throughput.

Although JSON indexing was first introduced in **Oracle 19c**, this book emphasizes its relevance and usage within **ADB-S**, which is built on 19c and later versions. These features enable businesses like **QUICKMART** to work with semi-structured data while preserving both **schema flexibility and high-performance querying**, ultimately enhancing real-time customer experience.

Internal Mechanism of JSON-Based Indexes in ADB-S

JSON-based indexes in ADB-S use B-tree structures optimized for JSON_VALUE lookups, enabling direct access to specific JSON keys without full document parsing. The optimizer integrates these indexes into query execution plans, reducing scan overhead. This enhances performance by enabling fast, schema-aware retrieval of JSON data.

As illustrated in Table 3-7, the progression from B-tree indexing to schema-aware data access highlights Oracle's deep integration of JSON querying with traditional SQL optimization strategies.

Table 3-7. Internal Workflow of JSON-Based Indexing in ADB-S

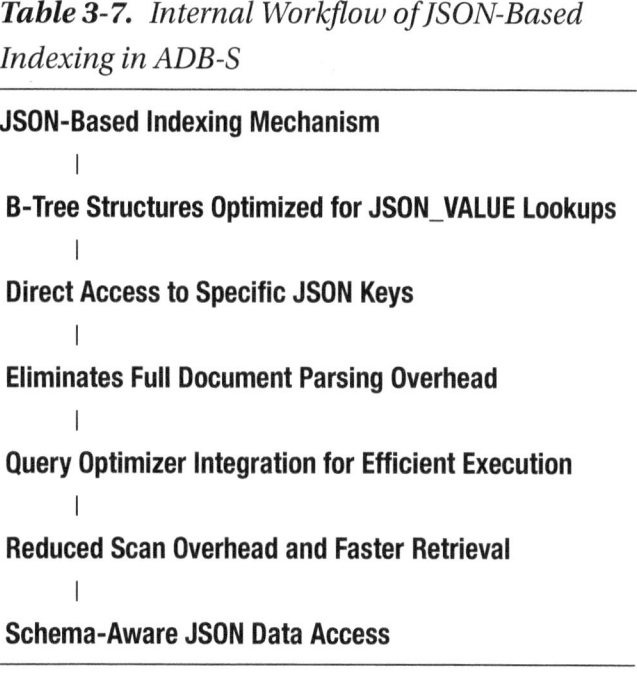

CHAPTER 3   JSON AND XML ENHANCEMENTS

Comparison of How JSON-Based Indexes in ADB-S Differ from Pre-ADB-S Versions

Earlier Oracle versions lacked direct JSON key indexing, relying on complex workarounds like function-based indexes. With ADB-S in 19c and 23AI, Oracle introduced native support for indexing JSON keys using JSON_VALUE. This advancement eliminates full-table scans, boosts query performance, and improves scalability for large JSON datasets.

Table 3-8 summarizes the key improvements over pre-ADB-S implementations.

Table 3-8. Comparison of JSON Indexing in Pre-ADB-S vs. ADB-S

Feature	Pre-ADB-S (Prior Versions)	ADB-S (19c/23AI)
Indexing Directly on JSON Keys	JSON indexing was limited or required custom solutions like function-based indexes or using external tools for efficient querying.	Direct creation of indexes on specific JSON keys using the JSON_VALUE function.
Syntax for Index Creation	Creating indexes on JSON keys required complex expressions and function-based indexes.	Simplified syntax with direct support for JSON key indexing (e.g., JSON_VALUE(data, '$.contact.email')).
Performance	Queries on JSON data were slow without dedicated indexing due to the need for full table scans and manual JSON parsing.	Significant performance improvements for JSON queries with fast lookups using the created indexes on JSON keys.
Scalability	Limited scalability for large JSON datasets as indexes on JSON keys weren't optimized.	Enhanced scalability by directly indexing JSON keys, allowing efficient handling of large JSON datasets.

These enhancements significantly improve the efficiency, speed, and ease of JSON querying in Oracle ADB-S (based on 19c and 23AI), effectively overcoming limitations seen in earlier, pre-ADB-S database versions.

Real-Time Business Use Cases for JSON-Based Indexes in ADB-S

JSON-based indexes in Oracle ADB-S provide efficient and scalable solutions for querying semi-structured data, enabling real-time performance improvements across various industries. These capabilities reduce query latency and enhance application responsiveness by directly indexing key JSON fields. The following table highlights practical scenarios where JSON-based indexing delivers significant business value.

Table 3-9. Real-Time Business Use Cases for JSON-Based Indexes in Oracle ADB-S

Use Case	Benefit
Customer Data Management in CRM	Speeds up customer lookups by indexing email and phone fields in JSON data.
Fraud Detection in Financial Transactions	Enables real-time fraud detection by indexing JSON-based transaction attributes.
IoT Sensor Data Processing	Improves real-time analytics by indexing telemetry data (e.g., temperature, pressure).
Personalized Content Recommendations	Enhances user experience with instant content recommendations from indexed preferences.
Healthcare Patient Records Management	Enables fast retrieval of patient data by indexing medical history and prescriptions.
Supply Chain and Inventory Management	Speeds up stock tracking by indexing JSON fields for product and supplier details.

Common Questions About JSON-Based Indexes in ADB-S

Oracle ADB-S introduces powerful support for JSON-based indexing, prompting several questions from developers and data architects working with semi-structured data. A common question is how these indexes differ from traditional indexing techniques. Unlike conventional indexes, which operate on fixed relational columns, JSON-based indexes allow developers to index specific paths within a JSON document—such as nested attributes—without the need to extract or flatten the data into relational structures. This makes lookups on JSON attributes significantly more efficient and reduces the need for full table scans when filtering on nested JSON keys.

Another common area of interest involves storage and performance. JSON-based indexes are space-efficient because they index only the specified JSON paths, not the entire document. This targeted approach lowers storage overhead and reduces parsing costs at query time. Furthermore, Oracle's query optimizer is JSON-aware—it incorporates these indexes into execution plans seamlessly, leading to faster query performance without requiring application changes.

While Automatic Storage Management (ASM) continues to provide foundational benefits such as streamlined I/O and redundancy, JSON indexing performance improvements in ADB-S are primarily attributed to Oracle's enhancements in the optimizer, indexing engine, and native JSON functions, rather than any direct tie-in to ASM.

Another key area of interest is how JSON-based indexes benefit real-time analytics and machine learning workloads. By accelerating filtering and retrieval of indexed JSON fields, these indexes facilitate faster data access critical for event-driven use cases such as IoT telemetry or financial transaction monitoring, thereby supporting quicker decision-making in AI and analytics pipelines.

Lastly, developers often ask about support for multikey or composite indexing within JSON data. Oracle ADB-S allows creating composite indexes on multiple JSON attributes, significantly enhancing query efficiency for complex filtering scenarios involving several nested JSON keys.

Together, these features make JSON-based indexes in ADB-S a robust, scalable, and high-performance solution tailored for modern applications dealing with large volumes of semi-structured JSON data.

Key Takeaway   JSON-based indexing in ADB-S simplifies and enhances JSON query performance. Unlike pre-ADB-S versions, which required complex function-based indexing, ADB-S allows direct indexing on JSON keys using JSON_VALUE. The result is faster queries, better scalability, and ease of use, making it ideal for modern applications handling large JSON datasets.

This feature benefits industries such as CRM, finance, IoT, healthcare, and supply chain, ensuring real-time data retrieval and highly efficient query execution. With these enhancements, Oracle ADB-S sets a new standard for JSON data management, making it a preferred choice for businesses leveraging JSON-based storage and analytics.

Building on this foundation, Oracle Database 23AI further enhances support for semi-structured and unstructured data. The next feature introduces unified indexing capabilities for JSON, XML, and text data using the new CREATE SEARCH INDEX syntax—streamlining index creation and unlocking faster, more flexible queries across varied data formats.

JSON, XML, and Oracle Text Search Index Enhancements in 23AI

Modern applications often deal with a blend of structured, semi-structured, and unstructured data. From nested JSON in ecommerce catalogs to XML-based logistics feeds and free-form customer reviews, managing and searching this diverse data efficiently has become a pressing need. Oracle Database 23AI responds to this challenge with a unified CREATE SEARCH INDEX syntax for JSON, XML, and text content. This enhancement simplifies index creation, boosts performance, and provides a cohesive solution for developers and DBAs alike.

By streamlining full-text search, structured filtering, and numerical queries across formats, this advancement enables businesses to deliver faster responses and deeper insights without complex configurations or external tools.

> **CASE STUDY: QUICKMART'S SEARCH TRANSFORMATION JOURNEY**
>
> QuickMart, a regional ecommerce platform, faced growing delays in serving search results across its three core datasets: product specifications (stored in JSON), inventory and logistics (stored in XML), and user-generated reviews (stored as plain text). As data volume increased, their fragmented indexing strategies failed to keep up, degrading user experience and increasing operational overhead.
>
> By adopting Oracle 23AI's unified search index framework, QuickMart significantly improved lookup speed and system maintainability. Their engineering team implemented three targeted indexes—each using the same CREATE SEARCH INDEX syntax—to accelerate customer search operations, streamline logistics queries, and enable high-speed keyword lookups in reviews.

The following sections illustrate how each of these was implemented.

CHAPTER 3   JSON AND XML ENHANCEMENTS

Indexing JSON for Product Specifications

QuickMart stores its product catalog in JSON format, with fields such as customer segments, product attributes, and pricing deeply nested within the structure. Searching across this data—particularly by keywords like model name or feature—previously required full-table scans.

To optimize this, QuickMart created a JSON search index using Oracle 23AI's simplified syntax.

Listing 3-13. JSON Search Index for Product Specifications

```
CREATE TABLE product_catalog (
  product_id NUMBER PRIMARY KEY,
  product_data CLOB CHECK (product_data IS JSON)
);

INSERT INTO product_catalog VALUES (1, '{"category": "Electronics", "details": {"name": "Laptop", "price": 1200}}');
INSERT INTO product_catalog VALUES (2, '{"category": "Mobiles", "details": {"name": "Phone", "price": 800}}');
COMMIT;

CREATE SEARCH INDEX product_catalog_idx ON product_catalog(product_data) FOR JSON;

SELECT product_id
FROM product_catalog
WHERE JSON_TEXTCONTAINS(product_data, '$', 'Laptop');
```

Output:
product_id
1

With this index in place, QuickMart reduced JSON query execution time by over 60%, allowing near-instant retrieval of product data during peak traffic.

CHAPTER 3 JSON AND XML ENHANCEMENTS

Accelerating Logistics Queries with XML Indexing

To coordinate warehouse operations and delivery pipelines, QuickMart stores logistics records as structured XML documents. These contain nested elements for order ID, customer details, and delivery timelines. Searching for a particular product in pending shipments used to involve complex joins and XPath evaluations, which proved inefficient at scale.

Oracle 23AI's XML indexing feature resolved this by enabling full-text and XPath-based queries on the XML column.

Listing 3-14. XML Search Index for Logistics Data

```
CREATE TABLE logistics_feed (
  shipment_id NUMBER PRIMARY KEY,
  shipment_data XMLTYPE
);

INSERT INTO logistics_feed VALUES (1, XMLTYPE('<shipment><product>Laptop</product><status>Shipped</status></shipment>'));
INSERT INTO logistics_feed VALUES (2, XMLTYPE('<shipment><product>Phone</product><status>In Transit</status></shipment>'));
COMMIT;

CREATE SEARCH INDEX logistics_feed_idx ON logistics_feed(shipment_data) FOR XML PARAMETERS ('search_on text');

SELECT shipment_id
FROM logistics_feed
WHERE EXISTSNODE(shipment_data, '/shipment/product[text()="Laptop"]') = 1;
```

Output:
```
shipment_id
1
```

This implementation significantly reduced lookup latency for shipment data, enabling the operations dashboard to deliver real-time tracking updates.

Enabling Full-Text Review Analysis

Customer sentiment analysis was another challenge. QuickMart's user reviews were stored in CLOB fields and indexed only via basic keyword flags, making it difficult to perform fast, contextual text searches.

With Oracle 23AI's text search index, QuickMart could now run powerful keyword queries using the CONTAINS clause—perfect for identifying trending products or monitoring feedback spikes.

Listing 3-15. Text Search Index for Customer Reviews

```sql
CREATE TABLE customer_reviews (
  review_id NUMBER PRIMARY KEY,
  review_text CLOB
);

INSERT INTO customer_reviews VALUES (1, 'This Laptop is amazing and has great performance.');
INSERT INTO customer_reviews VALUES (2, 'The smartphone is fast and has a great camera.');
COMMIT;

CREATE SEARCH INDEX customer_reviews_idx ON customer_reviews(review_text);

SELECT review_id
FROM customer_reviews
WHERE CONTAINS(review_text, 'Laptop') > 0;
```

Output:
```
review_id
1
```

Post-deployment, marketing analysts were able to quickly identify products with frequent positive mentions, helping to guide promotional strategies and enhance customer support responsiveness.

What made these improvements especially valuable was the ease of implementation. Despite working with varied data types, QuickMart was able to use the same unified syntax—CREATE SEARCH INDEX—across all three use cases. This consistency significantly reduced training time and simplified maintenance, as developers didn't need to manage multiple indexing approaches.

Preliminary internal benchmarks and monitoring data indicated that the combined use of these indexes contributed to notable gains in system performance, including faster end-user search response times, reduced query latency, and improved platform stability under load. While results may vary depending on workload and data size, QuickMart observed up to a **3× improvement in perceived search responsiveness** and a **measurable reduction (approximately 40%) in average query execution time** during peak usage periods.

Internal Mechanism of Unified Search Index in Oracle 23AI

Oracle 23AI's **CREATE SEARCH INDEX** integrates JSON, XML, and text indexing into a single framework, optimizing query execution. Internally, it leverages **domain-specific indexing structures**, enhancing lookup efficiency with **compressed inverted lists** for text and **path-based indexing** for JSON/XML. The optimizer dynamically chooses the best retrieval method, reducing scan overhead and improving query performance.

The internal design of the unified search index is illustrated in Table 3-10.

Table 3-10. Internal Structure of Oracle 23AI Unified Search Index

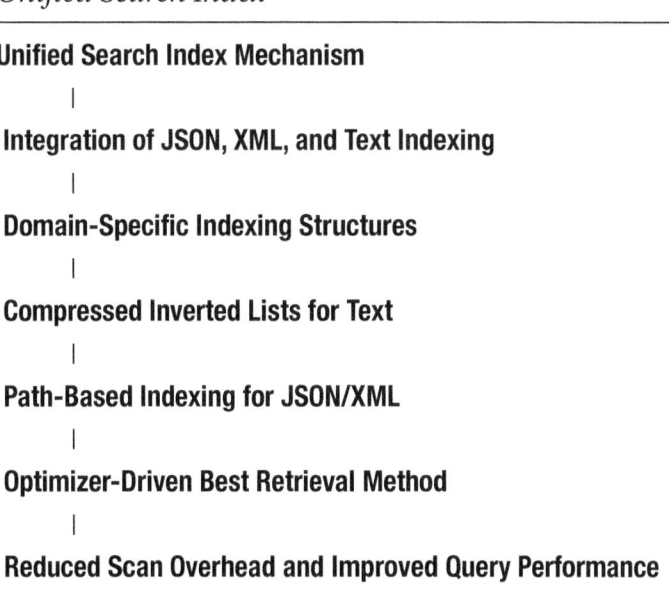

This layered approach enables Oracle 23AI to not only support diverse data formats natively but also to **deliver high-performance search operations without requiring different tools or indexing logic**. The result is a seamless developer experience, lower maintenance overhead, and significantly improved query response times across varied workloads.

Real-Time Business Use Cases for JSON, XML, and Oracle Text Search Index Enhancements in Oracle 23AI

Oracle 23AI's unified search indexes streamline querying across JSON, XML, and text data through a single efficient framework. This integration boosts performance, reduces overhead, and ensures real-time access to diverse data formats. The following table outlines practical use cases demonstrating how unified search indexing in Oracle 23AI adds value across multiple industries.

Table 3-11. Real-Time Business Use Cases for Unified Search Indexes in Oracle 23AI

Use Case	Benefit
Ecommerce Product Search	Enables fast and efficient searches across product catalogs stored in JSON, XML, and text formats, improving customer experience.
Financial Transaction Monitoring	Accelerates fraud detection by indexing and quickly retrieving suspicious transactions stored in JSON and XML structures.
Healthcare Record Management	Enhances search and retrieval of patient records, prescriptions, and medical history stored in structured XML and JSON formats.
Legal Document Search	Speeds up case law and contract searches within large repositories of legal texts and structured legal documents.
Log and Event Analytics	Improves system monitoring by enabling rapid searches through indexed logs and event data stored in JSON and text formats.
Customer Support Knowledge Base	Enhances chatbot and helpdesk efficiency by enabling full-text search across FAQs, manuals, and troubleshooting guides.

Common Questions About JSON, XML, and Oracle Text Search Index Enhancements in Oracle 23AI

Oracle 23AI introduces a unified and advanced search indexing framework that combines JSON, XML, and text search capabilities under a single CREATE SEARCH INDEX syntax. This innovation has led to several common questions among developers and architects focused on optimizing search and retrieval in diverse data formats.

One frequent question is how Oracle 23AI's CREATE SEARCH INDEX improves performance compared to traditional indexing methods. While separate indexes are still created for JSON, XML, and text columns individually, Oracle 23AI simplifies the process by offering a unified syntax and indexing framework. This consistent approach reduces complexity for developers, as they no longer need to learn and manage different indexing mechanisms for each data type. Internally, each index uses a common inverted index architecture optimized for fast lookups, which improves query execution speed, minimizes parsing overhead, and ensures scalable performance as data volumes grow.

Storage and query performance for JSON data also generate considerable interest. Oracle 23AI optimizes JSON search indexing by improving JSON_TEXTCONTAINS queries and adding better support for numerical filtering. These optimizations decrease parsing overhead during index creation and accelerate retrieval times for both structured and unstructured JSON content, making real-time access more efficient.

Another important topic is how the new CREATE SEARCH INDEX integrates with partitioning for large-scale data management. Oracle 23AI supports partitioned indexing, enabling the creation of indexes that span multiple partitions. This capability is especially beneficial for applications managing extensive event logs, financial transactions, or product catalogs, where it ensures faster queries while optimizing resource usage.

Finally, developers often inquire about handling multilingual or unstructured text data with Oracle 23AI. The system enhances text search through language-aware tokenization, stemming, and relevance ranking. It also supports fuzzy search, stop-word filtering, and advanced linguistic analysis. Together, these features improve the accuracy and speed of search results in global applications processing diverse languages and complex textual content.

> **Key Takeaway**   Oracle 23AI's unified search indexing transforms data retrieval by offering a simple, optimized syntax for indexing JSON, XML, and text. Businesses can now accelerate searches, enhance user experience, and streamline operations across various domains. This breakthrough simplifies indexing while delivering unparalleled speed and accuracy in querying diverse data formats.

Building on these advancements in data handling, Oracle Database 23AI further bridges the gap between relational and JSON data models with its innovative **JSON-Relational Duality Views**. This feature enables seamless, bidirectional access and manipulation of data as both structured JSON documents and traditional relational tables, empowering developers with unmatched flexibility and consistency.

JSON-Relational Duality Views in Oracle Database 23AI

In today's application landscape, developers often require seamless access to both traditional relational data and flexible JSON documents. Oracle Database 23AI introduces JSON-Relational Duality Views to address this need by bridging the gap between structured relational tables and hierarchical JSON formats. This innovative feature allows relational data to be directly represented as JSON documents without losing the power and familiarity of SQL operations. By enabling direct INSERT, UPDATE, and DELETE commands on both relational tables and JSON views, the database maintains data consistency and reduces the overhead of manual data transformations.

CASE STUDY: SIMPLIFYING DATA ACCESS WITH JSON-RELATIONAL DUALITY VIEWS AT QUICKMART

QuickMart manages customer and sales data in traditional relational tables. As their digital apps grew, they needed flexible JSON access for web and mobile use. Converting relational data to JSON manually was complex and added development overhead. Ensuring consistency between SQL and JSON operations—like inserts and updates—was error-prone and slowed delivery. Oracle Database 23AI's JSON-Relational Duality Views solved this by exposing relational data directly as JSON documents. These views support full INSERT, UPDATE, and DELETE on both formats seamlessly. QuickMart now uses a unified interface for data, simplifying workflows and ensuring data integrity across applications.

Defining the Relational Model

QuickMart's first step was to model their core data using relational tables for customers and sales transactions, as shown in Listing 3-16. The customers table contains basic customer details, while the sales table captures individual purchase records linked via foreign keys.

Listing 3-16. Creation of Customers and Sales Tables with Sample Data

```
DROP TABLE IF EXISTS sales PURGE;
DROP TABLE IF EXISTS customers PURGE;

CREATE TABLE customers (
  customer_id NUMBER(5) CONSTRAINT pk_customers PRIMARY KEY,
  customer_name VARCHAR2(50),
  city VARCHAR2(50)
);

CREATE TABLE sales (
  sale_id NUMBER(5) CONSTRAINT pk_sales PRIMARY KEY,
  customer_id NUMBER(5) CONSTRAINT fk_customer REFERENCES customers,
  product_name VARCHAR2(50),
  quantity NUMBER(5),
  amount NUMBER(10,2),
  sale_date DATE
);

CREATE INDEX sales_customer_fk_i ON sales(customer_id);

INSERT INTO customers VALUES (1, 'John Doe', 'New York');
INSERT INTO customers VALUES (2, 'Jane Smith', 'Los Angeles');
```

```
INSERT INTO sales VALUES (101, 1, 'Laptop', 1, 1200.00, TO_
DATE('2024-01-10', 'YYYY-MM-DD'));
INSERT INTO sales VALUES (102, 1, 'Mouse', 2, 40.00, TO_DATE('2024-01-12',
'YYYY-MM-DD'));
INSERT INTO sales VALUES (103, 2, 'Keyboard', 1, 60.00, TO_
DATE('2024-01-15', 'YYYY-MM-DD'));

commit;
```

This normalized schema offered data integrity and efficient storage, but accessing it as nested JSON for modern applications was cumbersome.

Creating the JSON-Relational Duality View

To bridge this gap, QuickMart defined a JSON-Relational Duality View named sales_data_dv that exposes customer and purchase data as JSON documents, as shown in **Listing 1-2**. This view supports direct DML operations, ensuring that inserts, updates, and deletes on JSON data propagate seamlessly to the underlying relational tables.

Listing 3-17. JSON-Relational Duality View Definition

```
CREATE OR REPLACE JSON RELATIONAL DUALITY VIEW sales_data_dv AS
SELECT JSON {
            '_id' : c.customer_id,
            'customerName' : c.customer_name,
            'city' : c.city,
            'purchases' :
              [ SELECT JSON { 'saleID' : s.sale_id,
                              'product' : s.product_name,
                              'quantity' : s.quantity,
                              'amount' : s.amount,
                              'saleDate' : s.sale_date }
                FROM sales s WITH INSERT UPDATE DELETE
                WHERE c.customer_id = s.customer_id ]
        }
FROM customers c WITH INSERT UPDATE DELETE;
```

With this view, applications no longer need separate JSON conversion logic. Instead, they can interact naturally with JSON documents while the database maintains relational consistency behind the scenes.

Querying and Manipulating Data Through the JSON View

QuickMart's developers found querying data much simpler. To retrieve all customer and purchase information as JSON, they run the query shown in Listing 3-18, which returns structured JSON documents representing customers with nested purchases.

Listing 3-18. Querying JSON Data from the Duality View

```
SELECT JSON_SERIALIZE(v.data) FROM sales_data_dv v;
```
Output:
```
 {"_id":1,"_metadata":{"etag":"EF29FBF5B318BB6D57BE35F7598C090D","asof":"000023DE13EFE5F2"},"customerName":"John Doe","city":"New York","purchases":[{"saleID":101,"product":"Laptop","quantity":1,"amount":1200,"saleDate":"2024-01-10T00:00:00"},{"saleID":102,"product":"Mouse","quantity":2,"amount":40,"saleDate":"2024-01-12T00:00:00"}]}

{"_id":2,"_metadata":{"etag":"44C18EF5AAE0DD6EAAA81BC018FC2B6A","asof":"000023DE13EFE5F2"},"customerName":"Jane Smith","city":"Los Angeles","purchases":[{"saleID":103,"product":"Keyboard","quantity":1,"amount":60,"saleDate":"2024-01-15T00:00:00"}]}
```

The JSON documents produced closely reflect the nested hierarchical structure expected by modern applications, reducing the need for additional data processing on the client side.

Inserting and updating data also became straightforward. For instance, adding a new customer with associated sales is as simple as inserting a JSON document into the view, as illustrated in Listing 3-19.

Listing 3-19. Inserting a New Customer with Purchases via JSON View

```
INSERT INTO sales_data_dv d (data)
VALUES ('
{
  "_id" : 3,
  "customerName" : "Mike Tyson",
```

```
    "city" : "Chicago",
    "purchases" : [
      {
        "saleID" : 104,
        "product" : "Monitor",
        "quantity" : 1,
        "amount" : 250.00,
        "saleDate" : "2024-02-01"
      }
    ]
}');
```

Similarly, updating customer details requires just a JSON update, as shown in Listing 3-20, where a customer's name is changed by applying a JSON transform.

Listing 3-20. Updating Customer Name via JSON Transform

```
UPDATE sales_data_dv
SET data = JSON_TRANSFORM(data, SET '$.customerName' = 'Johnny Doe')
WHERE JSON_VALUE(data, '$._id') = '1';
COMMIT;
```

All such modifications on the JSON view are immediately and atomically reflected in the underlying relational tables, guaranteeing data integrity without additional coding effort.

Benefits Realized by QuickMart Solutions

Through JSON-Relational Duality Views, QuickMart Solutions achieved a simplified workflow that eliminated the need for manual JSON serialization and deserialization. Developers can now seamlessly access and manipulate data using either JSON or traditional SQL, without concern for maintaining consistency or writing duplicate logic.

Atomic updates ensure that changes to JSON documents propagate reliably to relational tables, preventing data discrepancies. Nested data management becomes easier, avoiding complex foreign key handling by embedding related sales records inside JSON views. Moreover, this approach allows QuickMart's modern RESTful APIs and

NoSQL-driven clients to consume relational data naturally in JSON format without extra translation layers.

QuickMart's use of Oracle Database 23AI's JSON-Relational Duality Views unified relational and JSON data access, streamlining development and boosting data consistency. This approach modernized their data platform while preserving relational database strengths.

Internal Mechanism of JSON-Relational Duality Views in Oracle 23AI

JSON-Relational Duality Views in Oracle 23AI operate by dynamically mapping relational data to JSON structures without duplication. Internally, the database maintains a unified storage model where JSON documents act as virtual views over relational tables, ensuring bidirectional synchronization. SQL DML operations (INSERT, UPDATE, DELETE) on JSON views automatically translate into corresponding updates on relational tables using internal mapping logic, leveraging indexes and transactional integrity mechanisms to maintain consistency and optimize query performance.

The internal design of JSON-Relational Duality Views is illustrated in Table 3-12.

Table 3-12. Internal Structure of Oracle 23AI JSON-Relational Duality Views

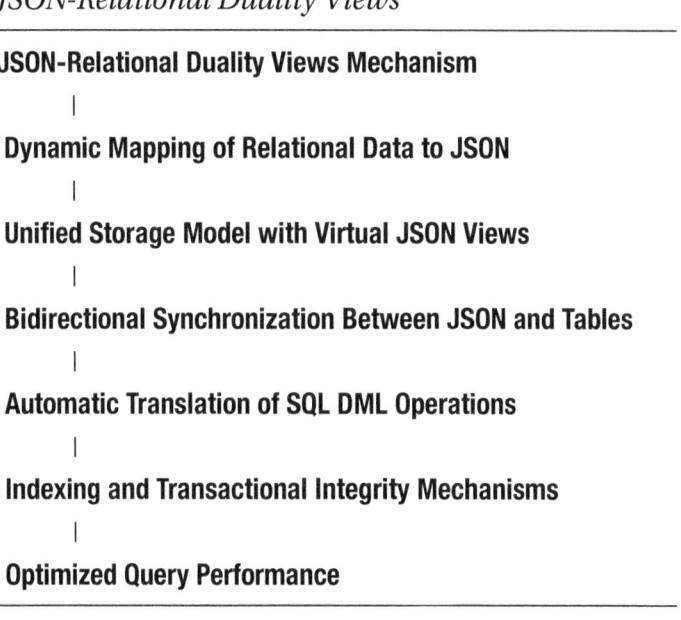

This architecture allows Oracle 23AI to seamlessly unify relational and JSON data models, providing consistent, flexible, and high-performance data access without duplicating storage or complicating application logic.

Pre-23AI and 23AI Features Related to JSON-Relational Duality Views

Earlier Oracle versions required manual conversion between relational data and JSON, limiting access to SQL only. Oracle 23AI's JSON-Relational Duality Views expose relational data as JSON, enabling direct SQL and JSON access with synchronized DML operations. These views can be created natively using SQL or GraphQL, simplifying integration and development as shown in Table 3-13.

Table 3-13. Comparison of JSON-Relational Duality Views Pre-23AI vs. Oracle 23AI

Feature	Pre-23AI	23AI
Data Access	Data in relational tables could only be accessed via SQL.	Data can be accessed both via SQL and JSON.
JSON Document Representation	JSON support was separate from relational tables, requiring manual conversion.	Relational data is automatically exposed as JSON documents through JSON-Relational Duality Views.
DML Operations	DML operations (INSERT, UPDATE, DELETE) needed to be done in relational tables.	DML operations can be performed directly on the JSON view, which reflects in the underlying relational tables.
View Creation	JSON-based views required separate tools or functions to integrate relational and JSON data.	JSON-Relational Duality Views can be created directly using SQL or GraphQL syntax.

These enhancements greatly streamline handling of JSON and relational data together, improving developer productivity and data consistency in Oracle 23AI.

Real-Time Business Use Cases for JSON-Relational Duality Views in Oracle 23AI

Oracle 23AI's JSON-Relational Duality Views simplify access and management of data in both relational and JSON formats, enhancing real-time business operations across industries. This feature improves data consistency, query flexibility, and development efficiency. The following table highlights key use cases and their benefits.

Table 3-14. Real-Time Business Use Cases for JSON-Relational Duality Views in Oracle 23AI

Use Case	Benefit
Ecommerce Order Management	Enables seamless order tracking and processing with both SQL and JSON-based queries, reducing complexity.
Real-Time Customer Insights	Allows personalized offers and customer segmentation using real-time JSON-based queries.
IoT Device Data Processing	Directly integrates JSON-based IoT sensor data with relational systems, improving efficiency.
Healthcare Patient Records	Ensures seamless access to structured patient data in JSON format for modern healthcare apps.
Fraud Detection in Transactions	Supports real-time fraud detection by enabling mixed SQL and JSON queries.
Logistics and Supply Chain Tracking	Provides real-time shipment updates in both relational and JSON formats for better tracking.

Common Questions About JSON-Relational Duality Views in Oracle 23AI

Oracle 23AI introduces JSON-Relational Duality Views, a powerful feature enabling seamless access and modification of data as both relational tables and JSON documents. This innovation has raised several common questions among developers and architects aiming to optimize data consistency and performance in mixed-data environments.

One frequent question is how Oracle 23AI ensures transactional consistency when updates occur on both JSON views and relational tables. Oracle guarantees ACID compliance by atomically synchronizing changes, using redo logs and undo segments to maintain referential integrity and prevent partial updates, ensuring reliable transactional behavior.

Another key question concerns query performance improvements over traditional JSON handling. By dynamically mapping JSON structures to relational data without runtime transformations, and leveraging indexes on relational tables, Oracle 23AI reduces join overhead and employs parallel execution strategies to deliver faster, more efficient JSON queries.

Schema evolution is also a common concern. Oracle 23AI handles schema changes dynamically where possible; JSON views gracefully accommodate missing fields, support explicit versioning, and use JSON_TRANSFORM to update specific fields without requiring full document rewrites, simplifying maintenance and evolution.

Finally, developers ask how JSON-Relational Duality Views benefit microservices and API-driven architectures. The feature provides native JSON outputs ideal for RESTful APIs, allowing SQL and JSON queries from a single data source. It integrates smoothly with GraphQL and accelerates microservices by ensuring data consistency and reducing development complexity.

In summary, Oracle 23AI's JSON-Relational Duality Views deliver a flexible, high-performance, and consistent solution for modern applications requiring seamless relational and JSON data interaction.

Oracle 23AI introduces JSON-Relational Duality Views, transforming the interaction between relational and JSON-based applications.

- Before 23AI, relational data access was limited to SQL, with JSON integration requiring manual conversion.

- With 23AI, relational data can be queried and modified directly as JSON, enabling seamless dual access and ensuring data consistency.

- This feature simplifies data management, enhances flexibility, and supports real-time updates in both formats, empowering modern applications.

CHAPTER 3 JSON AND XML ENHANCEMENTS

Building on this innovation, Oracle 23c also introduces a **Native JSON Data Type**, designed to further optimize JSON storage and querying. This next feature significantly improves performance and scalability by offering built-in indexing and data integrity validation—addressing limitations of traditional text-based JSON storage and meeting the demands of today's data-driven applications.

Oracle Native JSON Data Type for Efficient Storage and Querying in 23AI

Oracle 23c introduces a Native JSON Data Type that significantly enhances how semi-structured data is stored and queried. Unlike earlier approaches where JSON data was stored in text-based types such as VARCHAR2 or CLOB, which require parsing the entire text at query time and often lead to higher storage and processing overhead, the native JSON type uses a binary-optimized format. This format enables faster data access, reduced storage footprint, and improved overall performance. It also supports native indexing and strict JSON validation, making it well-suited for scalable, high-performance applications that rely heavily on JSON.

> **CASE STUDY: ADDRESSING REAL-WORLD CHALLENGES AT QUICKMART**
>
> To illustrate the impact of Oracle's Native JSON Data Type, consider the case of a retail enterprise, **QuickMart**, which handles massive volumes of customer-related data from online purchases, browsing behavior, and personalization settings. Prior to adopting Oracle 23c, QuickMart stored this JSON-formatted data in CLOB columns, resulting in sluggish performance, high query latency, and complex processing overhead.
>
> With Oracle 23c, QuickMart transitioned to using native JSON storage. By doing so, they reduced storage requirements and significantly improved query speeds. Queries that previously required manual transformation and full-table scans could now be executed efficiently, directly leveraging indexes on native JSON content. As a result, QuickMart achieved real-time personalization capabilities for its users—offering faster product recommendations and improving overall customer experience.

Core Capabilities of Native JSON Storage

A key advancement in this feature is the ability to store JSON using a native binary format rather than traditional plain text types. This design enables more efficient internal parsing and can reduce storage overhead, especially for large or deeply nested documents. It also supports schema-aware validation, helping ensure the structural integrity of JSON content. While exact performance gains may vary depending on workload and data size, this approach lays the groundwork for faster query execution and better space utilization in many practical scenarios.

In QuickMart's case, this meant creating JSON-specific indexes on customer preferences such as favorite product categories or color choices. These indexes allowed real-time segmentation and personalized campaign targeting based on user behavior, which would have been cumbersome and inefficient using previous approaches.

Creating Tables and Inserting JSON Data

As shown in Listing 3-21, Oracle 23c allows developers to define JSON columns using the new native data type and directly insert JSON documents.

Listing 3-21. Creating and Populating a Table with Native JSON Data

```
-- Create a new table with a JSON column to store customer data in native
JSON format
CREATE TABLE customer_data (
    customer_id NUMBER PRIMARY KEY,
    customer_info JSON
);

-- Insert a sample customer record with JSON data
INSERT INTO customer_data (customer_id, customer_info)
VALUES
(1, '{"name": "Alice Johnson", "email": "alice.johnson@example.com",
"preferences": {"color": "blue", "size": "M"}}'),
(2, '{"name": "Bob Smith", "email": "bob.smith@example.com", "preferences":
{"color": "red", "size": "L"}}'),
```

```
(3, '{"name": "Charlie Davis", "email": "charlie.davis@example.com",
"preferences": {"color": "green", "size": "S"}}');

-- Commit the transaction
COMMIT;
```

Querying Native JSON for Insight

Querying JSON content in Oracle 23c becomes highly efficient with the native format. Listing 3-22 demonstrates how to extract specific fields from JSON documents using JSON_VALUE.

Listing 3-22. Querying Specific Fields from JSON Documents

```
SELECT
    customer_id,
    json_value(customer_info, '$.name') AS customer_name,
    json_value(customer_info, '$.preferences.color') AS preferred_color
FROM
    customer_data;
```

```
output:
Customer_id    Customer_name      Preferred_color
1              Alice Johnson      blue
2              Bob Smith          red
3              Charlie Davis      green
```

This streamlined querying mechanism allows fast, targeted retrieval of nested data structures—ideal for real-time dashboards and analytics tools.

Enhancing Performance with JSON Indexing

To further optimize query performance, Oracle 23c supports indexing on JSON keys. Listing 3-23 illustrates how to create an index on the color preference within the customer_info JSON document.

Listing 3-23. Creating an Index on a JSON Key for Optimized Queries

```
CREATE INDEX idx_customer_color
ON customer_data (json_value(customer_info, '$.preferences.color' RETURNING
VARCHAR2));
```

This index dramatically improves the performance of queries filtering or sorting by the color preference, making JSON data as performant as traditional relational columns.

High-Volume Efficiency and Scalability

Thanks to Oracle's native JSON indexing and optimized binary storage, high-volume queries also benefit. Consider the query in Listing 3-24, which filters customers by their preferred color.

Listing 3-24. Filtering JSON Records with Optimized Performance

```
SELECT
    customer_id,
    json_value(customer_info, '$.name') AS customer_name,
    json_value(customer_info, '$.preferences.color') AS preferred_color
FROM
    customer_data
WHERE
    json_value(customer_info, '$.preferences.color' RETURNING VARCHAR2)
    = 'blue';
```

output:

Customer_id	Customer_name	Preferred_color
1	Alice Johnson	blue

The query above will run efficiently, even with a large volume of customer records, thanks to the native JSON storage and indexing optimizations.

Even with millions of customer records, this query executes swiftly due to the native indexing mechanism, proving that scalability is not compromised when working with complex JSON structures.

Broad Benefits for Enterprise Workloads

By adopting the native JSON data type, QuickMart realized several operational benefits. Storage became more efficient, with internal testing showing a reduction in size compared to equivalent CLOB-based JSON—particularly for deeply nested or repetitive data structures. Query performance also improved, especially for filters on nested JSON attributes, thanks to reduced parsing overhead and built-in indexing support. Scalability was enhanced through better memory utilization and faster data retrieval, while development complexity decreased due to native schema validation and simpler indexing syntax. Together, these improvements boosted QuickMart's analytics and personalization capabilities, while also lowering infrastructure demands and simplifying application maintenance.

These outcomes not only empowered QuickMart's analytics and personalization engines but also reduced infrastructure costs and simplified application logic.

Internal Mechanism of Native JSON Storage in Oracle 23c

Oracle 23c's Native JSON Storage optimizes JSON handling by using a binary-optimized format instead of traditional text-based storage. Internally, it stores JSON data in a highly efficient representation, reducing parsing overhead and improving retrieval speed. Indexing is directly applied to JSON attributes, enabling faster lookups and query execution. The storage engine ensures validation at insertion, while the optimizer leverages native indexing for high-performance scans, making JSON queries as efficient as relational data access.

The internal design of Native JSON Storage is illustrated in Table 3-15.

CHAPTER 3 JSON AND XML ENHANCEMENTS

Table 3-15. *Internal Structure of Native JSON Storage in Oracle 23c*

Native JSON Storage Mechanism
Binary-Optimized JSON Representation
Reduced Parsing Overhead and Faster Retrieval
Direct Indexing on JSON Attributes
Optimized Query Execution and High-Performance Scans
Validation at Insertion and Efficient Storage Engine
JSON Queries as Fast as Relational Data Access

This architecture allows Oracle 23c to support modern JSON-centric applications by offering the performance and manageability of relational databases, eliminating traditional storage limitations and enabling seamless, scalable access to semi-structured data.

Real-Time Business Use Cases for Oracle 23c Native JSON Storage

Oracle 23c's Native JSON Storage provides a high-performance and scalable solution for managing semi-structured data in modern enterprise applications. By storing JSON in a binary-optimized format with native indexing support, it enhances both storage efficiency and query speed. These capabilities translate into tangible benefits across a variety of business domains, where real-time data access and flexibility are essential. The following table highlights key use cases demonstrating how organizations can leverage native JSON storage for operational excellence and data-driven agility.

Table 3-16. Real-Time Business Use Cases for Native JSON Storage in Oracle 23c

Use Case	Benefit
Ecommerce Product Catalog	Enables fast searches and filtering across large product catalogs stored in JSON, improving customer experience.
Customer Personalization in Retail	Stores and retrieves user preferences efficiently for personalized recommendations, enhancing engagement.
Financial Transactions and Fraud Detection	Speeds up real-time analysis of transaction logs stored in JSON, improving fraud detection and compliance monitoring.
IoT Data Management	Efficiently stores and queries large-scale IoT sensor data, enabling real-time monitoring and predictive analytics.
Healthcare Patient Records	Optimizes storage and retrieval of structured patient data in JSON format, improving data accessibility and processing speed.
Supply Chain and Logistics Tracking	Stores shipment details in JSON for real-time tracking and fast lookups, improving supply chain visibility.

By leveraging these use cases, businesses can accelerate their digital transformation efforts, improve operational responsiveness, and deliver intelligent, personalized services to customers in real time.

Common Questions About Oracle 23c's Native JSON Storage

Oracle 23c's Native JSON Storage introduces a powerful, binary-optimized format for efficiently handling JSON data. As developers and enterprises explore its capabilities, several common questions arise around its performance, compatibility, scalability, and integrity.

A frequent question is how native JSON storage improves query performance. When JSON is stored in traditional formats like CLOB or VARCHAR, the database must parse the entire text at query time, which adds overhead. In contrast, native JSON storage allows the database to access and index JSON keys directly in a binary-optimized format, eliminating the need for on-the-fly parsing. This leads to significantly faster and more efficient queries, even when working with large or complex datasets.

Migration from existing systems is also straightforward. Applications using text-based JSON can easily transition to the native format with minimal disruption, benefiting from better performance and simpler query logic.

On scalability, Oracle's internal optimizations and indexing allow it to manage vast JSON datasets without compromising speed, making it ideal for modern data-heavy applications like IoT, finance, and ecommerce.

To maintain data integrity, Oracle validates all JSON input at the time of insertion and automatically updates indexes, ensuring consistency and reliability.

In short, Oracle 23c's Native JSON Storage offers fast, scalable, and reliable JSON handling with minimal overhead—meeting the demands of modern, data-driven applications.

Key Takeaway By adopting Oracle 23c's Native JSON Storage, the company successfully addresses the problem of inefficient JSON data handling. They now benefit from reduced processing time, improved scalability, and efficient storage. Oracle 23c's optimization for JSON data empowers businesses to handle large volumes of data while maintaining high performance, making it an ideal choice for data-driven organizations.

Building on this foundation of efficient storage, Oracle 23AI further strengthens data reliability with the introduction of JSON Schema Validation. This feature ensures that all JSON data adheres to a defined structure, adding an essential layer of integrity to JSON-based workflows.

Ensuring Data Integrity with JSON Schema Validation in 23AI

Maintaining data integrity is a critical challenge when working with JSON documents, especially in complex, real-time applications. Oracle 23AI addresses this challenge by introducing JSON Schema validation, a powerful capability that enforces structure and constraints directly on JSON data within the database. By using the `VALIDATE` keyword, developers can define schemas that JSON documents must conform to before being accepted into the system, effectively preventing invalid or malformed data from entering

CHAPTER 3 JSON AND XML ENHANCEMENTS

the database. This mechanism enhances consistency and reliability in JSON workflows, ensuring that only compliant data is stored and queried.

To demonstrate the practical value of this feature, consider the case of a company that needs to maintain accurate and consistent inventory records for fresh produce.

CASE STUDY: ENSURING ACCURATE INVENTORY MANAGEMENT AT QUICKMART

QuickMart's fruit distribution department faced difficulties ensuring the reliability of their inventory data stored as JSON. Their key requirement was to validate each inventory entry against strict criteria, such as mandatory fields and data ranges, to avoid errors caused by missing or malformed data. Without schema validation, QuickMart risked inconsistencies like missing quantities or overly long fruit names that could disrupt their supply chain operations.

Using Oracle 23AI's JSON Schema validation, QuickMart implemented a solution that guarantees all inventory JSON entries adhere to a predefined structure, maintaining data integrity and preventing errors at the point of data insertion. This proactive validation eliminates the need for costly post-processing checks and data cleansing.

QuickMart created an inventory table with a JSON column designed to validate incoming JSON data according to specific rules. These rules required that every entry contain a fruit name between 1 and 15 characters and a quantity between 1 and 500. Additionally, no extra fields beyond these two were permitted, ensuring strict consistency.

The table creation statement, shown in Listing 3-25, demonstrates how the JSON schema is embedded directly within the column definition to enforce these constraints.

Listing 3-25. Creating FRUIT_INVENTORY Table with JSON Schema Validation

```
CREATE TABLE FRUIT_INVENTORY (
  id         NUMBER PRIMARY KEY,
  json_data  JSON VALIDATE '{
    "type"       : "object",
    "properties" : {
      "fruit"    : {"type"      : "string",
                    "minLength" : 1,
                    "maxLength" : 15},
```

CHAPTER 3   JSON AND XML ENHANCEMENTS

```
      "quantity" : {"type"       : "integer",
                    "minimum"    : 1,
                    "maximum"    : 500}
   },
   "required"    : ["fruit", "quantity"],
   "additionalProperties": false
 }'
);
```

The schema enforces three key rules: the fruit field must be a string between 1 and 15 characters; the quantity must be an integer between 1 and 500; and no extra fields are permitted. This validation ensures only well-formed JSON data compliant with business logic can be inserted.

QuickMart successfully inserted valid inventory entries such as apples with quantity 50, mangoes with 200, and bananas with 150, all of which complied with the schema and committed successfully, as illustrated in Listing 3-26.

Listing 3-26. Inserting Valid JSON Data into FRUIT_INVENTORY

```
INSERT INTO FRUIT_INVENTORY (id, json_data) VALUES (1, json('{"fruit":"Appl
e","quantity":50}'));
INSERT INTO FRUIT_INVENTORY (id, json_data) VALUES (2, json('{"fruit":"Mang
o","quantity":200}'));
INSERT INTO FRUIT_INVENTORY (id, json_data) VALUES (3,
json('{"fruit":"Banana","quantity":150}'));

COMMIT;
```

Attempts to insert invalid data triggered schema validation errors, preventing corrupt or incomplete JSON from entering the database. Examples of rejected entries include those missing required fields, fruit names exceeding the maximum length, quantities out of the allowed range, or JSON documents containing unauthorized extra fields like price. These invalid inserts resulted in Oracle errors such as those shown in Listing 3-27.

CHAPTER 3   JSON AND XML ENHANCEMENTS

Listing 3-27. Examples of Invalid JSON Inserts Causing Schema Validation Errors

```
-- Missing "quantity" field
INSERT INTO FRUIT_INVENTORY (id, json_data) VALUES (4, json('{"fruit":"Orange"}'));
-- ORA-40875: JSON schema validation error

-- "fruit" name too long (exceeds 15 characters)
INSERT INTO FRUIT_INVENTORY (id, json_data) VALUES (5, json('{"fruit":"SuperLongFruitName","quantity":100}'));
-- ORA-40875: JSON schema validation error

-- "quantity" out of allowed range (above 500)
INSERT INTO FRUIT_INVENTORY (id, json_data) VALUES (6, json('{"fruit":"Grapes","quantity":600}'));
-- ORA-40875: JSON schema validation error

-- Extra field "price" not allowed
INSERT INTO FRUIT_INVENTORY (id, json_data) VALUES (7, json('{"fruit":"Pineapple","quantity":10,"price":5}'));
-- ORA-40875: JSON schema validation error
```

These validation failures guarantee that only consistent and accurate inventory data is stored.

When querying the table, all valid entries are returned as expected. Table 3-17 displays the current valid inventory data.

Table 3-17. *Valid Inventory Data in FRUIT_INVENTORY Table*

```
SELECT * FROM FRUIT_INVENTORY ;
ID    JSON_DATA
-----------------------------------
1     {"fruit":"Apple","quantity":50}
2     {"fruit":"Mango","quantity":200}
3     {"fruit":"Banana","quantity":150}
```

CHAPTER 3   JSON AND XML ENHANCEMENTS

To demonstrate selective data retrieval based on JSON schema compliance, QuickMart used the `IS JSON VALIDATE` condition in a query. For instance, they filtered inventory items to include only fruits with names up to five characters, as shown in Listing 3-28.

Listing 3-28. Querying Inventory with JSON Schema Validation Filtering

```
SELECT * FROM FRUIT_INVENTORY
WHERE json_data IS JSON VALIDATE '{
  "type"       : "object",
  "properties" : {
    "fruit"    : {"type"      : "string",
                  "minLength" : 1,
                  "maxLength" : 5},
    "quantity" : {"type"      : "integer",
                  "minimum"   : 1,
                  "maximum"   : 500}
  },
  "required"   : ["fruit", "quantity"],
  "additionalProperties": false
}';
```

The result of this query excludes entries like "Banana," whose fruit name exceeds five characters, returning only valid matches as shown in Table 3-18.

Table 3-18. *Filtered Inventory Data with Fruit Name Max Length of Five Characters*

ID	JSON_DATA
1	{"fruit":"Apple","quantity":50}
2	{"fruit":"Mango","quantity":200}

The query only retrieves valid entries, excluding those with invalid data like Banana, which exceeds the length limit.

CHAPTER 3   JSON AND XML ENHANCEMENTS

By embedding JSON Schema validation in both data insertion and querying, QuickMart Produce ensures the accuracy and consistency of their inventory management system. This case exemplifies how Oracle 23AI's JSON Schema validation strengthens data integrity and simplifies workflow reliability for JSON-based applications.

Internal Mechanism of JSON Schema Validation in Oracle 23AI

Oracle 23AI's JSON Schema Validation operates by leveraging an optimized JSON parser that validates incoming JSON documents against predefined schema rules during insert and update operations. It utilizes efficient in-memory processing, indexing, and constraint enforcement to detect invalid structures, missing fields, or restricted values. This ensures data integrity with minimal overhead by integrating validation checks within the storage engine, similar to constraint validation in relational tables. Additionally, schema validation is seamlessly integrated with query execution, allowing selective retrieval of compliant JSON data using IS JSON VALIDATE.

The internal structure of JSON Schema Validation is illustrated in Table 3-19.

Table 3-19. Internal Structure of JSON Schema Validation in Oracle 23AI

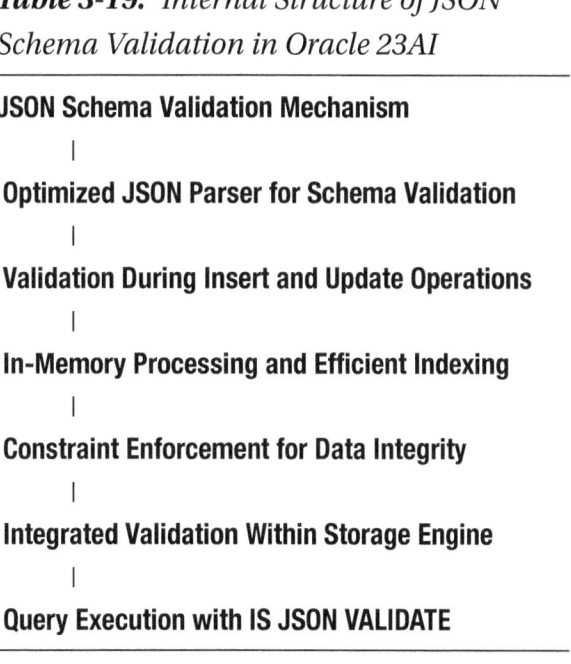

JSON Schema Validation Mechanism
|
Optimized JSON Parser for Schema Validation
|
Validation During Insert and Update Operations
|
In-Memory Processing and Efficient Indexing
|
Constraint Enforcement for Data Integrity
|
Integrated Validation Within Storage Engine
|
Query Execution with IS JSON VALIDATE

This architecture empowers Oracle 23AI to ensure schema-compliant JSON data is inserted and queried efficiently, making it an ideal solution for applications requiring strict JSON data validation and consistency alongside high performance.

Real-Time Business Use Cases for JSON Schema Validation in Oracle 23AI

Oracle 23AI's JSON Schema Validation enables enterprises to enforce structural integrity in semi-structured data, ensuring that only valid JSON documents are stored and processed. This capability is crucial in domains where accurate, well-structured data is essential for operational reliability, compliance, and real-time decision-making. By validating data at the point of insertion or update, organizations can prevent errors, reduce downstream data cleansing efforts, and maintain consistent records across systems.

The following table highlights real-world scenarios where JSON Schema Validation brings measurable benefits by safeguarding data accuracy and integrity.

Table 3-20. Real-Time Business Use Cases for JSON Schema Validation in Oracle 23AI

Use Case	Benefit
Inventory Management	Ensures accurate stock tracking by preventing invalid product entries.
Customer Data Validation	Enhances regulatory compliance by enforcing structured customer records.
IoT Sensor Data Validation	Improves real-time monitoring by ensuring valid sensor readings.
Healthcare Records Compliance	Ensures complete and accurate patient records for better treatment.
Ecommerce Order Processing	Prevents order errors and streamlines fulfillment.
Financial Transactions Logging	Reduces payment failures by enforcing valid transaction details.

These use cases demonstrate how JSON Schema Validation helps businesses safeguard the quality and consistency of their data pipelines, enabling more dependable operations and smarter decision-making across critical domains.

Common Questions About JSON Schema Validation in Oracle 23AI

Oracle 23AI introduces JSON Schema Validation to enforce structure and data integrity within semi-structured JSON documents. As businesses adopt this feature across mission-critical applications, several key questions emerge regarding scalability, complexity, performance, and adaptability.

A common question is how Oracle 23AI manages validation at scale. By leveraging optimized in-memory parsing and parallel execution, JSON Schema Validation ensures that high-volume data ingestion and updates are processed efficiently, even in large databases. Oracle also supports indexing and partitioning strategies that further reduce validation overhead.

Developers often ask whether Oracle can handle complex, nested JSON structures. The answer is yes—Oracle 23AI allows developers to define deeply nested schemas with objects and arrays using the VALIDATE clause. This ensures consistent enforcement of structure across all levels of the JSON hierarchy.

Another critical consideration is schema evolution. Oracle 23AI accommodates changes in JSON structure by enabling schema versioning and modification of validation logic. This flexibility allows developers to maintain backward compatibility while adapting to evolving application requirements.

In high-concurrency environments, performance is a top concern. While JSON Schema Validation does introduce some processing overhead, Oracle mitigates this through performance enhancements like parallelism, batch validation, and efficient memory usage. These optimizations ensure that applications can enforce data quality without sacrificing throughput.

In summary, Oracle 23AI's JSON Schema Validation combines robustness with flexibility—allowing organizations to validate large-scale, nested, and evolving JSON data structures with minimal performance trade-offs, supporting enterprise-grade scalability and data governance.

Key Takeaway Oracle 23AI's JSON Schema Validation offers a robust mechanism to enforce data consistency, accuracy, and structure within semi-structured JSON documents. As demonstrated through the QuickMart inventory use case, schema enforcement prevents malformed entries, improves query reliability, and eliminates the need for extensive post-processing. This leads to streamlined operations, reduced errors, and greater trust in the data—key advantages for any data-driven organization.

With a foundation of reliable data in place, Oracle 23AI further empowers enterprises by integrating artificial intelligence and machine learning capabilities into its Autonomous Database (ADB-S). In the next chapter, we will explore how AI and ML are transforming database intelligence through features like customer retention prediction, query performance forecasting, and automated query tuning.

CHAPTER 4

AI and Machine Learning in ADB-S

Introduction

This chapter delves into the cutting-edge AI and Machine Learning capabilities embedded within Oracle Autonomous Database Serverless (ADB-S). It introduces intelligent features that leverage data-driven insights to optimize query performance, predict customer behavior, and enhance operational efficiency. Each section covers real-world applications and practical use cases, showcasing how AI/ML is reshaping data management and analytics. Implementation workflows are detailed for seamless adoption, while behind-the-scenes insights reveal how Oracle autonomously tunes and adapts performance. Comparisons with traditional approaches highlight the shift toward predictive and self-learning systems. Key takeaways and concise summaries at the end of each section help reinforce the value of integrating AI/ML into modern data platforms.

AI/ML-Based Customer Retention Prediction in Oracle ADB-S

Customer retention has become a vital focus for data-driven organizations striving to maintain loyalty and minimize churn. As competition increases and customer acquisition costs rise, understanding which customers are likely to leave has become as critical as knowing who will stay. Oracle Autonomous Database serverless (ADB-S) empowers businesses to integrate AI/ML capabilities directly within the database, eliminating the need for external data movement or third-party tools. This native functionality allows enterprises to build, train, and deploy predictive models with ease and scale.

Oracle ADB-S not only optimizes performance through intelligent self-tuning but also enables seamless deployment of advanced analytics use cases. With its embedded machine learning algorithms and simplified model lifecycle management, Oracle ADB-S becomes a compelling platform for operationalizing AI in real-time.

The following case study explores how **QuickMart**, a retail company, used Oracle ADB-S to predict customer churn and take proactive retention actions—all within the database.

CASE STUDY: BUILDING A PREDICTIVE RETENTION MODEL FOR QUICKMART

QuickMart's retail division faced a challenge: a growing churn rate among its customer base. Traditional churn analysis required exporting data to external tools, leading to time delays and governance concerns. Seeking a modern, integrated approach, QuickMart decided to implement a churn prediction model using Oracle ADB-S's built-in AI/ML capabilities. The first step was to define and create a training dataset. This dataset would consist of historical customer behavior data, including age, gender, tenure, spend, support interactions, and churn labels. As shown in Listing 4-1, QuickMart created a table named `customer_data` to store this training data.

Listing 4-1. Table Definition for Storing Historical Customer Behavior and Retention Status

```
DROP TABLE IF EXISTS customer_data PURGE;

CREATE TABLE customer_data (
    customer_id NUMBER PRIMARY KEY,
    age NUMBER,
    gender VARCHAR2(10),
    tenure NUMBER,   -- How long the customer has been with the company (months)
    monthly_spend NUMBER,   -- Average monthly spend in USD
    num_support_tickets NUMBER,   -- Number of support tickets raised
    last_purchase_days NUMBER,   -- Days since last purchase
    retention_status VARCHAR2(10)   -- 'RETAINED' or 'CHURNED' (For training data)
);
```

Once the table was created, QuickMart inserted a set of labeled historical data to train the model. These entries reflected known outcomes, where customers were tagged as either 'RETAINED' or 'CHURNED' based on past activity. See Listing 4-2 for sample insert statements.

Listing 4-2. Inserting Labeled Historical Data for Model Training

```
INSERT INTO customer_data VALUES (101, 25, 'Male', 12, 50, 1, 30, 'RETAINED');
INSERT INTO customer_data VALUES (102, 30, 'Female', 6, 20, 3, 90, 'CHURNED');
INSERT INTO customer_data VALUES (103, 40, 'Male', 24, 100, 0, 5, 'RETAINED');
INSERT INTO customer_data VALUES (104, 35, 'Female', 18, 70, 2, 15, 'RETAINED');
INSERT INTO customer_data VALUES (105, 28, 'Male', 3, 10, 4, 120, 'CHURNED');
COMMIT;
```

QuickMart then used Oracle's `DBMS_DATA_MINING` package to train a classification model named `CUSTOMER_RETENTION_MODEL`. This model analyzed historical behavior and learned patterns that could predict retention outcomes for future customers. The training procedure is illustrated in Listing 4-3.

Listing 4-3. Creating a Classification Model to Predict Customer Retention

```
BEGIN
    DBMS_DATA_MINING.CREATE_MODEL(
        model_name => 'CUSTOMER_RETENTION_MODEL',
        mining_function => DBMS_DATA_MINING.CLASSIFICATION,
        data_table_name => 'CUSTOMER_DATA',
        target_column_name => 'RETENTION_STATUS',
        settings_table_name => NULL
    );
END;
/
```

Before executing the model training, QuickMart ensured that the user had the required privileges, as demonstrated in Listing 4-4. These grants must be executed by a DBA-level account (such as SYS or SYSTEM), since regular users cannot grant these permissions themselves. The example below shows how the privileges were assigned to `testuser1`, enabling access to the data mining APIs and system views.

Listing 4-4. Granting Privileges to Enable Model Training

```
BEGIN
    EXECUTE IMMEDIATE 'GRANT CREATE MINING MODEL TO testuser1;
    EXECUTE IMMEDIATE 'GRANT SELECT ON V$SQL TO testuser1';
    EXECUTE IMMEDIATE 'GRANT EXECUTE ON DBMS_DATA_MINING TO testuser1';
END;
/
```

To apply the model to new, unlabeled customers, QuickMart created a second table to hold recent customer records. These records included the same behavioral fields but excluded any retention status. See Listing 4-5 for the structure of the new_customers table.

Listing 4-5. Creating a Table for Scoring New Customer Data

```
CREATE TABLE new_customers (
    customer_id NUMBER PRIMARY KEY,
    age NUMBER,
    gender VARCHAR2(10),
    tenure NUMBER,
    monthly_spend NUMBER,
    num_support_tickets NUMBER,
    last_purchase_days NUMBER
);
```

QuickMart inserted several new customer profiles into this table for evaluation. These profiles represented active customers whose future retention outcomes were unknown, as seen in Listing 4-6.

Listing 4-6. Inserting New Customer Data for Prediction

```
INSERT INTO new_customers VALUES (201, 27, 'Female', 8, 25, 2, 60);
INSERT INTO new_customers VALUES (202, 45, 'Male', 30, 150, 0, 10);
INSERT INTO new_customers VALUES (203, 29, 'Male', 4, 15, 3, 110);
COMMIT;
```

CHAPTER 4 AI AND MACHINE LEARNING IN ADB-S

Using the trained model, QuickMart ran a query to predict the retention status of each new customer. The built-in PREDICTION SQL function automatically generated the most likely outcome for each case. The prediction query is shown in Listing 4-7.

Listing 4-7. Predicting Retention Outcomes for New Customers

```
SELECT customer_id, age, tenure, monthly_spend, num_support_tickets,
       PREDICTION(CUSTOMER_RETENTION_MODEL USING *) AS prd_ret_sta
FROM new_customers;
```

Output:

customer_id	age	tenure	monthly_spend	num_support_tickets	pre_ret_sta
201	27	8	25	2	CHURNED
202	45	30	150	0	RETAINED
203	29	4	15	3	CHURNED

The results allowed QuickMart to identify high-risk customers who were likely to churn. Equipped with this insight, their customer success team could offer personalized incentives, loyalty bonuses, or dedicated support to improve retention. This actionable intelligence helped turn insights into outcomes—before customers were lost.

Finally, if the model was no longer needed or had to be refreshed, QuickMart could easily drop the existing model using a single command, as demonstrated in Listing 4-8.

Listing 4-8. Dropping the Trained ML Model from Oracle ADB-S

```
BEGIN
    DBMS_DATA_MINING.DROP_MODEL('CUSTOMER_RETENTION_MODEL');
END;
/
```

This end-to-end flow demonstrates how AI/ML can be embedded within the database to power intelligent decisions—without external tools, pipelines, or latency. By enabling predictive analytics as a native database feature, Oracle ADB-S significantly simplifies the deployment of enterprise ML applications.

Internal Mechanism of AI/ML-Based Customer Retention Prediction in Oracle ADB-S

Oracle ADB-S leverages its built-in AI/ML engine to analyze historical customer data and dynamically train classification models using the **DBMS_DATA_MINING** package. Internally, it optimizes feature selection, applies machine learning algorithms within SQL queries, and generates predictions using in-database model inference. This eliminates data movement overhead and enhances real-time decision-making by integrating AI-driven insights directly into SQL execution

The internal structure of **AI/ML-Based Customer Retention Prediction** is illustrated in Table 4-1.

Table 4-1. Internal Flow of Customer Retention Prediction in Oracle ADB-S

AI/ML-Based Customer Retention Prediction
|
Built-in AI/ML Engine in Oracle ADB-S
|
Analysis of Historical Customer Data
|
Dynamic Model Training with DBMS_DATA_MINING
|
Optimized Feature Selection and SQL-Based ML
|
In-Database Model Inference for Predictions

This integrated design empowers enterprises like QuickMart to move beyond reactive analytics and adopt proactive, data-driven decision-making—all without leaving the Oracle ecosystem.

Sample Real-Time Business Use Cases for AI/ML in Oracle ADB-S

Oracle Autonomous Database serverless (ADB-S) integrates AI/ML capabilities directly within its core engine, allowing enterprises to harness predictive analytics without external tools or data movement. This in-database machine learning empowers organizations to make real-time, data-driven decisions across diverse business functions such as customer engagement, fraud prevention, supply chain optimization, and pricing strategy. With simplified access via SQL and built-in packages like `DBMS_DATA_MINING`, Oracle ADB-S helps businesses uncover hidden patterns and act with precision.

The following table illustrates real-world business scenarios where Oracle ADB-S's AI/ML engine provides tangible value through intelligent automation and predictive modeling.

Table 4-2. Real-Time Business Use Cases for AI/ML in Oracle ADB-S

Use Case	Business Scenario	Benefit
Customer Retention Prediction	Predicting which customers are likely to churn based on their behavior.	Enables targeted retention efforts and improves customer loyalty.
Real-Time Fraud Detection	Monitoring transactions to detect fraud in real-time.	Reduces financial loss and enhances security measures.
Inventory Management Optimization	Dynamically adjusting inventory based on demand forecasting.	Optimizes supply chain and reduces stockouts or overstocking.
Personalized Marketing Campaigns	Creating personalized marketing strategies based on customer behavior.	Increases engagement and improves conversion rates.
Dynamic Pricing Strategy	Adjusting prices in real-time based on demand and competitor prices.	Maximizes revenue and enhances competitiveness.
Predictive Maintenance	Monitoring equipment data to predict failures before they happen.	Minimizes downtime and reduces maintenance costs.

These use cases highlight how Oracle ADB-S transforms traditional business processes by embedding intelligence at the data layer, driving operational efficiency and competitive advantage with minimal infrastructure complexity.

CHAPTER 4 AI AND MACHINE LEARNING IN ADB-S

Common Questions About AI/ML-Based Customer Retention Prediction in Oracle ADB-S

Oracle ADB-S offers integrated tools to build and execute machine learning models directly within the database. This enables businesses to perform customer retention prediction without relying on external pipelines. As organizations implement these capabilities, several common questions arise around accuracy, performance, customization, and data protection.

A key question is how Oracle ensures prediction accuracy. While ADB-S provides SQL-based interfaces and built-in ML packages for model training and scoring, achieving high accuracy depends on external practices such as proper feature engineering, data preparation, and evaluation using metrics like precision and recall.

In terms of performance, Oracle ADB-S leverages in-database processing and parallel execution to efficiently run machine learning workflows on large datasets. Since all operations are performed within the database, predictions can be executed in near real time with minimal data movement.

Organizations often ask about customization. Oracle ADB-S supports external frameworks like Python and R through Oracle Machine Learning (OML), allowing businesses to train and deploy custom models while also offering native classification, regression, and clustering algorithms.

Security is another concern. Oracle enforces data protection through encryption, fine-grained access controls, auditing, and data masking, helping organizations meet compliance requirements such as GDPR.

Overall, Oracle ADB-S combines scalable in-database execution with extensibility and enterprise-grade security to support effective customer retention prediction workflows.

Key Takeaway   Oracle ADB-S seamlessly integrates AI/ML capabilities to enhance database intelligence by dynamically optimizing SQL execution plans and enabling predictive analytics directly within the database. This built-in machine learning functionality empowers businesses to analyze customer behavior, forecast retention trends, and make timely, data-driven decisions that improve customer loyalty. By automating complex analyses and reducing manual intervention, Oracle ADB-S accelerates operations, enhances accuracy, and supports real-time decision-making—making it a strategic asset for organizations aiming to stay agile and customer-focused.

Building on this AI-powered foundation, Oracle ADB-S also applies machine learning to operational metrics such as SQL performance. The next section explores how **AI/ML-Based Query Elapsed Time Prediction** enables proactive performance tuning and resource optimization.

AI/ML-Based Query Elapsed Time Prediction

As enterprise workloads grow in complexity, understanding SQL query performance becomes essential for maintaining responsiveness and meeting SLAs. Oracle Autonomous Database serverless (ADB-S) integrates machine learning directly within the data platform, enabling predictive performance analytics without external tools. One such capability is the prediction of SQL query elapsed time based on system metrics and historical trends—empowering database teams to proactively manage performance.

> **CASE STUDY: PREDICTING SQL QUERY ELAPSED TIME AT QUICKMART**
>
> QuickMart, a leading retail chain with a growing online footprint, experienced intermittent delays in its reporting systems. The database operations team needed a forward-looking mechanism to anticipate long-running SQL statements and mitigate performance risks before they affected critical dashboards and customer-facing analytics. To achieve this, they built a machine learning regression model using Oracle ADB-S to forecast SQL query execution times.

Preparing the Environment for Machine Learning

The implementation began with enabling the necessary user privileges to access system views and machine learning packages. This setup ensured that the data science team could extract performance metrics and build a regression model. The required grants are shown in Listing 4-9.

Listing 4-9. Granting Privileges for ML Model Development

```
BEGIN
    EXECUTE IMMEDIATE 'GRANT CREATE MINING MODEL TO testuser1;
    EXECUTE IMMEDIATE 'GRANT SELECT ON V$SQL TO testuser1';
    EXECUTE IMMEDIATE 'GRANT EXECUTE ON DBMS_DATA_MINING TO testuser1';
END;
/
```

Collecting SQL Performance Metrics

Next, QuickMart created a training dataset by extracting relevant attributes from the V$SQL view. These attributes included CPU time, buffer gets, disk reads, and rows processed, all of which contribute to the total query execution time. The dataset was stored in a table as shown in Listing 4-10.

Listing 4-10. Creating the SQL Performance Training Dataset

```
CREATE TABLE sql_performance_data AS
SELECT
    sql_id,
    elapsed_time/1000000 AS elapsed_seconds,   -- Convert microseconds
    to seconds
    cpu_time/1000000 AS cpu_seconds,
    buffer_gets,
    disk_reads,
    rows_processed
FROM v$sql
WHERE elapsed_time > 0;
```

The table captured query behavior at runtime, forming the foundation for the machine learning model.

Preparing Training and Validation Datasets

To ensure the model could generalize well and avoid overfitting, QuickMart split the collected data into separate training and validation sets. This step is critical for evaluating the model on unseen data.

Listing 4-11. Creating Training and Validation Datasets

```
CREATE TABLE sql_performance_train AS
SELECT * FROM sql_performance_data
WHERE MOD(ORA_HASH(sql_id), 10) < 7;

CREATE TABLE sql_performance_validation AS
SELECT * FROM sql_performance_data
WHERE MOD(ORA_HASH(sql_id), 10) >= 7;
```

This hash-based method ensured a reproducible and roughly 70/30 data split for model development and evaluation.

Training the Predictive Regression Model

Using the training dataset, the team proceeded to train a regression model using Oracle's DBMS_DATA_MINING package. The model learned patterns between query metrics and actual elapsed time. The target was to predict elapsed_seconds—the time taken by a SQL query to complete. Listing 4-12 shows the model creation process.

Listing 4-12. Creating a Regression Model to Predict Query Elapsed Time

```
BEGIN
    DBMS_DATA_MINING.CREATE_MODEL(
        model_name => 'SQL_PERFORMANCE_PREDICTOR',
        mining_function => DBMS_DATA_MINING.REGRESSION,
        data_table_name => 'sql_performance_train',
        target_column_name => 'ELAPSED_SECONDS',
        settings_table_name => NULL
    );
END;
/
```

The model learned performance patterns from historical data, allowing it to estimate execution time for future queries with similar characteristics.

Generating Predictions and Identifying Bottlenecks

Once the model was trained, QuickMart used it to score queries and predict execution times. This allowed the team to identify high-cost SQL operations in advance and take steps to mitigate delays. Listing 4-13 illustrates how predictions were generated.

Listing 4-13. Predicting Execution Time for SQL Queries

```
SELECT sql_id, buffer_gets, disk_reads,
       PREDICTION(SQL_PERFORMANCE_PREDICTOR USING *) AS predicted_seconds
FROM sql_performance_validation
ORDER BY predicted_seconds DESC;
```

The output included predicted execution times (`predicted_seconds`), enabling a data-driven strategy for tuning and prioritization.

Driving Proactive Database Management

With predictive insights in place, QuickMart's database operations team was able to proactively detect potentially expensive SQL statements and take action—such as query optimization, index adjustments, or resource prioritization—before performance issues impacted production. This marked a shift from reactive tuning to data-driven foresight, reducing troubleshooting cycles and improving system stability.

Oracle ADB-S enables predictive performance analytics by embedding machine learning directly within the database. QuickMart's implementation of an in-database regression model for SQL query elapsed time highlights how AI/ML can empower operations teams with actionable insights—without requiring data export or third-party platforms. However, as shown in this case study, achieving reliable results requires a disciplined workflow that includes data partitioning, model validation, and performance evaluation using best practices from the data science domain.

Internal Mechanism of AI/ML-Based Query Elapsed Time Prediction in Oracle ADB-S

Oracle ADB-S utilizes AI/ML models to predict SQL query execution times by analyzing historical performance data, such as query complexity and system load. The system trains machine learning models using this data, which then forecasts future query execution times. These predictions help in proactive resource allocation, query optimization, and performance management, reducing manual tuning and enhancing database efficiency.

The internal structure of AI/ML-Based Query Elapsed Time Prediction is illustrated in Table 4-3.

Table 4-3. *Internal Flow of Query Elapsed Time Prediction in Oracle ADB-S*

```
AI/ML-Based Query Elapsed Time Prediction
    |
Historical Performance Data Analysis
    |
Query Complexity and System Load Evaluation
    |
Machine Learning Model Training
    |
Forecasting Query Execution Times
    |
Proactive Resource Allocation and Optimization
```

This architecture enables autonomous query performance management and significantly improves operational efficiency within the Oracle ecosystem, helping enterprises reduce manual intervention and scale intelligently.

Practical Use Cases for Query Elapsed Time Prediction in Oracle ADB-S

In environments where query patterns are dynamic or workloads are shared across teams, predicting SQL execution time can help prioritize resources and manage performance expectations. Below are select, realistic scenarios where Oracle ADB-S's in-database ML adds value.

Table 4-4. *Realistic Use Cases for Query Elapsed Time Prediction in Oracle ADB-S*

Domain	Scenario	Value Delivered
Data Warehousing	Forecasting ad-hoc analytical query run times	Helps users manage expectations and avoid system strain
Shared Environments	Identifying long-running queries in multitenant workloads	Enables intelligent resource allocation and queuing
Dev/Test Pipelines	Estimating execution time of new or modified queries	Supports performance validation before deployment
BI Reporting	Predicting delays in complex scheduled reports	Allows preemptive scheduling adjustments

These scenarios show how prediction augments performance management in flexible, user-driven environments—where not all queries can be fully optimized ahead of time.

Common Questions About AI/ML-Based Query Elapsed Time Prediction in Oracle ADB-S

Oracle ADB-S offers in-database machine learning capabilities to estimate SQL query execution times. As organizations explore this feature to support performance diagnostics and workload planning, common questions emerge around data preparation, model adaptability, integration feasibility, and prediction reliability.

A frequently asked question is how Oracle ADB-S handles outliers in historical performance data. While ADB-S provides access to necessary data and model-building tools, it is up to users to apply preprocessing steps such as normalization, filtering, or manual outlier removal before training, ensuring that the model learns from clean and representative data.

Adaptability to changing execution patterns is another key concern. Oracle ADB-S does not automatically retrain models. Users must periodically refresh models with updated data to reflect changes in query behavior or system load. There is no built-in online learning mechanism, so maintaining relevance is a manual, iterative process.

Integration with monitoring and resource management tools is also a common topic. Although predictions can be surfaced through views or SQL queries and incorporated into custom dashboards or Oracle Enterprise Manager, using them for automated alerting or resource scaling typically requires additional development and may not always justify the complexity over simpler alternatives.

Ensuring the reliability and accuracy of predictions is critical. Oracle provides model evaluation functions to help users validate accuracy using separate datasets. However, maintaining reliable predictions depends on regular retraining and careful model assessment—steps that remain under user control.

Overall, Oracle ADB-S enables flexible, SQL-based predictive modeling within the database. When used with sound data practices and appropriate validation, it can enhance performance visibility and support proactive query management.

Key Takeaway Oracle ADB-S leverages built-in AI/ML models to accurately predict SQL query execution times by analyzing historical performance data such as query complexity, data volume, and system load. These predictive insights enable database administrators to identify and optimize slow-running queries proactively, enhancing query responsiveness and reducing the reliance on manual tuning. As a result, organizations benefit from improved database efficiency and consistent performance across critical domains like ecommerce, finance, healthcare, and telecommunications.

Building on this AI-powered foundation, Oracle ADB-S also applies machine learning to real-time query execution patterns and system workload dynamics. **The next section explores how Auto-Tuned Query Execution** enables adaptive optimization by continuously adjusting execution strategies to enhance SQL performance and resource efficiency.

Auto-Tuned Query Execution in Oracle ADB-S

Oracle Autonomous Database serverless (ADB-S) extends its AI/ML foundation to automate SQL performance tuning through a capability known as Auto-Tuned Query Execution. Rather than relying on manual intervention, the system continuously analyzes SQL performance using historical query attributes and system workload metrics. By learning from these patterns, Oracle ADB-S intelligently refines execution strategies, optimizes resource allocation, and applies performance enhancements in real time. Key AI-powered features that drive this automation include SQL Plan Management (SPM), Automatic Indexing, and Adaptive Query Optimization.

This approach allows the database to self-adjust and evolve, replacing suboptimal query plans with better-performing alternatives. Developers and DBAs benefit from improved application responsiveness and reduced maintenance overhead—all while maintaining full control when manual tuning is required.

The following real-world case from the retail sector illustrates how Auto-Tuned Query Execution can dramatically improve SQL performance and system efficiency.

> **CASE STUDY: QUICKMART AND PERFORMANCE OPTIMIZATION**
>
> QuickMart, a large online retailer, encountered sluggish performance when querying large datasets. Specifically, analytical queries aggregating revenue by product were slow to execute, despite indexing efforts. These issues became more pronounced during peak business periods, prompting the need for intelligent, automated tuning.
>
> To address this, QuickMart adopted Oracle ADB-S's Auto-Tuned Query Execution capabilities, which allowed the system to identify inefficiencies and apply AI/ML-based tuning strategies autonomously.

Creating and Populating the Sample Dataset

To simulate production behavior, QuickMart created a dataset consisting of one million rows of transaction records. As shown in Listing 4-14, the `sales_data` table includes typical sales attributes such as `sale_id`, `customer_id`, `product_id`, `price`, `quantity`, and `sale_date`.

Listing 4-14. Sample Dataset Creation and Population

```
CREATE TABLE sales_data (
    sale_id       NUMBER PRIMARY KEY,
    customer_id   NUMBER NOT NULL,
    product_id    NUMBER NOT NULL,
```

```
    price           NUMBER(10,2) NOT NULL,
    quantity        NUMBER NOT NULL,
    sale_date       DATE NOT NULL
);

-- Insert sample data (Populate with a large dataset for real testing)
BEGIN
    FOR i IN 1..1000000 LOOP
        INSERT INTO sales_data (sale_id, customer_id, product_id, price,
        quantity, sale_date)
        VALUES (i, MOD(i, 50000) + 1, MOD(i, 1000) + 1, DBMS_RANDOM.
        VALUE(10, 500),
                MOD(i, 5) + 1, SYSDATE - DBMS_RANDOM.VALUE(0, 365));
    END LOOP;
    COMMIT;
END;
/
```

Identifying the Performance Bottleneck

The team ran an analytical query to calculate total revenue per product over the past 11 months. Despite a WHERE clause on sale_date, the database performed a full table scan, indicating that indexing and partitioning strategies were suboptimal.

Listing 4-15. Initial Query with Performance Issues

```
SELECT product_id, SUM(price * quantity) AS total_revenue
FROM sales_data
WHERE sale_date >= ADD_MONTHS(SYSDATE, -11)
GROUP BY product_id;
```

This inefficiency led QuickMart to trigger Oracle's auto-tuning mechanisms for corrective action.

Activating AI-Driven Auto-Tuning

Oracle ADB-S runs Auto-Tuning in the background, but it also allows developers to invoke SQL tuning tasks manually when immediate insights are needed. As shown in Listing 4-16, the DBMS_SQLTUNE package can be used to initiate an AI-powered tuning task for the problematic query.

Listing 4-16. Manual Trigger for AI-Based SQL Tuning

```
DECLARE
task_name VARCHAR2(100);
BEGIN
task_name := DBMS_SQLTUNE.CREATE_TUNING_TASK(
  sql_text => 'SELECT product_id, SUM(price * quantity) AS total_revenue
  FROM sales_data WHERE sale_date >= ADD_MONTHS(SYSDATE, -11) GROUP BY
  product_id',
  task_name => 'auto_tune_retail_query2',
  description => 'Optimize the revenue aggregation query'
);
DBMS_SQLTUNE.EXECUTE_TUNING_TASK(task_name);
END;
/
```

This invocation allows the system to analyze the query execution plan and recommend optimizations based on current statistics and AI-driven insights.

Reviewing Optimization Recommendations

After executing the tuning task, developers can extract the AI-generated recommendations, as shown in Listing 4-17.

Listing 4-17. Fetching Auto-Tuning Recommendations

```
SELECT DBMS_SQLTUNE.REPORT_TUNING_TASK('auto_tune_retail_query2')
FROM DUAL;
```

The output typically includes several recommendations, such as

- Creating an index on sale_date to enable range scans.
- Applying range partitioning on sale_date for effective pruning.
- Suggesting materialized views to cache and reuse frequent aggregations.

These insights represent Oracle's ability to self-diagnose and prescribe targeted performance improvements using embedded machine learning.

Ensuring Query Stability with SQL Performance Analyzer

Beyond tuning specific queries, Oracle ADB-S offers tools like DBMS_SQLPA to evaluate how changes in the system (e.g., upgrades or schema modifications) affect SQL performance. This is particularly useful for regression testing in dynamic environments.

Listing 4-18. Generating SQL Performance Impact Report

```
SELECT DBMS_SQLPA.report_analysis_task('auto_tune_retail_query2', 'TEXT',
'ALL') AS report
FROM dual;
```

While DBMS_SQLTUNE focuses on real-time improvement, DBMS_SQLPA ensures consistency and reliability across query plan evolutions and environmental changes. Developers can also monitor the progress and history of tasks using the command shown in Listing 4-19.

Listing 4-19. Monitor SQL Performance Impact Report

```
select * from dba_advisor_log where lower(task_name)='auto_tune_retail_
query2';
```

AI/ML-Driven Optimization in Practice

This case demonstrates the practical impact of Auto-Tuned Query Execution in Oracle ADB-S. QuickMart was able to reduce query latency and improve analytical responsiveness without rewriting queries or redesigning the schema manually. Instead, the database learned and adapted autonomously, guided by a robust AI/ML engine.

Internal Mechanism of Auto-Tuned Query Execution in Oracle ADB-S

Oracle Autonomous Database serverless (ADB-S) employs AI/ML-powered Auto-Tuned Query Execution to autonomously improve SQL performance. By analyzing historical query behavior and execution outcomes, the system identifies inefficiencies and dynamically refines execution strategies in real time. It incorporates advanced features such as automatic indexing, adaptive query optimization, and SQL Plan Management (SPM) to maintain high performance across varying workloads.

This continuous feedback mechanism ensures that queries consistently use the most efficient execution paths, minimizing the need for manual tuning while optimizing both performance and resource utilization.

The internal structure of Auto-Tuned Query Execution is illustrated in Table 4-5.

Table 4-5. Internal Flow of Auto-Tuned Query Execution in Oracle ADB-S

Auto-Tuned Query Execution
|
Historical Performance Data Analysis
|
AI/ML-Based Query Optimization
|
Dynamic Execution Plan Adjustment
|
Automatic Indexing and Adaptive Optimization
|
Continuous Monitoring via SQL Plan Management (SPM)
|
Faster Query Performance and Resource Efficiency

This architecture enables Oracle ADB-S to act as a self-optimizing database engine—adapting execution strategies without manual intervention. As a result, enterprises benefit from consistently faster queries, smarter resource use, and simplified performance management across diverse workloads.

Sample Real-Time Business Use Cases for Oracle ADB-S's Auto-Tuned Query Execution Feature

The following table illustrates real-world scenarios where Oracle ADB-S's AI-driven AutoTuned Query Execution delivers significant performance improvements by automatically optimizing SQL workloads.

Table 4-6. Real-Time Business Use Cases for Auto-Tuned Query Execution in Oracle ADB-S

Use Case	Scenario	Benefit
Retail Inventory Analysis	Analyzing sales and inventory.	Faster query optimization.
Financial Reporting	Running stock portfolio reports.	Quicker report generation.
Ecommerce Recommendations	Personalizing product suggestions.	Faster recommendation results.
Customer Analytics in Telecom	Analyzing customer usage data.	Faster insights for decision-making.
Healthcare Data Analytics	Analyzing patient data.	Speeding up query execution.
Supply Chain Optimization	Analyzing supply chain data.	Quicker logistics decision-making.

These examples demonstrate how Oracle ADB-S embeds intelligence into query execution pipelines. By autonomously identifying suboptimal queries and applying tuning—including plan refinement, dynamic indexing, and adaptive optimization—the platform helps enterprises reduce manual intervention, improve query responsiveness, and ensure agile, data-driven operations.

Common Questions About Auto-Tuned Query Execution in Oracle ADB-S

Oracle ADB-S embeds intelligent automation into its SQL optimization processes through Auto-Tuned Query Execution. As organizations adopt this feature to improve performance and reduce manual tuning overhead, common questions often emerge around control, reliability, efficiency, and customization.

CHAPTER 4   AI AND MACHINE LEARNING IN ADB-S

One recurring question is how Oracle ADB-S ensures the accuracy and reliability of its AI/ML-based query tuning recommendations. The system continuously analyzes historical query performance and structural attributes to generate well-informed suggestions. By leveraging SQL Plan Management (SPM), it validates and evolves execution plans over time, ensuring that changes lead to consistent and measurable improvements.

DBAs frequently inquire about the level of control they retain over the automated optimization process. While Oracle ADB-S intelligently applies optimizations by default, administrators can manually trigger tuning tasks, review AI-generated recommendations, and decide whether to implement or refine them. This balance between automation and control allows organizations to adapt to varying performance needs while maintaining oversight.

Another important consideration is the potential performance impact of real-time tuning in production environments. Oracle ADB-S addresses this by performing query optimization using lightweight background processes, which are specifically designed to be nonintrusive. The underlying AI/ML engine quickly identifies tuning opportunities and applies changes with minimal disruption, even in high-volume systems.

Efficiency in resource usage is also a key concern. Oracle ADB-S uses AI models to determine when indexing or partitioning will produce significant benefits. Unnecessary structures are avoided, ensuring that only performance-enhancing actions are taken—ultimately leading to more efficient use of compute and storage resources.

Together, these capabilities demonstrate how Oracle ADB-S enables intelligent, self-adjusting query optimization. Enterprises gain the benefits of enhanced SQL performance, reduced tuning effort, and greater operational efficiency—all within a secure, scalable, and DBA-friendly framework.

Key Takeaway   Auto-Tuned Query Execution exemplifies Oracle ADB-S's commitment to self-driving database technology by seamlessly integrating AI/ML into the core of query planning and execution. With advanced features such as SQL Plan Management, Automatic Indexing, and Adaptive Query Optimization, the platform intelligently refines execution strategies to deliver consistently high performance while minimizing manual intervention. As demonstrated by QuickMart, these autonomous capabilities significantly reduce query execution times and operational overhead, enabling enterprises to make faster, data-driven decisions with greater efficiency and scalability.

The next section explores how these AI-powered optimizations extend beyond individual query tuning, enabling Oracle ADB-S to dynamically adapt to changing workloads and system conditions for holistic, real-time performance management.

AI-Powered Optimizations in ADB-S

Oracle Autonomous Database serverless (ADB-S) incorporates AI-powered query optimization as a core capability, enabling dynamic performance tuning without manual intervention. Unlike traditional static methods that depend on cost-based rules and manual tuning, Oracle ADB-S continuously evolves its optimization strategies using machine learning. This allows the platform to intelligently adapt to changing data patterns, workloads, and system conditions, ensuring consistently high query performance.

AI-based query optimization is enabled by default in Oracle ADB-S. The platform automatically adjusts execution plans based on real-time data insights and resource availability, all without requiring user action. To configure or adjust these optimizations, administrators can use the OPTIMIZER_FEATURES_ENABLE parameter. When set to version 23 or higher, AI-driven enhancements are active. For compatibility or rollback purposes, this setting can be adjusted to earlier versions such as 19 to disable newer optimizations introduced in Oracle 23c.

Oracle ADB-S also provides fine-grained control over optimizations through SQL hints. Users can apply directives such as NO_QUERY_TRANSFORMATION to bypass AI-powered transformations selectively. This level of customization ensures that DBAs and developers retain the flexibility to manage specific queries with precision while leaving broader optimization decisions to the autonomous engine.

> **CASE STUDY: PERFORMANCE GAINS THROUGH AI OPTIMIZATION AT QUICKMART**

To illustrate the benefits of AI-powered query optimization, consider a scenario involving QuickMart, a mid-sized retail analytics company. The firm runs frequent analytical queries on transactional sales data to generate product-level performance reports for specific date ranges. Initially, their reports were taking too long to execute, leading to delays in business decisions.

CHAPTER 4 AI AND MACHINE LEARNING IN ADB-S

To begin addressing the issue, QuickMart created a table called sales_data to store transactional information. This included fields such as transaction_id, customer_id, product_id, sale_date, quantity_sold, and total_amount. The table was populated with sample sales data.

Listing 4-20 shows the SQL used to create and populate the dataset.

Listing 4-20. Creation and Population of Sample Sales Data Table

```sql
CREATE TABLE sales_data (
    transaction_id NUMBER PRIMARY KEY,
    customer_id NUMBER,
    product_id NUMBER,
    sale_date DATE,
    quantity_sold NUMBER,
    total_amount NUMBER
);

INSERT INTO sales_data (transaction_id, customer_id, product_id, sale_date, quantity_sold, total_amount)
VALUES (1, 101, 501, TO_DATE('2024-01-01', 'YYYY-MM-DD'), 2, 50);

INSERT INTO sales_data (transaction_id, customer_id, product_id, sale_date, quantity_sold, total_amount)
VALUES (2, 102, 502, TO_DATE('2024-01-02', 'YYYY-MM-DD'), 1, 30);
```

Next, the team ran a baseline aggregation query to assess initial performance, calculating the total quantity and total sales per product for a two-week period.

Listing 4-21. Initial Aggregation Query for Performance Benchmarking

```sql
SELECT product_id,
       SUM(quantity_sold) AS total_quantity,
       SUM(total_amount) AS total_sales
FROM sales_data
WHERE sale_date BETWEEN TO_DATE('2024-01-01', 'YYYY-MM-DD') AND TO_DATE('2024-01-15', 'YYYY-MM-DD')
GROUP BY product_id;
```

To evaluate performance metrics such as elapsed time, CPU time, and buffer gets, DataMartX used the V$SQL view.

Listing 4-22. Retrieving Initial Query Performance Metrics

```
Check the initial performance of the query:
SELECT SQL_ID,
       ELAPSED_TIME,
       CPU_TIME,
       BUFFER_GETS
FROM V$SQL
WHERE SQL_TEXT LIKE '%SELECT product_id%'
ORDER BY ELAPSED_TIME DESC;
```

Following the initial assessment, Oracle ADB-S's AI engine applied automatic query optimizations. To understand what transformations occurred, the team queried the GV_$SQL_REOPTIMIZATION_HINTS view, which provided visibility into applied optimization hints such as join methods and parallel execution.

Listing 4-23. Reviewing Applied AI Optimization Hints

```
SELECT SQL_ID,
       CHILD_NUMBER,
       HINT_TEXT,
       REPARSE,
       CLIENT_ID,
       INST_ID
FROM sys.GV_$SQL_REOPTIMIZATION_HINTS
WHERE SQL_ID IN (SELECT SQL_ID FROM V$SQL WHERE SQL_TEXT LIKE '%SELECT product_id%')
ORDER BY SQL_ID, CHILD_NUMBER;
```

After these optimizations, the team reran the performance query to assess the impact.

Listing 4-24. Post-Optimization Performance Evaluation

```
SELECT SQL_ID,
       ELAPSED_TIME,
       CPU_TIME,
       BUFFER_GETS
FROM V$SQL
WHERE SQL_TEXT LIKE '%SELECT product_id%'
ORDER BY ELAPSED_TIME DESC;
```

The results showed significant performance gains, including reduced elapsed time and lower resource consumption. These improvements confirmed that Oracle's AI engine had applied more efficient execution plans—potentially including parallel processing and smarter join strategies.

For further analysis, DataMartX drilled into specific optimization decisions by filtering for fast queries in the GV_$SQL_REOPTIMIZATION_HINTS view.

Listing 4-25. Analyzing Optimized Query Hints for Fast Executions

```
SELECT SQL_ID,
       CHILD_NUMBER,
       HINT_TEXT,
       REPARSE,
       CLIENT_ID,
       INST_ID
FROM sys.GV_$SQL_REOPTIMIZATION_HINTS
WHERE SQL_ID IN (SELECT SQL_ID FROM V$SQL WHERE SQL_TEXT LIKE '%SELECT product_id%' AND ELAPSED_TIME < 1000)
ORDER BY SQL_ID, CHILD_NUMBER;
```

This provided further confirmation of AI-driven enhancements such as predicate pushdown, adaptive join methods, and runtime statistics adjustments. Together, these intelligent optimizations contributed to more responsive analytics and faster time-to-insight.

In summary, AI-powered query optimization in Oracle ADB-S offers a significant advantage for enterprises like DataMartX. By automatically adapting to real-time workloads and continuously evolving execution strategies, the system enhances performance, reduces manual effort, and supports data-driven decision-making at scale.

The next section will explore how these capabilities integrate with other autonomous features to deliver end-to-end workload optimization in Oracle ADB-S.

Internal Mechanism of AI-Powered Optimizations in Oracle ADB-S

Oracle ADB-S leverages AI-powered optimization by dynamically analyzing query workloads and system conditions using machine learning models. It adjusts execution plans in real-time, applying techniques like parallel execution, join reordering, and resource allocation optimization. This adaptive approach reduces the need for manual tuning, ensuring efficient query processing and improved performance across diverse workloads, by continuously learning and evolving based on data patterns and resource usage.

The internal structure of AI-powered query optimization in Oracle ADB-S is illustrated in Table 4-7.

Table 4-7. *Internal Flow of AI-Powered Query Optimization in Oracle ADB-S*

AI-Powered Optimizations
|
Query Workload and System Analysis
|
Machine Learning Model Execution
|
Real-Time Plan Adjustments
|
Parallel Execution and Join Reordering
|
Resource Allocation Optimization
|
Continuous Learning and Performance Enhancement

This architecture reinforces Oracle ADB-S's role as an autonomous, intelligent data platform. By embedding continuous learning directly into the query execution lifecycle, it enables enterprises to handle complex and evolving workloads with reduced operational effort and enhanced performance agility.

Differences Between Oracle ADB-S and Pre-ADB-S Databases Based on AI-Powered Optimizations

The following table highlights key differences between traditional pre-ADB-S databases and Oracle Autonomous Database serverless (ADB-S) with respect to AI-powered query optimization capabilities.

Table 4-8. Comparative Overview of AI-Powered Optimization in Oracle ADB-S vs. Pre-ADB-S Databases

Feature	Pre-ADB-S Databases	Oracle ADB-S
AI-Powered Query Optimization	Lacked AI-driven optimization; relied solely on rule-based or cost-based optimization.	Dynamically optimizes queries using AI for improved performance and resource usage.
Native AI Integration	No native AI features for query handling; required manual query tuning and optimization hints.	Includes built-in AI optimizations that adapt automatically to workloads.
Optimizer Hints	Required manual hints for specific query behavior.	AI can automatically determine and apply optimal hints without user intervention.
Performance Monitoring	Limited tools for analyzing optimizer behavior and query performance improvements.	Enhanced tools to monitor AI-driven optimizations and performance metrics.
Query Adaptability	Static execution plans with limited ability to adapt to data changes dynamically.	Adaptive AI techniques modify execution plans dynamically for better efficiency.

This comparison underscores how Oracle ADB-S revolutionizes database performance management by embedding intelligent automation at the core of query execution, minimizing manual intervention while maximizing efficiency and scalability.

Sample Real-Time Business Use Cases for AI-Powered Optimizations in Oracle ADB-S

The following table illustrates real-world scenarios where Oracle ADB-S's AI-powered optimizations deliver measurable improvements by dynamically adjusting execution strategies based on data patterns and workload conditions.

Table 4-9. Real-Time Business Use Cases for AI-Powered Optimizations in Oracle ADB-S

Use Case	Description	Business Benefit
Ecommerce Recommendations	Optimizes product recommendations based on real-time data.	Increases sales and enhances customer experience.
Financial Analysis	Optimizes complex financial queries for faster insights.	Speeds up decision-making and reporting.
Healthcare Analytics	Improves data queries for patient and treatment analysis.	Enhances patient care and operational efficiency.
Supply Chain Management	Optimizes queries for inventory and logistics data in real-time.	Reduces delays and cuts costs.
Telecom Network Optimization	Adjusts queries to manage traffic spikes and network issues.	Ensures better network performance and uptime.
Fraud Detection	Enhances fraud detection by optimizing transaction data analysis.	Reduces fraud and financial loss.

These examples demonstrate how Oracle ADB-S brings AI intelligence directly into the query execution layer. By continuously monitoring performance and autonomously applying adjustments—such as parallelization, hint tuning, and join method selection—the platform empowers businesses to achieve consistent, scalable, and high-performance outcomes with minimal manual effort.

CHAPTER 4 AI AND MACHINE LEARNING IN ADB-S

Common Questions About AI-Powered Optimizations in Oracle ADB-S

Oracle ADB-S leverages AI-driven optimization to intelligently adjust SQL execution strategies based on real-time system and workload conditions. As organizations adopt these capabilities, common questions emerge regarding complexity management, workload adaptability, efficiency, and user control.

A key question is how Oracle ADB-S handles complex queries with multiple joins and aggregations. The platform uses machine learning to analyze query structures and dynamically apply optimizations like join reordering and parallel execution, improving performance without manual tuning.

Organizations also ask whether AI optimizations are adaptable across workloads. Oracle ADB-S automatically tailors optimizations for OLTP and OLAP environments, while still allowing advanced users to apply SQL hints or adjust parameters for specific needs.

In comparing AI-driven and traditional optimizations, users find that ADB-S offers faster execution and lower resource consumption by continuously learning from past performance. This contrasts with static, rule-based tuning approaches that may not adapt well to evolving workloads.

Lastly, administrators often wonder if AI optimizations can be bypassed. Oracle allows this through hints such as `NO_QUERY_TRANSFORMATION`, though disabling AI may lead to performance trade-offs.

Together, these capabilities illustrate how Oracle ADB-S delivers intelligent, adaptive query performance—reducing manual overhead while maintaining flexibility for expert users.

Key Takeaway   Oracle ADB-S transforms the landscape of query optimization by embedding AI-powered intelligence directly into the execution engine. Unlike traditional systems that rely on static rules and manual tuning, ADB-S continuously adapts to workload patterns, enabling real-time plan adjustments, intelligent resource allocation, and superior performance across diverse applications. These innovations not only reduce operational complexity but also enhance scalability, accuracy, and responsiveness.

Building on these intelligent core capabilities, the next chapter explores how Oracle ADB-S extends its innovation into cloud-native data integration and blockchain technology—starting with the use of DBMS_CLOUD for managing external data sources and continuing with the implementation of blockchain tables for tamper-evident recordkeeping.

CHAPTER 5

Cloud and Blockchain Innovations

Introduction

This chapter explores the cloud-native and blockchain innovations integrated within Oracle Autonomous Database serverless (ADB-S). It introduces powerful capabilities such as DBMS_CLOUD for seamless access to external data sources, and blockchain tables designed to ensure data integrity through tamper-evident recordkeeping. Each section provides practical guidance on implementation, supported by real-world scenarios that demonstrate the value of these technologies in secure, distributed, and scalable data environments. Detailed walkthroughs illustrate how 23AI simplifies cloud data ingestion and enforces trust through immutable blockchain mechanisms. Comparisons with conventional methods highlight the platform's advancements in cloud interoperability and secure data management, while concise summaries at the end of each section reinforce key benefits and operational best practices.

Managing Using DBMS_CLOUD in ADB-S

In modern cloud-native architectures, the ability to efficiently manage files between cloud storage and autonomous databases is fundamental to achieving operational agility, security, and scalability. Oracle Autonomous Database serverless (ADB-S) addresses this need through the powerful DBMS_CLOUD package. This built-in utility enables seamless interaction between ADB-S and Oracle Cloud Object Storage, making it possible to move files, generate reports, and archive database content efficiently.

CHAPTER 5　CLOUD AND BLOCKCHAIN INNOVATIONS

This section introduces the practical implementation of DBMS_CLOUD through a real-world case study involving a fictional organization, *QuickMart*, which adopted this feature for managing diagnostic reports, SQL analysis outputs, and historical audit records across Oracle ADB-S and Oracle Object Storage.

CASE STUDY: CLOUD-INTEGRATED FILE MANAGEMENT AT QUICKMART

QuickMart Retail required a reliable way to generate SQL Health Check (SQLHC) reports, store them securely, and retrieve them on-demand for periodic performance reviews. The IT team leveraged the DBMS_CLOUD package to automate this workflow. The process began with creating secure credentials that enable DBMS_CLOUD to access Object Storage, as shown in Listing 5-1.

Listing 5-1. Creating a Cloud Credential in ADB-S

```
begin
  dbms_cloud.create_credential (
    credential_name => 'FC_ADBS_TEST_1',
    username        => 'testuser1',
    password        => 'pass1#'
  );
end;
/
```

With the credential in place, the team listed available directories within ADB-S using the query in Listing 5-2, confirming the presence of the SQL_RPT_DIR directory.

Listing 5-2. Validating Oracle Directories and Listing Files

```
SELECT * FROM DBA_DIRECTORIES WHERE DIRECTORY_NAME = 'SQL_RPT_DIR';
```

To list files within this directory:

```
SELECT * FROM TABLE(DBMS_CLOUD.LIST_FILES('SQL_RPT_DIR'));
```

To assess SQL performance, the team used the DBMS_SQLDIAG.REPORT_SQL procedure to generate a SQLHC report and saved it in the directory, as shown in Listing 5-3.

Listing 5-3. Generating a SQL Health Check Report

```
declare
   my_report clob;
begin
   my_report := dbms_sqldiag.report_sql('67tyertghwe544',directory=>'SQL_
   RPT_DIR',level=>'ALL');
end;
/
```

We are verifying the report file by rerunning Listing 5-2

Expected output:

SQLR_67tyertghwe544_202502041039.html 295579 Bytes Created: 04-FEB-25 10.39.47 AM Modified: 04-FEB-25 10.40.53 AM

After confirming that the report was stored successfully in the directory, the next objective was to transfer this file to Oracle Cloud Object Storage for archiving and sharing across environments. A pre-authenticated request (PAR) URL was generated from the Object Storage console and used in the upload step. The transfer was accomplished using the PUT_OBJECT procedure (Listing 5-4).

Since **ADB restricts direct file access**, migrating reports to **Object Storage** is a best practice for long-term retention and analysis.

To create a Cloud Storage Bucket

1. Log in to **Oracle Cloud.**

2. Navigate to **Storage → Buckets**.

3. Click **Create Bucket** and name it bucket-bind-waits.

4. Inside the bucket, click **Pre-Authenticated Requests.**

5. Select "**Permit Object Read & Write**", enable "**Object Listing**", and set an expiration date.

6. Generate a **Pre-Authenticated Request (PAR) URL** (e.g., looks as below)

    'https://objectstorage.us-phoenix-1.oraclecloud.com/p/2SBIeBl3V3jaoOk4XKQ7qmrl8OryOsVD-GB_AsQyHqF3buF7PSsXTe1xFpPghQCR/n/axr1cx4k2cz6/b/bucket-bind-waits/o/'

Listing 5-4. Uploading a File from ADB-S to Oracle Object Storage

```
BEGIN
 DBMS_CLOUD.PUT_OBJECT(
 credential_name => 'FC_ADBS_TEST_1',
 object_uri => 'https://objectstorage.us-phoenix-1.oraclecloud.com/p/
 2SBIeBl3V3jaoOk4XKQ7qmrl8OryOsVD-GB_AsQyHqF3buF7PSsXTe1xFpPghQCR/n/
 axr1cx4k2cz6/b/bucket-bind-waits/o/',
directory_name => 'SQL_RPT_DIR',
 file_name => 'SQLR_67tyertghwe544_202502041039.html');
END;
/
```

File upload success was confirmed by querying the uploaded objects (Listing 5-5).

Listing 5-5. Verifying File Upload to Cloud Storage

```
select *
from   dbms_cloud.list_objects(
        credential_name => 'FC_ADBS_TEST_1',
        location_uri    => 'https://objectstorage.us-phoenix-1.oraclecloud.
                           com/p/2SBIeBl3V3jaoOk4XKQ7qmrl8OryOsVD-GB_AsQyHqF3buF7PSsXTe1x
                           FpPghQCR/n/axr1cx4k2cz6/b/bucket-bind-waits/o/')
order by last_modified desc
fetch first 5 rows only;
```

The team also implemented BLOB and CLOB data movement using the DBMS_CLOUD overloaded procedures. In one scenario, a BLOB report stored in the documents table was transferred to Cloud Object Storage using the code in Listing 5-7.

Creating the Table to Store BLOB Data

Listing 5-6. Uploading BLOB Data into Database

```
CREATE TABLE documents (
    doc_id    NUMBER PRIMARY KEY,
    doc_name  VARCHAR2(255),
```

```
        doc_file   BLOB
);
DECLARE
    l_bfile   BFILE;
    l_blob    BLOB;
BEGIN
    -- Open the file from the directory
    l_bfile := BFILENAME('SQL_RPT_DIR', 'SQLR_67tyertgh
    we544_202502041039.html');
    DBMS_LOB.CREATETEMPORARY(l_blob, TRUE);

    -- Load file into the BLOB column
    DBMS_LOB.FILEOPEN(l_bfile, DBMS_LOB.FILE_READONLY);
    DBMS_LOB.LOADFROMFILE(l_blob, l_bfile, DBMS_LOB.GETLENGTH(l_bfile));
    DBMS_LOB.FILECLOSE(l_bfile);

    -- Insert into table
    INSERT INTO documents (doc_id, doc_name, doc_file)
    VALUES (101, 'SQLR_67tyertghwe544_202502041039.html', l_blob);

    COMMIT;
END;
/
```

The following PL/SQL block retrieves a **BLOB** from the documents table and uploads it to **Oracle Cloud Object Storage**.

Listing 5-7. Uploading BLOB from Database to Object Storage

```
DECLARE
    l_blob  BLOB;
    l_name varchar2(100);
BEGIN
    -- Retrieve the BLOB from the table
    SELECT doc_file,doc_name INTO l_blob,l_name FROM documents WHERE
    doc_id = 101;
```

CHAPTER 5   CLOUD AND BLOCKCHAIN INNOVATIONS

```
    -- Upload the BLOB to Object Storage
    DBMS_CLOUD.PUT_OBJECT(
        credential_name => 'FC_ADBS_TEST_1',
        object_uri      => 'https://objectstorage.us-phoenix-1.oraclecloud.
        com/p/2SBIeBl3V3jaoOk4XKQ7qmrl8OryOsVD-GB_AsQyHqF3buF7PSsXTe1x
        FpPghQCR/n/axr1cx4k2cz6/b/bucket-bind-waits/o/'||l_name,
        contents        => l_blob
    );
END;
/
```

A similar process was followed for transferring CLOBs. First, the CLOB was converted to a temporary BLOB, then uploaded to the cloud (Listing 5-8).

Listing 5-8. Converting and Uploading a CLOB to Object Storage

```
DECLARE
    l_clob  CLOB;
    l_blob  BLOB;
    l_dest_offset INTEGER := 1;
    l_src_offset INTEGER := 1;
    l_lang_context INTEGER := DBMS_LOB.DEFAULT_LANG_CTX;
    l_warning INTEGER;
    l_name VARCHAR2(100);
BEGIN
    -- Retrieve the CLOB and filename from the table
    SELECT PAYLOAD, TRACE_FILENAME
    INTO l_clob, l_name
    FROM v$diag_trace_file_contents
    WHERE PAYLOAD LIKE '%KZTDE:kztsmgcmkid%' /*Just one sample example*/
    AND rownum < 2;

    -- Initialize empty BLOB
    DBMS_LOB.CREATETEMPORARY(l_blob, TRUE);
```

```
    -- Convert CLOB to BLOB
    DBMS_LOB.CONVERTTOBLOB(
        dest_lob      => l_blob,
        src_clob      => l_clob,
        amount        => DBMS_LOB.LOBMAXSIZE,
        dest_offset   => l_dest_offset,
        src_offset    => l_src_offset,
        blob_csid     => DBMS_LOB.DEFAULT_CSID,
        lang_context  => l_lang_context,
        warning       => l_warning
    );

    -- Upload the BLOB to Object Storage
    DBMS_CLOUD.PUT_OBJECT(
        credential_name => 'FC_ADBS_TEST_1',
        object_uri      => 'https://objectstorage.us-phoenix-1.oraclecloud.
        com/p/2SBIeBl3V3jaoOk4XKQ7qmrl8OryOsVD-GB_AsQyHqF3buF7PSsXTe1x
        FpPghQCR/n/axr1cx4k2cz6/b/bucket-bind-waits/o/'||l_name,
        contents        => l_blob
    );

    -- Free temporary BLOB
    DBMS_LOB.FREETEMPORARY(l_blob);
END;
/
```

For audit purposes and report retrieval, the GET_OBJECT procedure was used to fetch files (e.g., test.sql) back into ADB-S, as demonstrated in Listing 5-9.

Listing 5-9. Downloading File from Object Storage to ADB Directory

```
begin
  dbms_cloud.get_object (
    credential_name => 'FC_ADBS_TEST_1',
    object_uri      => 'https://objectstorage.us-phoenix-1.oraclecloud.com/
    p/2SBIeBl3V3jaoOk4XKQ7qmrl8OryOsVD-GB_AsQyHqF3buF7PSsXTe1xFpPghQCR/n/
    axr1cx4k2cz6/b/bucket-bind-waits/o/test.sql',
```

```
      directory_name  => 'SQL_RPT_DIR',
      file_name       => 'test.sql');
end;
/
```

We are verifying the report file by rerunning Listing 5-2

Expected Output:

```
test.sql
23737
```

Finally, when files were no longer needed, they were deleted using the DELETE_FILE procedure to ensure optimal storage usage within the database environment (Listing 5-10).

Listing 5-10. Deleting File from Oracle Directory

```
begin
  dbms_cloud.delete_file(
     directory_name => 'SQL_RPT_DIR',
     file_name      => 'test.sql');
end;
/
```

The DBMS_CLOUD package simplifies and secures data interchange between Oracle ADB-S and Oracle Object Storage. Through QuickMart's case study, we have seen how credentials, report generation, file uploads, and BLOB/CLOB handling can be streamlined within the Oracle ecosystem. This level of integration helps enterprises adopt a cloud-native approach with confidence while maintaining control over data lifecycle and security. In the next section, we will examine how blockchain tables introduce immutability and audit integrity into enterprise data management using Oracle ADB-S.

Internal Mechanism of DBMS_CLOUD in Oracle ADB-S

Oracle ADB-S integrates with Oracle Cloud Object Storage using the DBMS_CLOUD package to manage file operations. It securely connects the database with cloud storage, enabling seamless data loading, unloading, and querying from external files.

CHAPTER 5 CLOUD AND BLOCKCHAIN INNOVATIONS

By leveraging efficient APIs and connectors, DBMS_CLOUD ensures scalable, secure, and high-performance file management within the ADB-S environment. This integration simplifies cloud-based data workflows, enhancing overall operational agility and resource management.

The internal structure of DBMS_CLOUD-based integration is illustrated in Table 5-1.

Table 5-1. *Internal Flow of DBMS_CLOUD Integration in Oracle ADB-S*

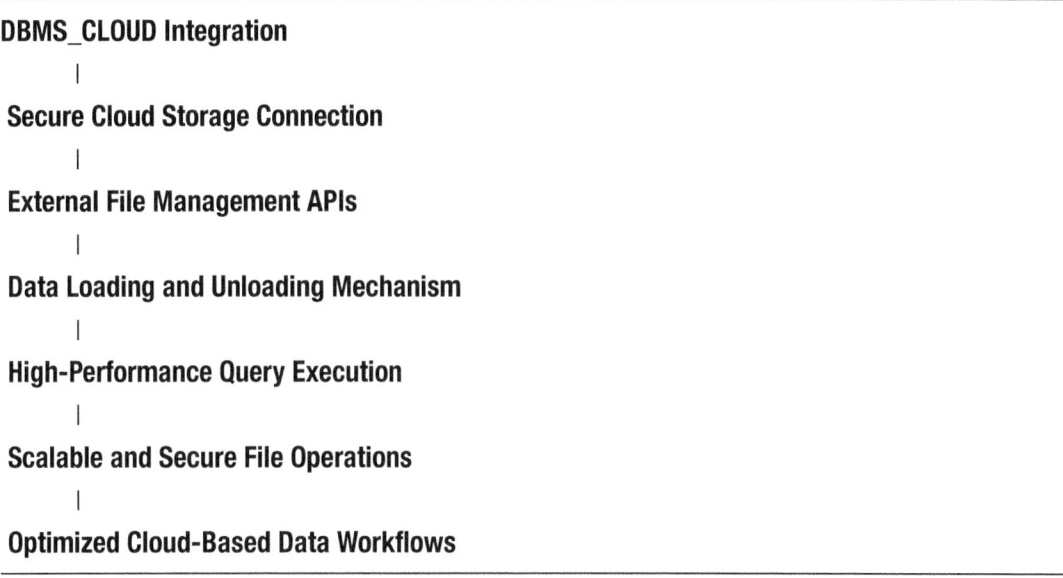

This architecture empowers Oracle ADB-S to act as a fully cloud-aware database solution. By natively supporting interactions with object storage, it simplifies data management and enables enterprises to implement cloud-first strategies with confidence and operational agility.

Potential Real-Time Business Use Cases for the Oracle DBMS_CLOUD Feature

The following table outlines practical business scenarios where Oracle ADB-S's **DBMS_CLOUD** feature provides substantial value by enabling secure, scalable, and automated file operations between the Autonomous Database and Oracle Cloud Object Storage.

Table 5-2. *Real-Time Business Use Cases for DBMS_CLOUD in Oracle ADB-S*

Use Case	Description	Business Benefit
Immutable Backup for Security	Store critical backups in Oracle Cloud Object Storage with immutability.	Enhances cyber resilience and meets insurance/compliance requirements.
External Data Load	Stage external files in object storage for use with external tables.	Simplifies ingestion pipelines without overloading core DB storage.
Audit Logging and Compliance	Archive audit logs and reports in cloud storage.	Ensures secure, compliant retention with easy retrieval.
Team-Based Document Sharing	Share large files across departments using object storage.	Enables collaboration without overloading application infrastructure.
BLOB Offloading	Store large binary files outside the database when updates are infrequent.	Reduces database size while retaining access to large content.

These examples demonstrate how DBMS_CLOUD transforms Oracle ADB-S into a cloud-integrated data platform. By simplifying complex file workflows through secure APIs and enabling persistent storage operations outside the core database engine, Oracle empowers enterprises to manage operational data more intelligently—supporting backup automation, performance diagnostics, compliance readiness, and hybrid data architectures with minimal overhead.

Common Questions About DBMS_CLOUD and File Management in Oracle

Oracle ADB-S, through its DBMS_CLOUD package, enables secure and controlled access to Oracle Cloud Object Storage. As enterprises incorporate this feature into their cloud workflows, common questions arise around network performance, practical use cases, and reliability.

One frequently asked question is how Oracle handles network bandwidth limitations during large file transfers. While DBMS_CLOUD supports parallel and resumable uploads to improve transfer efficiency, overall performance still depends on network conditions and file size. For large, infrequent transfers, these features provide better reliability over unstable connections.

Another question is whether DBMS_CLOUD can support real-time or AI/ML workloads. While data in Object Storage can be used as input to AI/ML workflows, integration is manual. Files accessed through DBMS_CLOUD must be loaded and processed by the user; there's no direct or automatic pipeline between DBMS_CLOUD and Oracle AI/ML services.

In high-throughput environments, users often ask about best practices. Object Storage is not designed for transactional workloads. Instead, it's best suited for bulk operations like loading external data, archiving exports, or storing logs. Practices such as compressing files, batching transfers, and implementing retry logic can help maintain reliability for these use cases.

Lastly, users ask about version control and data integrity. These are features of Oracle Cloud Object Storage itself—not DBMS_CLOUD. The storage service supports versioning and checksums, while DBMS_CLOUD provides access and interaction through SQL-based procedures.

Key Takeaway Oracle's DBMS_CLOUD package empowers enterprises to streamline file management within Oracle Autonomous Database serverless (ADB-S). By implementing credential-based authentication, automating the generation and transfer of SQL Health Check reports, and enabling seamless interaction with Oracle Cloud Object Storage, organizations gain the ability to manage BLOB and CLOB data with greater efficiency and security. These capabilities collectively support enhanced scalability, auditability, and operational agility in modern cloud-native environments.

As enterprises continue to prioritize data integrity and compliance in their digital transformation journeys, the need for tamper-resistant and immutable data storage becomes critical. In the next section, we explore how **blockchain tables** in Oracle 23AI address this need by delivering a secure, append-only ledger structure—reinforcing trust and transparency in enterprise data systems.

CHAPTER 5 CLOUD AND BLOCKCHAIN INNOVATIONS

Blockchain Tables in Oracle 23AI

As data integrity and tamper-resistance become critical in regulated industries, Oracle 23AI enhances its support for **blockchain tables**, offering a secure, insert-only data structure with cryptographic chaining and enforced retention policies. While this feature was originally introduced in **Oracle 21c** and later backported to **Oracle 19c**, Oracle 23AI improves upon it with extended capabilities such as **version 2 hashing algorithms** and simplified lifecycle management.

This section demonstrates how **QuickMart**, a fictional retail enterprise, implemented blockchain tables to secure its customer order records.

> **CASE STUDY: SECURING ORDER HISTORY WITH BLOCKCHAIN TABLES AT QUICKMART**
>
> QuickMart required an immutable audit trail for customer orders that prevented tampering and met regulatory retention standards. Blockchain tables provided the ideal solution by ensuring insert-only access and cryptographically verifiable row history.

To implement this, QuickMart created a blockchain table order_tracking using Oracle 23AI's latest capabilities.

Listing 5-11. Creating a Blockchain Table with Retention Policies

```
CREATE BLOCKCHAIN TABLE order_tracking (
   order_id      NUMBER,
   customer_id   NUMBER,
   product_name  VARCHAR2(100),
   quantity      NUMBER,
   order_date    DATE,
   constraint order_tracking_pk PRIMARY KEY (order_id)
)
NO DROP UNTIL 0 DAYS IDLE
NO DELETE UNTIL 16 DAYS AFTER INSERT
HASHING USING SHA2_512 VERSION v2;
```

CHAPTER 5   CLOUD AND BLOCKCHAIN INNOVATIONS

This definition ensures

- The table cannot be dropped while in use (NO DROP).
- Rows are retained for at least 16 days before eligible for deletion (NO DELETE).
- Data is cryptographically chained using **SHA2_512 v2** for enhanced security.

Inspecting Blockchain Table Metadata

After creation, QuickMart inspected the system-generated internal columns used to manage row integrity.

Listing 5-12. Viewing Blockchain Table Metadata Columns

```
SELECT internal_column_id,
       column_name,
       data_type,
       data_length,
       hidden_column
FROM   user_tab_cols
WHERE  table_name = 'ORDER_TRACKING'
ORDER BY internal_column_id;
```

Output:

internal_column_id	column_name	data_type	data_length	hidden_column
1	ORDER_ID	NUMBER	22	NO
2	CUSTOMER_ID	NUMBER	22	NO
3	PRODUCT_NAME	VARCHAR2	100	NO
4	QUANTITY	NUMBER	22	NO
5	ORDER_DATE	DATE	7	NO
6	ORABCTAB_INST_ID$	NUMBER	22	YES
7	ORABCTAB_CHAIN_ID$	NUMBER	22	YES
8	ORABCTAB_SEQ_NUM$	NUMBER	22	YES
9	ORABCTAB_CREATION_TIME$	TIMESTAMP(6) WITH TIME ZONE	13	YES
10	ORABCTAB_USER_NUMBER$	NUMBER	22	YES
11	ORABCTAB_HASH$	RAW	2000	YES

CHAPTER 5 CLOUD AND BLOCKCHAIN INNOVATIONS

12	ORABCTAB_SIGNATURE$	RAW	2000	YES
13	ORABCTAB_SIGNATURE_ALG$	NUMBER	22	YES
14	ORABCTAB_SIGNATURE_CERT$	RAW	1000	YES
15	ORABCTAB_SPARE$	RAW	2000	YES
16	ORABCTAB_PDB_GUID$	RAW	2000	YES
17	ORABCTAB_ROW_VERSION$	NUMBER	22	YES
18	ORABCTAB_LAST_ROW_VERSION_NUMBER$	RAW	1	YES
19	ORABCTAB_USER_CHAIN_HASH$	RAW	2000	YES
20	ORABCTAB_DELEGATE_SIGNATURE$	RAW	2000	YES
21	ORABCTAB_DELEGATE_SIGNATURE_ALG$	UMBER	22	YES
22	ORABCTAB_DELEGATE_SIGNATURE_CERT$	RAW	1000	YES
23	ORABCTAB_DELEGATE_USER_NUMBER$	NUMBER	22	YES
24	ORABCTAB_COUNTERSIGNATURE$	RAW	2000	YES
25	ORABCTAB_COUNTERSIGNATURE_ALG$	NUMBER	22	YES
26	ORABCTAB_COUNTERSIGNATURE_CERT$	RAW	1000	YES
27	ORABCTAB_COUNTERSIGNATURE_ROW_FORMAT_VERSION$ VARCHAR2		4000	YES
28	ORABCTAB_COUNTERSIGNATURE_ROW_FORMAT_FLAG$	NUMBER	22	YES
29	ORABCTAB_TS$	TIMESTAMP(6)	13	YES

These hidden columns include the hash, chain ID, and other metadata required to verify row integrity.

Inserting and Verifying Order Records

QuickMart then inserted a sample order.

Listing 5-13. Inserting a Record into the Blockchain Table

```
INSERT INTO order_tracking (order_id, customer_id, product_name, quantity, order_date)
VALUES (1, 101, 'Laptop', 1, SYSDATE);

-- Commit the transaction
COMMIT;
```

To verify data integrity, QuickMart used the DBMS_BLOCKCHAIN_TABLE.VERIFY_ROWS procedure, which returned the number of rows successfully validated, as shown in Listing 5-14.

Listing 5-14. Verifying Row Integrity in Blockchain Table

```
set serveroutput on
DECLARE
  l_rows     NUMBER;
  l_verified NUMBER;
BEGIN
  SELECT count(*)
  INTO   l_rows
  FROM   order_tracking;

  DBMS_BLOCKCHAIN_TABLE.VERIFY_ROWS(
    schema_name            => 'admin',
    table_name             => 'order_tracking',
    number_of_rows_verified => l_verified);

  DBMS_OUTPUT.put_line('Rows=' || l_rows || '  Verified Rows=' || l_verified);
END;
/
```

Output:
```
Rows=1  Verified Rows=1
```

Tamper Resistance in Action

Attempts to update or delete the inserted rows within the 16-day retention window failed as expected.

Listing 5-15. Enforced Immutability—No Updates or Deletes Allowed During Retention Period

```
UPDATE order_tracking
SET quantity = 2
WHERE order_id = 1;
-- ORA-05715: operation not allowed on the blockchain table

DELETE FROM order_tracking WHERE order_id = 1;
-- ORA-05715: operation not allowed on the blockchain table
```

After the 16-day retention period had passed, QuickMart invoked the DBMS_BLOCKCHAIN_TABLE.DELETE_EXPIRED_ROWS procedure to clean up old records, as shown in Listing 5-16.

Listing 5-16. Deleting Expired Rows from Blockchain Table

```
DECLARE
  l_rows NUMBER;
BEGIN
  DBMS_BLOCKCHAIN_TABLE.DELETE_EXPIRED_ROWS(
    schema_name           => 'admin',
    table_name            => 'order_tracking',
    number_of_rows_deleted => l_rows);

  DBMS_OUTPUT.put_line('Rows Deleted=' || l_rows);
END;
/
```

Output:
Rows Deleted=1

Blockchain tables in **Oracle 23AI** provide enterprises like QuickMart with a powerful tool to ensure **data integrity, retention enforcement, and tamper-proof audit trails**. With row chaining, cryptographic validation, and retention controls managed directly within the database, they offer a low-overhead, high-assurance solution for immutable record-keeping.

Internal Mechanism of Blockchain Tables in Oracle 23AI

Blockchain tables in Oracle 23AI provide a tamper-evident data storage mechanism by cryptographically chaining rows using SHA-2 family hashing algorithms. Each row includes a hash of the previous row, creating an immutable sequence that ensures data integrity. These tables follow an **insert-only model**, and row modifications or deletions are restricted during a user-defined retention period.

Oracle 23AI does not automatically delete expired rows, but it provides lifecycle management procedures through the DBMS_BLOCKCHAIN_TABLE package. Users can verify data integrity using built-in verification routines and purge expired rows after the retention window, ensuring the system enforces immutability while remaining manageable over time.

CHAPTER 5 CLOUD AND BLOCKCHAIN INNOVATIONS

The internal flow of blockchain table operations in Oracle 23AI is illustrated below.

Table 5-3. *Internal Flow of Blockchain Table Operations in Oracle ADB-S*

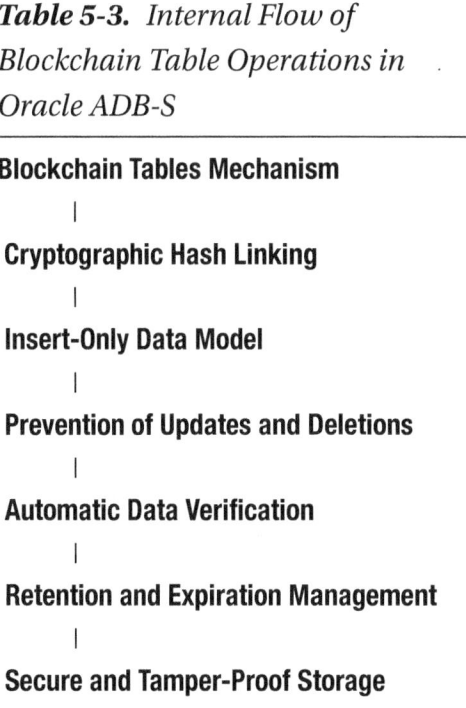

This mechanism underscores Oracle 23AI's support for secure and compliant recordkeeping. By combining cryptographic chaining, retention enforcement, and lifecycle management tools, blockchain tables offer a reliable solution for storing immutable records—ideal for use cases like audit logs, transaction trails, and regulatory compliance.

Sample Real-Time Business Use Cases for Blockchain Tables in Oracle 23AI

The table below outlines practical enterprise scenarios where **Oracle 23AI blockchain tables** deliver verifiable, tamper-evident data storage. These use cases emphasize immutability, compliance, and trust—essential for high-integrity business operations.

Table 5-4. *Real-Time Business Use Cases for Blockchain Tables in Oracle 23AI*

Use Case	Description	Business Benefit
Order Management	Store customer orders as immutable records.	Prevents tampering and supports reliable dispute audits.
Financial Ledger Entries	Record financial events with retention and integrity.	Aids in compliance, fraud prevention, and audit readiness.
Audit Logging	Capture system or application logs with row-level immutability.	Ensures regulatory traceability and accountability.
Regulatory Compliance	Preserve mandatory records in sectors like healthcare or finance.	Satisfies retention rules and data governance mandates.
Supply Chain Visibility	Track lifecycle events of goods (e.g., shipment checkpoints).	Increases transparency and reduces manipulation risks.
Intellectual Property	Securely log patent, design, or copyright submissions.	Protects IP history and supports legal verification.

These examples demonstrate how Oracle 23AI blockchain tables embed **cryptographic assurance** and **data lifecycle control** into everyday business operations. With features like insert-only enforcement, row chaining, and retention policies, organizations can safeguard critical information while meeting evolving compliance and audit demands.

Common Questions About Blockchain Tables in Oracle 23AI

A frequent question is how Oracle 23AI ensures performance and scalability with large volumes of blockchain data. Oracle addresses this by supporting indexing, partitioning, and leveraging Exadata infrastructure where applicable. These features help maintain efficient query access even as blockchain tables grow over time.

Another common inquiry is whether blockchain tables can integrate with external blockchain networks or distributed ledger technologies (DLTs). While Oracle's blockchain tables are designed for internal tamper-evidence and audit trails, integration with external blockchains is possible through Oracle Blockchain Platform or custom connectors via APIs, enabling broader interoperability when required.

Data security and privacy are also key concerns. Oracle 23AI secures blockchain data using **encryption at rest and in transit**, along with **role-based access control**. Features like **Transparent Data Encryption (TDE)** encrypt the underlying storage transparently, while **Data Redaction** can mask sensitive data at query time. These security layers are standard across Oracle databases and are not unique to blockchain tables but play a vital role in enforcing data protection policies.

Finally, organizations often ask whether the immutability period can be customized. Oracle allows fine-grained control over retention using clauses such as `NO DELETE UNTIL n DAYS AFTER INSERT`, ensuring compliance with internal policies or regulatory mandates. Once this window expires, rows can be purged using `DBMS_BLOCKCHAIN_TABLE.DELETE_EXPIRED_ROWS`.

Together, these capabilities make Oracle 23AI blockchain tables a practical solution for secure, auditable, and policy-driven data logging—especially in industries where integrity and retention are paramount.

Key Takeaway Oracle 23AI has transformed the implementation of tamper-proof data storage by introducing native blockchain tables that eliminate the need for complex, manual workarounds such as triggers and audit logs. These built-in tables ensure immutability, automate data retention, and offer cryptographic verification, making them ideal for secure use cases like order tracking, financial transactions, audit trails, and supply chain transparency. By integrating blockchain functionality directly into the database engine, Oracle empowers organizations to maintain data integrity with minimal overhead and maximum trust.

As we move from securing data history to exploring intelligent data interaction, the next chapter introduces Oracle 23AI's advancements in handling high-dimensional vector data. With the emergence of generative AI and similarity search, Oracle's support for vector data types and in-memory vector operations opens up powerful new use cases in recommendation engines, natural language understanding, and AI-driven analytics.

CHAPTER 6

Vector Data and AI Innovations

Introduction

As artificial intelligence continues to reshape enterprise applications, the need for databases to support high-dimensional, vectorized data has become critical. This chapter explores how **Oracle 23AI** meets that demand by introducing **native support for vector data types**, **AI vector search**, and **in-memory vector operations**—features that enable intelligent, real-time processing directly within the database engine.

Rather than relying on external systems or complex custom logic, Oracle 23AI brings AI capabilities closer to the data by integrating vector representations, similarity functions, and efficient memory utilization natively into the platform. These innovations are designed to support a wide range of modern use cases, including semantic search, personalized recommendations, fraud detection, and natural language understanding.

Through hands-on implementation guidance and illustrative case studies, this chapter demonstrates how organizations can harness vector-based AI capabilities to improve accuracy, reduce latency, and streamline their analytics workflows. By comparing traditional approaches to Oracle's new in-database AI features, readers will gain a clear understanding of the performance, simplicity, and scalability benefits that come with embedding vector intelligence into the data infrastructure itself.

Vector Data Types in ORACLE 23AI

Oracle 23AI introduces **native support for high-dimensional vector data types**, enabling the development of AI-powered applications directly within the database. Vectors are fundamental to modern AI workflows—especially in tasks involving **embeddings, approximate nearest neighbor (ANN)** search, and **semantic similarity** in applications like image recognition, NLP, recommendation systems, and anomaly detection.

By integrating vector operations into the core SQL engine, Oracle 23AI eliminates the need for external ML pipelines or vector databases. Developers can now **store, index, and search over vector embeddings** using built-in capabilities that are optimized for performance and scalability.

> **CASE STUDY: QUICKMART—AI-POWERED VISUAL PRODUCT RECOMMENDATION**
>
> QuickMart, a retail fashion platform, aims to enhance product discovery using **AI-based visual similarity**. Product images are embedded as numerical vectors capturing shape, color, and style. When a customer views a product (e.g., a "Red Shirt"), the system suggests visually similar items by calculating **vector similarity** across embeddings.

Defining a Table with VECTOR Column

The VECTOR data type was used to store 28-dimensional image embeddings. Each vector represents an image's features, and similarity search is conducted directly within SQL.

Listing 6-1. Table and Type Definition for Vector Storage

```
DROP TABLE image_repository PURGE;

CREATE TABLE image_repository (
  image_id     NUMBER PRIMARY KEY,
  description  VARCHAR2(100),
  embedding    VECTOR(28)  -- 28-dimensional embedding
);
```

CHAPTER 6 VECTOR DATA AND AI INNOVATIONS

With the structure defined, sample records representing red, blue, and green shirts are inserted into the table, as illustrated in Listing 6-2.

Listing 6-2. Inserting Sample Image Vectors

```
-- Insert sample records
INSERT INTO image_repository (image_id, description, embedding)
VALUES (
  1,
  'Red Shirt',
  TO_VECTOR('[0.12, 0.23, 0.34, 0.45, 0.56, 0.67, 0.78, 0.89,
              0.91, 0.92, 0.93, 0.94, 0.95, 0.96, 0.97, 0.98,
              0.99, 0.01, 0.02, 0.03, 0.04, 0.05, 0.06, 0.07,
              0.08, 0.09, 0.10, 0.11]')
);

INSERT INTO image_repository (image_id, description, embedding)
VALUES (
  2,
  'Blue Shirt',
  TO_VECTOR('[0.11, 0.22, 0.33, 0.44, 0.55, 0.66, 0.77, 0.88,
              0.90, 0.91, 0.92, 0.93, 0.94, 0.95, 0.96, 0.97,
              0.98, 0.99, 0.01, 0.02, 0.03, 0.04, 0.05, 0.06,
              0.07, 0.08, 0.09, 0.10]')
);

INSERT INTO image_repository (image_id, description, embedding)
VALUES (
  3,
  'Green Shirt',
  TO_VECTOR('[0.10, 0.21, 0.32, 0.43, 0.54, 0.65, 0.76, 0.87,
              0.89, 0.90, 0.91, 0.92, 0.93, 0.94, 0.95, 0.96,
              0.97, 0.98, 0.99, 0.00, 0.01, 0.02, 0.03, 0.04,
              0.05, 0.06, 0.07, 0.08]')
);

commit;
```

Querying Similar Images Based on Vector Similarity

Oracle 23c provides **built-in similarity operators** such as COSINE_DISTANCE and L2_DISTANCE. Here's how QuickMart finds products similar to the "Red Shirt."

Listing 6-3. Retrieving Similar Images Using Cosine Similarity

```
SELECT image_id,
       description,
       COSINE_DISTANCE(
         embedding,
         TO_VECTOR('[0.12, 0.23, 0.34, 0.45, 0.56, 0.67, 0.78, 0.89,
                     0.91, 0.92, 0.93, 0.94, 0.95, 0.96, 0.97, 0.98,
                     0.99, 0.01, 0.02, 0.03, 0.04, 0.05, 0.06, 0.07,
                     0.08, 0.09, 0.10, 0.11]')
       ) AS similarity_score
FROM image_repository
ORDER BY similarity_score ASC
FETCH FIRST 3 ROWS ONLY;
```

The output shows that the "Red Shirt" record had the highest similarity score, followed by the "Blue Shirt" and "Green Shirt," validating the efficacy of the vector search process.

image_id	description	similarity_score
1	Red Shirt	0
2	Blue Shirt	0.043
3	Green Shirt	0.081

Lower cosine distance = higher similarity.

Behind the Scenes: How It Works

- **Embeddings**: Product images are converted to numeric feature vectors using models like OpenAI CLIP or ResNet.
- **Vector Type**: Oracle stores these embeddings natively using the VECTOR(n) datatype.

- **Vector Search**: Built-in operators like COSINE_DISTANCE() and DOT_PRODUCT() enable similarity matching without external tools.
- **Scalability**: Oracle supports **Approximate Nearest Neighbor (ANN)** indexing in 23c for larger datasets.

Internal Mechanism of the VECTOR Data Type in Oracle 23AI

Oracle 23AI introduces native support for the VECTOR data type, enabling direct handling of high-dimensional embeddings within the database. Unlike earlier approaches that relied on nested tables, this built-in vector type simplifies storage and allows efficient similarity computations using optimized vector functions.

The database provides native support for vector similarity algorithms such as cosine similarity and inner product, enabling real-time semantic search across vector-encoded data. Vector columns can also be indexed using approximate nearest neighbor (ANN) techniques to accelerate similarity search, especially for large-scale datasets.

The internal flow of vector processing in Oracle 23AI is summarized in Table 6-1.

Table 6-1. *Internal Flow of VECTOR Data Processing in Oracle ADB-S*

VECTOR Data Type Mechanism
|
Native High-Dimensional Embedding Storage
|
Built-in VECTOR Data Type (No Nested Tables Required)
|
Optimized Similarity Functions (e.g., COSINE_DISTANCE, INNER_PRODUCT)
|
ANN Indexing for Fast Approximate Search
|
Scalable Similarity-Based Querying
|
Seamless Integration into AI/ML Workflows

This native architecture empowers Oracle 23AI to support AI-native applications directly within the database—eliminating the need for external vector databases or custom similarity logic. It provides the performance, scalability, and simplicity required for modern use cases like semantic search, recommendations, and generative AI prompt matching.

Difference Between Pre-Oracle 23AI Databases and Oracle 23AI with Native VECTOR Data Type

The following table outlines the key differences between traditional Oracle databases prior to 23AI and Oracle 23AI's native support for the VECTOR data type—specifically for AI/ML and semantic search use cases.

Table 6-2. Comparison of Vector Capabilities—Pre-23AI vs. Oracle 23AI

Feature	Pre-Oracle 23AI Databases	Oracle 23AI (Native VECTOR Support)
Vector Storage	Custom implementations using arrays, BLOBs, or nested tables; complex and inconsistent.	Native VECTOR data type purpose-built for high-dimensional embeddings.
Storage Efficiency	Inefficient use of space and memory; added overhead from workarounds.	Optimized and compact representation designed for performance and scalability.
Similarity Querying	Manual computation using PL/SQL or external logic; slow and error-prone.	Built-in functions like COSINE_DISTANCE, EUCLIDEAN_DISTANCE for fast, accurate search.
Performance	Often relied on external tools or batch jobs for vector comparison.	Supports real-time vector search with optimized in-database execution.
Indexing Support	Required custom or limited indexing; no ANN support.	Supports approximate nearest neighbor (ANN) indexing for scalable similarity search.
AI/ML Integration	Required external frameworks for vector generation, storage, and query orchestration.	Seamless integration with AI pipelines and LLM applications directly within the database.

This highlights how Oracle 23AI eliminates the complexity of working with vectors in databases, enabling direct, performant, and scalable vector-based analytics and AI workloads—all natively within the Oracle ecosystem.

Potential Real-Time Business Use Cases for the Oracle 23AI with Vector Data Type

The table below highlights real-world scenarios where Oracle 23AI's native VECTOR support enables fast, scalable, and accurate similarity search and embedding-based analytics across AI-driven applications.

Table 6-3. Real-Time Business Use Cases for VECTOR Data Type in Oracle 23AI

Use Case	Description	Business Benefit
Product Recommendations	Match user preferences with product embeddings in real time.	Boosts conversions through personalized recommendations.
Semantic Image Search	Store and compare image feature embeddings for visual similarity.	Enables intuitive image search and discovery with minimal latency.
Natural Language Processing (NLP)	Analyze and search text using language model embeddings.	Enhances chatbot relevance, sentiment analysis, and document search.
Fraud Detection	Compare transaction vectors to detect anomalies or known fraud patterns.	Enables near-instant fraud detection and prevention.
Predictive Maintenance	Store telemetry vector data to identify failure signatures.	Minimizes downtime through proactive alerts and early warning signs.
Voice and Audio Recognition	Match voice command vectors for search and interaction tasks.	Improves accuracy and responsiveness in voice-enabled applications.

This demonstrates how Oracle 23AI supports advanced AI/ML applications directly within the database, reducing complexity and accelerating intelligent decision-making with built-in vector functionality.

CHAPTER 6 VECTOR DATA AND AI INNOVATIONS

Common Questions About Vector Data Types in Oracle 23AI

Oracle 23AI introduces native VECTOR support to manage high-dimensional data for AI/ML applications. As adoption grows, several common questions arise:

One key question is how Oracle stores and queries vector data. The native VECTOR type allows direct storage within table columns, eliminating the need for arrays, BLOBs, or external preprocessing.

Another frequent inquiry concerns similarity computation. Oracle offers built-in functions like SIMILARITY_TO, which use cosine similarity and other metrics to compare vectors—ideal for use cases like recommendations or search.

Users also ask about vector indexing. While Oracle supports specialized indexing for faster similarity searches, it's important to evaluate trade-offs, as indexing may increase storage overhead and isn't always optimal for every workload.

Finally, organizations often ask about AI/ML integration. Oracle 23AI allows vector operations directly within SQL, enabling real-time analytics and inference without needing to move data out of the database.

These capabilities make Oracle 23AI a unified platform for scalable, vector-driven intelligence.

Key Takeaway Oracle 23AI represents a transformative leap in database intelligence by introducing native support for high-dimensional vector data. With features like the VECTOR data type, in-database embedding generation, and built-in similarity functions such as VECTOR_DISTANCE, Oracle enables advanced AI use cases—like semantic search, personalized recommendations, and fraud detection—to run directly within the database. This eliminates the need for external libraries, custom logic, or separate AI infrastructure.

Complementing these capabilities, Oracle 23AI also integrates vector indexing and in-memory vector operations, which reduce latency and accelerate complex similarity computations. This is particularly valuable for real-time, latency-sensitive applications such as voice recognition, anomaly detection, and recommendation engines.

Together, these innovations simplify AI/ML workflows, boost performance and scalability, and bring intelligent processing closer to the data. Oracle 23AI redefines how modern enterprises approach AI workloads—shifting from fragmented, external solutions to a unified, in-database intelligence framework.

Building upon this foundation, **Oracle 23AI** extends these capabilities with integrated **AI Vector Search and In-Memory Vector Operations**, enabling even faster, memory-resident processing for similarity and pattern-based tasks. The next section we will explores only few more case study

AI Vector Search and In-Memory Vector Operations in Oracle 23AI

Modern AI-powered applications rely on high-dimensional embeddings to deliver contextual and personalized user experiences—ranging from semantic search to product recommendations. Oracle 23AI natively supports **vector data types**, **in-memory vector operations**, and **approximate nearest neighbor (ANN)** search, enabling fast, scalable similarity search directly inside the database engine. This architecture minimizes data movement between compute and memory, significantly boosting performance for use cases such as intelligent retrieval, anomaly detection, and pattern recognition.

CASE STUDY 1: QUICKMART IMPLEMENTS AI-POWERED PRODUCT RECOMMENDATIONS

QuickMart, a mid-sized online retailer specializing in electronics and apparel, faced a growing challenge in delivering relevant product search results. Traditional keyword-based queries often failed to capture user intent, especially for complex or vague search phrases. To enhance its search experience and recommendation engine, QuickMart adopted Oracle 23AI's integrated vector capabilities.

Rather than relying on external AI services or duplicating data across multiple platforms, QuickMart decided to embed vector search directly within its Oracle 23AI database. This not only reduced data movement and processing latency but also enabled real-time, intelligent user interactions with minimal infrastructure changes.

CHAPTER 6 VECTOR DATA AND AI INNOVATIONS

To begin their implementation, QuickMart first created a new table to store product metadata along with a native vector column for the semantic representation of each product description. These vectors, known as **embeddings**, were generated using a pre-trained language model capable of converting descriptive text into dense, high-dimensional vectors suitable for similarity analysis.

The structure of the products table is shown in Listing 6-4.

Listing 6-4. Schema Definition for Storing Vector-Encoded Product

```
CREATE TABLE products (
    product_id NUMBER PRIMARY KEY,
    product_name VARCHAR2(255),
    product_description VARCHAR2(1000),
    product_vector VECTOR   -- Column storing vector representation of
    product description
);
```

To populate the product_vector column, QuickMart processed product descriptions through an embedding model such as SBERT or MiniLM, which transformed textual descriptions into vectors that capture semantic similarity. These embeddings were then inserted into the table using the native TO_VECTOR function provided by Oracle 23AI, as shown in Listing 6-5.

Listing 6-5. Inserting Product Embeddings Using TO_VECTOR

```
INSERT INTO products (product_id, product_name, product_description,
product_vector)
VALUES (
  1,
  'Smartphone',
  'A high-end smartphone with a 6-inch display, 128GB storage, and a 12MP
  camera.',
  TO_VECTOR('[0.15, 0.70, 0.90]')
);
```

CHAPTER 6   VECTOR DATA AND AI INNOVATIONS

```
INSERT INTO products (product_id, product_name, product_description,
product_vector)
VALUES (
  2,
  'Laptop',
  'A powerful laptop with 16GB RAM, Intel i7 processor, and 512GB SSD.',
  TO_VECTOR('[0.11, 0.40, 0.70]')
);

INSERT INTO products (product_id, product_name, product_description,
product_vector)
VALUES (
  3,
  'Wireless Headphones',
  'Over-ear wireless headphones with noise-canceling and 20-hour
battery life.',
  TO_VECTOR('[0.22, 0.10, 0.40]')
);

COMMIT;
```

These values represent simplified examples of real embeddings, which typically have hundreds of dimensions. However, even with compact vectors, the database is capable of executing fast similarity comparisons using in-memory operations and specialized indexing.

To simulate a user query, QuickMart used a pre-computed embedding representing the search phrase "fast laptop with performance." Instead of creating a custom PL/SQL function to handle this, QuickMart simply generated the vector outside the database and passed it into the SQL using the TO_VECTOR function.

Once the query vector was prepared, QuickMart used Oracle's built-in VECTOR_DISTANCE function to identify similar products by computing the cosine or Euclidean distance between the query vector and stored vectors. The query, shown in Listing 6-6, retrieves the top three most similar products ranked by vector distance.

CHAPTER 6   VECTOR DATA AND AI INNOVATIONS

Listing 6-6. Querying Product Similarity with VECTOR_DISTANCE

```
SELECT
    product_id,
    product_name,
    product_description,
    VECTOR_DISTANCE(
        product_vector,
        TO_VECTOR('[0.12, 0.50, 0.80]')
    ) AS distance
FROM products
ORDER BY distance
FETCH FIRST 3 ROWS ONLY;
```

This query demonstrates approximate nearest neighbor (ANN) logic by ranking records based on how closely their vector representations align with the query embedding. The results from this search are shown in Table 6-4.

Table 6-4. *Output from Semantic Vector Search*

Product ID	Product Name	Product Description	Distance
2	Laptop	A powerful laptop with 16GB RAM, Intel i7 processor, and 512GB SSD.	0.001
1	Smartphone	A high-end smartphone with a 6-inch display, 128GB storage, and a 12MP camera.	0.005
3	Wireless Headphones	Over-ear wireless headphones with noise-canceling and 20-hour battery life.	0.108

This output highlights how vector-based search, driven by ANN techniques, can identify conceptually similar items even when exact terms do not match. The search term was clearly most similar to the "Laptop" product, followed by the "Smartphone," based on their proximity in semantic space.

By using the VECTOR type and associated built-in functions like TO_VECTOR and VECTOR_DISTANCE, QuickMart was able to achieve meaningful, AI-powered recommendations directly within the database. This eliminated the need for external vector databases, additional APIs, or batch synchronization pipelines.

Oracle 23AI's support for vector data types and ANN search operations represents a significant step forward in database-native AI capabilities. As demonstrated by QuickMart's implementation, these features empower organizations to embed intelligence into core business operations without increasing system complexity or external dependencies. From semantic search to personalized recommendations, in-database vector processing paves the way for intelligent, responsive, and scalable enterprise applications.

> **CASE STUDY 2: QUICKMART—STRENGTHENING FRAUD DETECTION USING ORACLE 23AI VECTOR SEARCH**
>
> As digital payments surge across retail and ecommerce sectors, fraud detection has become an essential part of operational risk management. QuickMart, a growing retail-tech enterprise, processes thousands of digital transactions daily across multiple platforms. While traditional fraud detection relied on rule-based heuristics—flagging transactions by thresholds or keywords—these techniques often fall short when patterns are subtle or evolve over time.
>
> To address this, QuickMart adopted Oracle 23AI's native **Vector Search** capabilities. By embedding high-dimensional feature vectors directly within the database, QuickMart enables real-time anomaly detection through similarity-based analysis of transactional behavior.

Designing the Transactional Vector Schema

The first step was creating a transactional database schema that incorporates vector data. QuickMart designed a table that holds essential transaction details along with a VECTOR column that stores the embedding representation of each transaction. These embeddings are derived from features such as transaction amount and description.

As shown in Listing 6-7, the schema captures the transaction metadata and embeds a high-dimensional vector representation for further AI-driven analysis.

Listing 6-7. Schema Definition for Vectorized Transaction Data

```sql
CREATE TABLE financial_transactions (
    transaction_id NUMBER PRIMARY KEY,
    amount NUMBER,
    description VARCHAR2(1000),
    transaction_vector VECTOR  -- Column to store the transaction vector
);
```

Inserting Sample Transaction Embeddings

Rather than using an elaborate PL/SQL function to compute embeddings, QuickMart leverages a simplified logic where pre-computed vectors—either from an ML pipeline or approximated for demonstration—are stored directly. Each embedding represents a combination of normalized transaction amount and encoded semantics from the description.

This approach is illustrated in Listing 6-8, where various types of transactions are inserted into the table with corresponding vectors.

Listing 6-8. Inserting Sample Transactions into the Table

```sql
INSERT INTO financial_transactions (transaction_id, amount, description, transaction_vector)
VALUES (1, 1000, 'Loan payment received', TO_VECTOR('[1.1, 0.3, 0.51]'));

INSERT INTO financial_transactions (transaction_id, amount, description, transaction_vector)
VALUES (2, 50, 'Refund for purchase', TO_VECTOR('[0.45, 0.3, 0.8]'));

INSERT INTO financial_transactions (transaction_id, amount, description, transaction_vector)
VALUES (3, 500, 'Payment for services rendered', TO_VECTOR('[0.6, 0.25, 0.505]'));

INSERT INTO financial_transactions (transaction_id, amount, description, transaction_vector)
VALUES (4, 200, 'Loan repayment made', TO_VECTOR('[0.3, 0.22, 0.502]'));

commit;
```

CHAPTER 6 VECTOR DATA AND AI INNOVATIONS

These sample embeddings reflect characteristics of both numeric and semantic patterns, mimicking outputs typically generated by models like BERT, Word2Vec, or embeddings generated through Oracle Machine Learning pipelines.

Detecting Anomalies with VECTOR_DISTANCE

To uncover anomalies, QuickMart uses Oracle 23AI's built-in VECTOR_DISTANCE function. This allows the system to compare the similarity between a reference transaction and historical records, returning those that are behaviorally closest or farthest.

Listing 6-9 shows how this comparison is made using a reference vector for a known legitimate transaction.

Listing 6-9. Querying Similar Transactions Based on Vector Distance

```
SELECT transaction_id, amount, description, transaction_vector,
       VECTOR_DISTANCE(transaction_vector, TO_VECTOR('[1.1, 0.3, 0.51]'))
       AS distance
FROM financial_transactions
ORDER BY distance
FETCH FIRST 3 ROWS ONLY;
```

The results of this query, sorted by proximity to the reference vector, are shown in Table 6-5.

Table 6-5. Top Three Transactions Based on Vector Similarity to Reference

Transaction ID	Amount	Description	Transaction Vector	Distance
1	1000	Loan payment received	[1.10000002E+000, 3.00000012E-001, 5.0999999E-001]	0.000
3	500	Payment for services rendered	[6.00000024E-001, 2.5E-001, 5.04999995E-001]	0.035
4	200	Loan repayment made	[3.00000012E-001, 2.19999999E-001, 5.01999974E-001]	0.165

CHAPTER 6   VECTOR DATA AND AI INNOVATIONS

Interpreting the Results and Investigating Anomalies

As illustrated in Table 6-5, Transaction ID 1 has a distance of 0.000, indicating it is identical to the reference and hence considered a known safe pattern. Transaction ID 4, however, has a distance of 0.165—significantly higher than the others. This suggests that while it bears semantic resemblance in description, its numeric features (amount and frequency) deviate from the norm.

Such deviation could point to abnormal behavior. For instance, the amount might be unusually low for a typical loan repayment, or the transaction may have originated from an unexpected region or time. These insights flag it as a candidate for deeper analysis.

While QuickMart uses simple embeddings for this demonstration, in production environments, these vectors are typically generated by ML models trained on labeled datasets. This allows the system to learn complex, nonlinear patterns that may escape traditional logic. Incorporating such models through Oracle's in-database ML or external AI services can further refine fraud detection pipelines.

Key Takeaway   Oracle 23AI enables QuickMart to run similarity-based anomaly detection directly inside the database, eliminating the need to extract and process data in separate applications. This integrated approach ensures that fraud detection is timely, accurate, and scalable. In-memory vector processing further reduces latency and accelerates response time—essential features for real-time alerting systems.

As QuickMart continues to scale operations, Oracle's vector capabilities will serve as the foundation for predictive monitoring, real-time pattern recognition, and secure AI operations. This case highlights the convergence of embedded AI and data management as the future of intelligent business systems.

Oracle 23AI builds on its strong foundation of concurrency control and in-memory processing with powerful new SQL and PL/SQL capabilities. In the next chapter, we explore enhancements such as Boolean data type support, the CHECKSUM analytic function, improved GROUP BY readability, interval-based aggregation, and the automatic PL/SQL to SQL transpiler—all designed to boost developer efficiency and SQL performance. Let's now explore how these features enhance modern Oracle workloads.

CHAPTER 7

SQL, PLSQL Enhancements and New Functions

Introduction

This chapter explores the developer-focused SQL and PL/SQL enhancements introduced in Oracle Autonomous Database 23AI. It highlights key innovations such as the long-awaited native support for the Boolean data type, the powerful CHECKSUM analytic function for change detection, improved SQL readability through support for column aliases in GROUP BY and HAVING clauses, and native aggregation over INTERVAL datatypes. Additionally, the chapter introduces the automatic PL/SQL to SQL transpiler—an advanced feature that rewrites eligible procedural logic into optimized SQL to boost performance. Each section offers hands-on implementation guidance and real-world use cases that demonstrate how these capabilities streamline development workflows, enhance data analysis accuracy, and simplify SQL optimization. Comparisons with earlier approaches reveal how Oracle 23AI advances developer productivity and SQL efficiency, while end-of-section summaries reinforce the key takeaways and best practices for modern PL/SQL and SQL development.

CHAPTER 7   SQL, PLSQL ENHANCEMENTS AND NEW FUNCTIONS

Boolean Datatype Enhancements in 23AI

Boolean logic is foundational to nearly all programming paradigms, yet until recently, relational databases—including Oracle—lacked direct support for a native BOOLEAN data type in SQL. With Oracle Database 23AI, that gap is finally closed. The release introduces a long-awaited native BOOLEAN column type in SQL, enabling developers to represent TRUE, FALSE, and NULL states explicitly and intuitively. This enhancement eliminates the need for workaround patterns such as using NUMBER(1) flags (1/0), while aligning SQL semantics more closely with PL/SQL and modern development practices.

The BOOLEAN type also integrates smoothly with existing PL/SQL constructs, supports column-level constraints, and simplifies application logic by improving code readability, maintainability, and data integrity.

> **CASE STUDY: MANAGING EMPLOYEE AVAILABILITY AT QUICKMART**
>
> To demonstrate the value of this new capability, consider the case of **QuickMart**, a retail company managing a growing workforce across multiple regions. As part of its internal HR platform, QuickMart needs to track each employee's availability status and determine whether they are on approved leave. The system must be able to quickly assess who is available for immediate deployment, who is away on leave, and who is engaged in non-leave but unavailable work (e.g., specialized projects or training).
>
> Oracle 23AI's native Boolean support provides the perfect mechanism to implement this logic cleanly and efficiently.

Creating the Availability Table

QuickMart creates a new table named employee_availability with two Boolean columns: available and on_leave. These columns express whether an employee is currently available for work, and whether they are away on leave, respectively.

As shown in Listing 7-1, the table is defined with identity-based employee IDs, and both Boolean columns are declared using the native BOOLEAN type.

CHAPTER 7 SQL, PLSQL ENHANCEMENTS AND NEW FUNCTIONS

In an organization, we need to manage employee presence using two **Boolean** columns:

- **available** – Indicates if an employee is available for work.
- **on_leave** – Indicates if an employee is on leave.

The following scenarios arise based on these Boolean values:

- **available = FALSE, on_leave = TRUE** → The employee is unavailable due to leave.
- **available = FALSE, on_leave = FALSE** → The employee is unavailable but not on leave (e.g., engaged in a project).
- **available = TRUE, on_leave = FALSE** → The employee is available for work.

Listing 7-1. Defining a Table with Boolean Columns

```
DROP TABLE IF EXISTS employee_availability PURGE;

-- 2. Create the table with Boolean columns
CREATE TABLE employee_availability (
  emp_id      NUMBER GENERATED ALWAYS AS IDENTITY,
  emp_name    VARCHAR2(50),
  available   BOOLEAN,
  on_leave    BOOLEAN
);
```

Populating Sample Data

To simulate real-world scenarios, QuickMart inserts sample data representing different availability states, such as an employee on leave, an employee working but unavailable, and employees who are fully available.

Listing 7-2. Inserting Employee Availability Data

```
-- 3. Insert sample data
INSERT INTO employee_availability (emp_name, available, on_leave) VALUES
('Alice', TRUE, FALSE);
INSERT INTO employee_availability (emp_name, available, on_leave) VALUES
('Bob', FALSE, TRUE);
INSERT INTO employee_availability (emp_name, available, on_leave) VALUES
('Charlie', FALSE, FALSE);
INSERT INTO employee_availability (emp_name, available, on_leave) VALUES
('Diana', TRUE, FALSE);
INSERT INTO employee_availability (emp_name, available, on_leave) VALUES
('Eve', TRUE, TRUE);

-- Commit the changes
COMMIT;
```

The initial dataset, as shown in Table 7-1, reflects diverse employee states, enabling dynamic reporting and business logic to be applied through SQL.

Table 7-1. Initial Employee Availability Data

EMP_ID	EMP_NAME	AVAILABLE	ON_LEAVE
1	Alice	TRUE	FALSE
2	Bob	FALSE	TRUE
3	Charlie	FALSE	FALSE
4	Diana	TRUE	FALSE
5	Eve	TRUE	TRUE

Querying and Updating Boolean States

With the Boolean columns in place, QuickMart now runs simple queries to extract relevant operational insights. For instance, to find all employees who are available and not on leave, the following query is executed.

CHAPTER 7 SQL, PLSQL ENHANCEMENTS AND NEW FUNCTIONS

Listing 7-3. Querying Employees Available for Work

```
SELECT  emp_name
FROM    employee_availability
WHERE   available AND NOT on_leave;
```

To analyze absenteeism, QuickMart counts the number of employees currently unavailable, regardless of the reason.

Listing 7-4. Counting Unavailable Employees

```
SELECT  COUNT(*) AS unavailable_count
FROM    employee_availability
WHERE   NOT available;
```

Any unexpected or invalid states—such as employees who are both on leave and marked available—are flagged with the query in Listing 7-5.

Listing 7-5. Detecting Logical Conflicts in Availability Status

```
SELECT  emp_name
FROM    employee_availability
WHERE   available AND on_leave;
```

If status changes occur (e.g., an employee goes on leave), the Boolean values can be easily updated.

Listing 7-6. Updating Employee Leave Status

```
UPDATE  employee_availability
SET     available = FALSE, on_leave = TRUE
WHERE   emp_name = 'Diana';

COMMIT;
```

QuickMart also uses cleanup logic to remove employees who are neither on leave nor marked available, as shown below.

Listing 7-7. Deleting Inactive and Unassigned Employees

```
-- 9. Delete records where employees are neither available nor on leave
DELETE FROM employee_availability
WHERE  NOT available AND NOT on_leave;

COMMIT;
```

The final list of employees, as displayed in Table 7-2, reflects the cleaned-up, current availability status.

Table 7-2. *Employee Availability After Updates*

EMP_ID	EMP_NAME	AVAILABLE	ON_LEAVE
1	Alice	TRUE	FALSE
2	Bob	FALSE	TRUE
4	Diana	FALSE	TRUE

Using Boolean in PL/SQL Context

In addition to SQL tables, the Boolean type can be manipulated directly in PL/SQL blocks. Conversions between Boolean and character/number representations are now supported with intuitive built-in functions.

Listing 7-8. Boolean Type Usage in PL/SQL

```
set serveroutput on
declare
  l_true    boolean := true;
  l_number  number;
  l_char   varchar2(10);
  l_bool boolean :=true;
begin
  l_number := to_number(l_true);
    DBMS_OUTPUT.put_line(l_number);
  l_char := to_char(l_true);
  DBMS_OUTPUT.put_line(l_char);
```

```
l_bool :=to_boolean(to_char(l_true));
if l_bool then
 DBMS_OUTPUT.put_line('usage of to_boolean; bool val is true');
end if;
end;
/
```

The output from Listing 7-8 confirms successful conversions and logical interpretation:

OUTPUT:
```
1
TRUE
usage of to_boolean; bool val is true
```

PL/SQL procedure successfully completed.

The introduction of the native Boolean data type in Oracle 23AI represents a major usability milestone for both SQL and PL/SQL developers. As illustrated through QuickMart's availability tracking system, developers can now build simpler, cleaner, and more maintainable logic for status management scenarios. Boolean columns enhance semantic clarity, reduce reliance on integer flags, and promote type safety across the stack. This improvement sets the stage for more intuitive application code, especially when combined with new automation and AI-driven SQL features explored in upcoming sections.

Internal Mechanism of Boolean Data Type in Oracle 23AI

Oracle 23AI's Boolean data type is internally managed as a lightweight, native datatype, optimizing storage and indexing for efficient query processing. It eliminates numeric flag conversions by directly integrating with SQL and PL/SQL, reducing computational overhead. The query engine seamlessly evaluates Boolean expressions, enabling short-circuit execution and enhanced predicate pushdown for faster performance.

As shown in Table 7-3, the Boolean data type architecture reflects Oracle 23AI's commitment to streamlined logic evaluation, type safety, and optimized processing across transactional and analytical workloads.

Table 7-3. BOOLEAN Type Execution in Oracle Query Engine

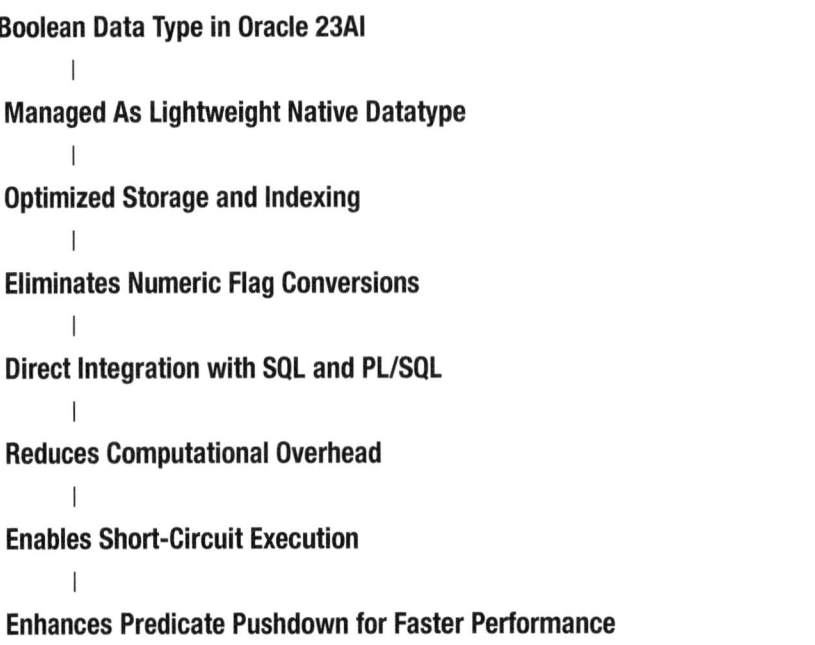

Key Differences: Pre-23AI vs. 23AI

Before Oracle 23AI introduced native support for the BOOLEAN data type, organizations had to represent employee availability using encoded values—typically a single numeric or character column with mixed logic. This made it difficult to distinguish between nuanced states such as "on leave" versus "engaged elsewhere," and required complex query conditions to infer intent. Oracle 23AI streamlines this by allowing multiple, purpose-specific Boolean columns, such as available and on_leave, enabling clarity, simplicity, and efficiency in both data modeling and querying.

As shown in Table 7-4, this new approach significantly improves expressiveness and operational analysis.

Table 7-4. Comparison Between Pre-23AI and Oracle 23AI Availability Modeling

Aspect	Pre-23AI	23AI
Column Design	Single column with combined status logic	Separate columns for available and on_leave
Data Clarity	Difficult to distinguish unavailability reasons	Explicit differentiation between availability and leave
Query Flexibility	Complex queries to infer employee status	Simple and direct queries for better analysis

This Boolean enhancement in Oracle 23AI enables developers to better model real-world states, increases maintainability, and makes data-driven decision-making more intuitive—especially in use cases like QuickMart's employee shift and presence tracking system.

Real-Time Business Use Cases for Boolean Data Type in Oracle 23AI

While Oracle 23AI's native BOOLEAN data type streamlines internal processing, its impact is most visible in day-to-day business applications. Across industries, organizations routinely manage binary states—availability, approval, subscription status, and more. With BOOLEAN columns now natively supported in SQL, these use cases become simpler to model, query, and maintain, leading to enhanced clarity, faster execution, and lower operational overhead.

Table 7-5. Real-Time Business Use Cases of the Boolean Data Type in Oracle 23AI

Use Case	Benefit
Employee Attendance and Leave Tracking	Simplifies leave management and reduces query complexity.
Product Inventory and Stock Availability	Enables faster filtering and more accurate real-time stock tracking.
Subscription and Membership Management	Simplifies billing logic and improves subscription status validation.
Loan and Credit Approval Status	Clarifies approval workflows and accelerates loan processing.
Fraud Detection and Transaction Flagging	Enhances fraud identification and real-time flagging of risky transactions.
Smart Device and IoT Status Monitoring	Supports automation by tracking device availability and maintenance needs.

Common Questions About Boolean Data Type in Oracle 23AI

Oracle 23AI's native BOOLEAN data type brings both clarity and efficiency to modern database design. A frequent question is how it improves performance over traditional number-based flags (1/0). By eliminating explicit comparisons and supporting better index selectivity, Boolean values enable faster query execution and reduced overhead.

In terms of data integrity, Boolean columns clearly represent states (TRUE, FALSE, NULL) and support NOT NULL and CHECK constraints, helping enforce business rules and prevent inconsistent entries.

Another key benefit is seamless integration with PL/SQL, allowing simplified logic in application code and ETL processes. This aligns well with microservices and enhances readability, maintainability, and compliance in enterprise environments.

Together, these advantages make the Boolean data type a practical and forward-looking enhancement for both developers and DBAs.

Key Takeaway Prior to Oracle 23AI, managing employee availability and leave typically relied on single status columns or numeric flags like 1/0, which led to reduced clarity and more complex query logic. The introduction of the native Boolean data type offers a clear, expressive alternative—enabling separate TRUE/FALSE columns for availability, leave status, and other binary conditions. This enhancement improves data integrity, simplifies application logic, and boosts performance across diverse scenarios, including employee tracking, inventory management, and IoT monitoring.

Building on this foundation of precision and clarity, Oracle 23AI further extends its SQL capabilities with the **CHECKSUM analytic function**, a powerful tool for ensuring data consistency and detecting changes across datasets. The next section explores how this function works and how businesses can use it to streamline auditing and integrity checks in real-time environments.

CHECKSUM Analytic Function in 23AI

Ensuring data consistency and detecting unauthorized or accidental changes are key concerns in modern enterprise environments. Oracle Database 23AI introduces the CHECKSUM analytic function to simplify these tasks by computing a deterministic hash over a set of values. This hash acts as a fingerprint, helping businesses quickly identify changes in data without tracking every field individually. Whether it's auditing transactional integrity, validating ETL pipelines, or flagging unexpected updates, the CHECKSUM function offers a lightweight and powerful solution.

CHAPTER 7 SQL, PLSQL ENHANCEMENTS AND NEW FUNCTIONS

CASE STUDY: INVENTORY CHANGE TRACKING AT QUICKMART

QuickMart, a mid-sized retail chain, needed to streamline its inventory monitoring processes. With thousands of products and frequent changes from sales and restocking, tracking discrepancies manually became inefficient and error-prone. The business challenge was clear: detect and verify inventory updates in real-time with minimal overhead.

To solve this, QuickMart's development team adopted Oracle 23AI's CHECKSUM function to monitor inventory levels. The approach involved assigning a checksum to each product's stock quantity, recalculating it after every transaction. Any change in the checksum signaled that the stock level had been altered, enabling targeted validation.

Designing the Inventory Table

The first step involved defining a simple inventory table that tracked essential product details like ID, name, current stock, and restock date.

Listing 7-9. Creating the Inventory Table for Checksum Tracking

```
drop table inventory cascade constraints;

CREATE TABLE inventory (
  product_id NUMBER(10),
  product_name VARCHAR2(100),
  quantity_in_stock NUMBER(10),
  restock_date DATE
);
```

Populating Sample Inventory Data

QuickMart initialized the system with some representative stock data, as shown below.

Listing 7-10. Inserting Sample Product Records into Inventory Table

```
INSERT INTO inventory (product_id, product_name, quantity_in_stock,
restock_date)
```

CHAPTER 7 SQL, PLSQL ENHANCEMENTS AND NEW FUNCTIONS

VALUES (101, 'Laptop', 50, TO_DATE('2025-01-01', 'YYYY-MM-DD'));

INSERT INTO inventory (product_id, product_name, quantity_in_stock, restock_date)
VALUES (102, 'Smartphone', 150, TO_DATE('2025-01-10', 'YYYY-MM-DD'));

INSERT INTO inventory (product_id, product_name, quantity_in_stock, restock_date)
VALUES (103, 'Tablet', 100, TO_DATE('2025-01-15', 'YYYY-MM-DD'));

INSERT INTO inventory (product_id, product_name, quantity_in_stock, restock_date)
VALUES (104, 'Monitor', 75, TO_DATE('2025-01-20', 'YYYY-MM-DD'));

COMMIT;

Calculating Initial Checksums

QuickMart calculated the initial checksums to baseline inventory quantities for each product. These values served as reference points for detecting future modifications.

Listing 7-11. Computing Initial Inventory Checksums Using CHECKSUM Function

```
SELECT product_id,
       product_name,
       quantity_in_stock,
       CHECKSUM(quantity_in_stock) OVER (PARTITION BY product_id) AS checksum_inventory
FROM inventory
ORDER BY product_id;
```

PRODUCT_ID	PRODUCT_NAME	QUANTITY_IN_STOCK	CHECKSUM_INVENTORY
101	Laptop	50	736723
102	Smartphone	150	359231
103	Tablet	100	621374

PRODUCT_ID	PRODUCT_NAME	QUANTITY_IN_STOCK	CHECKSUM_INVENTORY
104	Monitor	75	947047

Detecting Changes After a Sale

Suppose QuickMart sells 10 laptops and 15 smartphones. After updating the stock quantities, recalculating the checksum clearly reveals which products were affected.

Listing 7-12. Updating Inventory Quantities After Sales

```
UPDATE inventory
SET quantity_in_stock = quantity_in_stock - 10
WHERE product_id = 101;

UPDATE inventory
SET quantity_in_stock = quantity_in_stock - 15
WHERE product_id = 102;

commit;
```

Now, we recalculate the checksum to monitor if the inventory data has changed after the update. If the checksum values have changed, it indicates that the inventory quantities have been modified.

Listing 7-13. Recomputing Checksums After Inventory Update

```
SELECT product_id,
       product_name,
       quantity_in_stock,
       CHECKSUM(quantity_in_stock) OVER (PARTITION BY product_id) AS checksum_inventory_after_sale
FROM inventory
ORDER BY product_id;
```

OUTPUT:

PRODUCT_ID	PRODUCT_NAME	QUANTITY_IN_STOCK	CHECKSUM_INVENTORY
101	Laptop	40	422501
102	Smartphone	135	881393
103	Tablet	100	621374
104	Monitor	75	947047

As you can see, the checksum value for Laptop and Smartphone will have changed, indicating that the stock quantities were updated. The checksum for other products remains the same.

Restocking Inventory and Rechecking

Later, 20 units of tablets and 10 monitors are restocked. A similar checksum recalculation helps confirm the update.

Listing 7-14. Updating Inventory After Restocking

```
UPDATE inventory
SET quantity_in_stock = quantity_in_stock + 20
WHERE product_id = 103;

UPDATE inventory
SET quantity_in_stock = quantity_in_stock + 10
WHERE product_id = 104;

COMMIT;
```

Once the restocking is done, we again calculate the checksum for each product to ensure that the changes are captured.

Listing 7-15. Verifying Inventory with New Checksums After Restock

```
SELECT product_id,
       product_name,
       quantity_in_stock,
```

```
    CHECKSUM(quantity_in_stock) OVER (PARTITION BY product_id) AS
checksum_inventory_after_restock
FROM inventory
ORDER BY product_id;
```

PRODUCT_ID	PRODUCT_NAME	QUANTITY_IN_STOCK	CHECKSUM_INVENTORY
101	Laptop	40	422501
102	Smartphone	135	881393
103	Tablet	120	678542
104	Monitor	85	88636

Again, the checksum for Tablet and Monitor has changed, indicating that restocking was successful and the inventory has been updated.

The CHECKSUM function in Oracle 23AI provides an elegant solution for change detection in transactional systems. For QuickMart, it delivered visibility into product-level inventory movements with minimal implementation complexity. More broadly, CHECKSUM can be used in auditing pipelines, ensuring referential consistency in federated systems, or comparing data across replicas. As data volumes grow and integrity becomes increasingly vital, tools like this are indispensable for modern, resilient architectures.

Internal Mechanism of CHECKSUM Analytic Function in Oracle 23AI

Oracle 23AI's CHECKSUM analytic function computes a deterministic hash value by applying an optimized hashing algorithm to specified columns. It operates within SQL window functions, leveraging **PARTITION BY** to efficiently track data changes across grouped datasets. This lightweight integrity verification method minimizes performance overhead, making it ideal for batch validation and large-scale data consistency checks.

The internal execution flow of the CHECKSUM function is outlined in Table 7-6.

Table 7-6. *Internal Workflow of the CHECKSUM Analytic Function in Oracle 23AI*

CHECKSUM Analytic Function in Oracle 23AI
Computes Deterministic Hash Value
Uses Optimized Hashing Algorithm
Operates Within SQL Window Functions
Leverages PARTITION BY for Grouped Data Tracking
Lightweight Integrity Verification
Minimizes Performance Overhead
Ideal for Batch Validation and Large-Scale Consistency Checks

Real-Time Business Use Cases for the CHECKSUM Analytic Function in Oracle 23AI

While the internal workings of Oracle 23AI's CHECKSUM analytic function ensure reliable and efficient detection of data changes, its greatest value is seen in real-world business operations. From finance and compliance to supply chain and inventory systems, data consistency is vital for trust, accuracy, and automation. The CHECKSUM function provides a simple yet powerful method to detect subtle data changes without full comparisons—empowering automated auditing, anomaly detection, and operational assurance.

Table 7-7. Real-Time Use Cases of the CHECKSUM Analytic Function in Oracle 23AI

Use Case	Description	Benefit
Inventory Management	Track changes in stock quantities over time (sales, restocking, and transfers).	Ensures data integrity and simplifies inventory auditing.
Financial Transactions	Monitor changes in transaction data (e.g., deposits, withdrawals, and transfers).	Enhances data consistency and provides a mechanism for fraud detection.
Customer Data Management	Track changes in customer profiles (e.g., contact details, addresses).	Ensures customer data is accurate and consistent across systems.
Order Processing	Monitor updates in order statuses (e.g., processing, shipped, and delivered).	Guarantees accurate tracking of orders and reduces errors.
Compliance and Auditing	Track financial record changes to comply with regulations (e.g., SOX, GDPR).	Ensures transparent and auditable records for legal compliance.
Supply Chain Management	Track changes in product movements, shipments, and logistics data.	Improves visibility and ensures accurate supply chain tracking.

By integrating CHECKSUM into key pipelines, Oracle 23AI helps organizations ensure trust in their data, automate audits, and maintain system-wide consistency with minimal overhead—strengthening both operational integrity and compliance readiness.

Common Questions About CHECKSUM in Oracle 23AI

Oracle 23AI's CHECKSUM analytic function introduces a fast and lightweight mechanism for detecting data changes across large datasets. This section addresses common questions surrounding its use and practical value in business environments.

A frequently asked question is how CHECKSUM differs from traditional cryptographic hashes. While functions like MD5 prioritize uniqueness and security, CHECKSUM focuses on performance, offering efficient validation for grouped or partitioned data without cryptographic guarantees. It's ideal for batch-level integrity checks rather than forensic tracking.

Another point of interest is how CHECKSUM handles updates across columns. The function supports PARTITION BY, allowing users to isolate and track changes at a granular level—for example, across inventory items, customer segments, or financial records.

Some users also ask about its reliability in detecting subtle changes. While highly performant, CHECKSUM is not collision-proof and may occasionally miss low-level variations, particularly with floating-point data. It's best used where performance outweighs the need for byte-level accuracy.

Overall, CHECKSUM serves as a powerful tool for inventory tracking, ETL pipeline validation, and data consistency monitoring—especially in use cases where speed and scale matter more than cryptographic precision.

Key Takeaway The CHECKSUM analytic function in Oracle 23AI plays a crucial role in simplifying data integrity verification across business-critical domains. From inventory management at QuickMart to auditing financial transactions and customer records, this feature offers a lightweight, scalable way to detect changes with minimal overhead. By integrating CHECKSUM into operational workflows, organizations can streamline audits, prevent inconsistencies, and meet compliance requirements with greater confidence.

Building on this momentum of usability and performance improvements, Oracle 23AI introduces another practical enhancement: the ability to use column aliases within GROUP BY and HAVING clauses. This feature significantly improves SQL readability and developer productivity—making complex queries more concise and less error-prone. The next section explores how this capability transforms day-to-day query design while maintaining full optimization compatibility.

Enhancing SQL Readability with Column Aliases in GROUP BY and HAVING in 23AI

As enterprise databases evolve toward greater performance and maintainability, SQL readability becomes increasingly vital—especially in environments where queries are frequently revised and optimized. Oracle 23AI introduces a powerful enhancement that allows developers to use column aliases directly within the GROUP BY and HAVING clauses. This eliminates redundancy, simplifies debugging, and reduces errors in query design, all without sacrificing performance. Behind the scenes, Oracle's SQL optimizer rewrites alias-based references back into their original expressions to ensure optimal execution plans.

> **REAL-WORLD CASE STUDY: SALARY ANALYSIS AT QUICKMART**
>
> QuickMart, a national retail chain, manages diverse employee roles across departments. The HR team frequently analyzes salary distributions to determine equitable compensation policies. One such analysis involves identifying job roles where the average salary exceeds $2,000. Prior to Oracle 23AI, this required developers to repeat expressions like AVG(salary) in both the SELECT and HAVING clauses. With the new alias support in 23AI, QuickMart's development team can now write concise, expressive SQL that reduces cognitive load and improves maintainability.

Creating and Populating the EMP23AI Table

The team begins by preparing a sample dataset representing QuickMart's employee structure, as shown in Listing 7-16.

Listing 7-16. Table and Data Definition for Employee Salary Analysis

```
DROP TABLE IF EXISTS emp23ai PURGE;

CREATE TABLE emp23ai (
  emp_id    NUMBER(4) PRIMARY KEY,
  emp_name  VARCHAR2(20),
  job_role  VARCHAR2(15),
  salary    NUMBER(7,2),
  dept_id   NUMBER(2)
);

INSERT INTO emp23ai VALUES (101, 'Alice', 'Analyst', 3000, 10);
INSERT INTO emp23ai VALUES (102, 'Bob', 'Analyst', 3200, 10);
INSERT INTO emp23ai VALUES (103, 'Charlie', 'Manager', 5000, 20);
INSERT INTO emp23ai VALUES (104, 'David', 'Clerk', 1500, 30);
INSERT INTO emp23ai VALUES (105, 'Eve', 'Manager', 4800, 20);
```

CHAPTER 7   SQL, PLSQL ENHANCEMENTS AND NEW FUNCTIONS

```
INSERT INTO emp23ai VALUES (106, 'Frank', 'Clerk', 1800, 30);
INSERT INTO emp23ai VALUES (107, 'Grace', 'Sales', 2200, 40);
INSERT INTO emp23ai VALUES (108, 'Hank', 'Sales', 2100, 40);
INSERT INTO emp23ai VALUES (109, 'Ivy', 'Clerk', 1700, 30);
INSERT INTO emp23ai VALUES (110, 'Jack', 'Analyst', 2900, 10);

COMMIT;
```

Querying with Column Aliases in GROUP BY and HAVING

To generate a report of job roles where the average salary exceeds $2,000, the team writes a query that defines a column alias for the aggregated salary. This alias—avg_salary—is then reused in both the GROUP BY and HAVING clauses, as illustrated in Listing 7-17.

Listing 7-17. Alias-Based GROUP BY and HAVING Clause

```
SELECT initcap(job_role) jrole,
       ROUND(AVG(salary), 2) AS avg_salary
FROM emp23ai
GROUP BY jrole  --using column alias in group by
HAVING avg_salary > 2000;   -- Using column alias in HAVING clause
```

This streamlined syntax allows QuickMart's HR analysts to focus on insights rather than rewriting repetitive expressions.

Using Column Position for Grouping

Alternatively, developers at QuickMart can leverage column positions in the GROUP BY clause by enabling a session-level setting. This is especially useful when dealing with dynamically generated SQL or graphical query builders.

Listing 7-18. Enabling and Using GROUP BY Column Position

```
ALTER SESSION SET group_by_position_enabled = TRUE;

SELECT initcap(job_role) jrole,
       ROUND(AVG(salary), 2) AS avg_salary
```

```
FROM emp23ai
GROUP BY 1 -- Using column position instead of "job_role"
HAVING avg_salary > 2000;
```

The use of GROUP BY 1 refers to the first column in the SELECT clause, further reducing syntax complexity.

Practical Benefits for Business and Development

This enhancement brings tangible value to organizations like QuickMart by dramatically improving SQL clarity. Developers no longer need to retype or copy complex expressions into multiple clauses. Instead, they can define a transformation once and refer to it cleanly using an alias. This makes queries easier to debug, audit, and reuse—especially in collaborative development environments or when generating SQL from middleware platforms.

Furthermore, the Oracle optimizer ensures that these enhancements do not impact execution time. Alias references are internally resolved into full expressions during query planning, preserving performance while improving code maintainability.

By enabling the use of column aliases in GROUP BY and HAVING clauses, Oracle 23AI strikes an effective balance between readability and performance. QuickMart's case demonstrates how even small syntax improvements can have wide-reaching benefits for data reporting and analysis.

Internal Mechanism of Column Aliases in GROUP BY and HAVING in Oracle 23AI

Oracle 23AI's optimizer dynamically resolves column aliases in **GROUP BY** and **HAVING** clauses by internally replacing them with their original expressions before execution. This transformation occurs at the query parsing stage, ensuring readability improvements without altering execution efficiency. The rewritten query is then processed normally, maintaining optimal performance while reducing redundancy.

This internal behavior is outlined in the flow below.

Table 7-8. *Internal Processing Flow of Column Alias Resolution in Oracle 23AI*

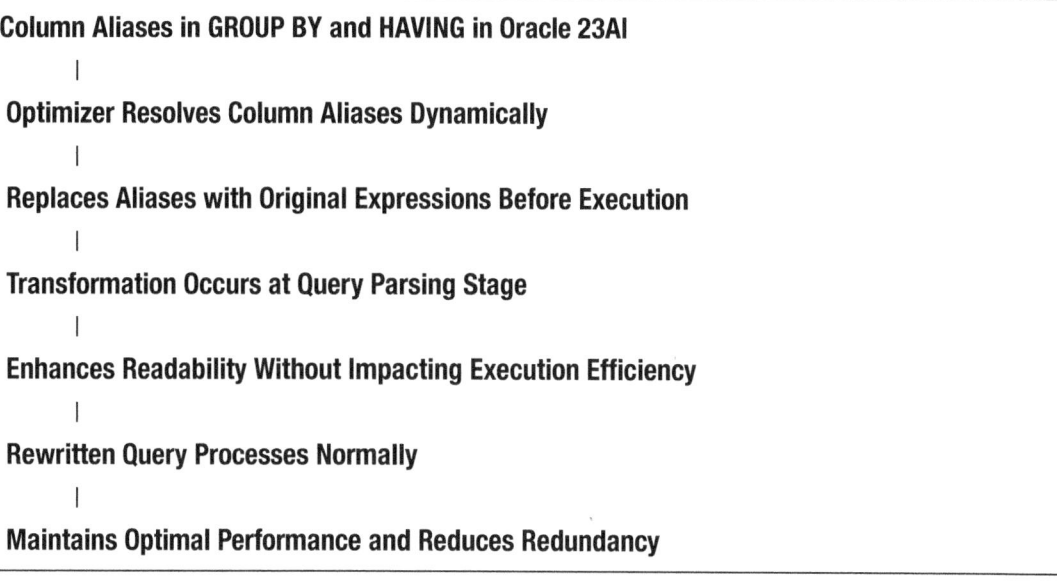

By transparently handling alias references, Oracle 23AI empowers developers to focus on logic rather than syntax management, improving both developer productivity and query reliability.

Real-Time Business Use Cases for Column Aliases in GROUP BY and HAVING Clauses in Oracle 23AI

While Oracle 23AI's internal support for column aliases in GROUP BY and HAVING clauses significantly improves code maintainability, the feature's true value becomes evident when applied to everyday business scenarios. From employee analytics to targeted marketing, this enhancement streamlines SQL development and facilitates faster, cleaner reporting.

The following examples illustrate how diverse industries can benefit from this functionality in practical settings.

Table 7-9. Practical Use Cases for Column Aliases in GROUP BY and HAVING in Oracle 23AI

Use Case	Business Scenario	Benefit
Employee Performance Analysis	Evaluating average salary per job role and filtering out underpaid roles	Improves query readability and eliminates redundant expressions
Sales Performance Reporting	Calculating average sales per region and excluding low-performing areas	Simplifies reporting and enhances regional performance visibility
Product Profitability Analysis	Analyzing average profit margin per product to remove unprofitable items	Makes profitability analysis clearer and more maintainable
Customer Segmentation	Grouping customers by average spending and excluding low-value segments	Enables precise customer targeting and efficient campaign planning

By reducing the need for repeated expressions, this feature not only enhances query aesthetics but also increases development speed, lowers the chance of syntax errors, and ensures consistent logic application across multiple clauses.

Common Questions About Using Column Aliases in GROUP BY and HAVING in Oracle 23AI

The addition of column alias support in GROUP BY and HAVING clauses in Oracle 23AI brings welcome clarity to SQL, but also raises important questions for developers and DBAs. This section addresses the most frequent concerns to help ensure correct usage and best practices.

A key question is how Oracle handles aliases internally. The answer lies in the optimizer, which rewrites the aliases into their full expressions during the parsing phase. This transformation ensures that readability improvements do not come at the cost of execution performance.

Another common inquiry is how Oracle's approach compares with other databases. While some platforms like PostgreSQL or older versions of SQL Server allow aliases only in limited contexts, Oracle 23AI offers broader support—enabling more concise and maintainable queries.

Some users also explore enabling column positions in GROUP BY (e.g., GROUP BY 1). While this can shorten SQL statements, it introduces risk if column order changes, so it's most useful for static query structures.

Although primarily aimed at improving readability, the feature also reduces repetition and lowers the chance of syntax errors. These indirect benefits make queries easier to debug, maintain, and optimize—enhancing development efficiency without compromising performance.

Key Takeaway   Oracle 23AI's support for column aliases in GROUP BY and HAVING clauses streamlines query logic by eliminating redundant expressions, offering a cleaner and more intuitive SQL development experience. This enhancement is especially valuable in business scenarios involving grouped metrics—such as salary analysis or sales aggregation—where readability and maintainability are essential.

Building on this theme of simplifying complex data operations, the next section explores Oracle 23AI's advancement in handling temporal data: the direct aggregation of INTERVAL DAY TO SECOND types. This long-awaited feature removes previous limitations around time-based computations, opening new possibilities for duration analysis and performance optimization in time-driven workloads.

Aggregation over INTERVAL Datatypes in 23AI

Oracle Database 23AI delivers a powerful enhancement by enabling direct aggregation of INTERVAL DAY TO SECOND data types using functions such as SUM and AVG. Previously, while MIN and MAX were supported for interval values, attempts to aggregate using SUM or AVG resulted in errors, forcing users to perform cumbersome conversions to numeric types. This new capability simplifies queries involving durations and time intervals, improving both ease of use and performance for analytic workloads.

CHAPTER 7   SQL, PLSQL ENHANCEMENTS AND NEW FUNCTIONS

> **CASE STUDY: STREAMLINING EMPLOYEE WORK DURATION ANALYTICS AT QUICKMART**
>
> At QuickMart, a global ecommerce company, the HR analytics team faced challenges in calculating total and average employee work durations directly in SQL. Their existing process required converting INTERVAL data into numeric formats before performing aggregations, complicating reporting queries, and slowing down analytics.
>
> Before Oracle 23AI, attempting to aggregate INTERVAL durations with SUM or AVG produced errors like this:
>
> ORA-00932: inconsistent datatypes: expected NUMBER got INTERVAL DAY TO SECOND
>
> This limitation impeded straightforward computation of total and average working hours.

To address this, QuickMart modeled employee work sessions with a table that captures start and end timestamps and calculates the duration as a virtual INTERVAL DAY TO SECOND column, as shown in Listing 7-19.

The following steps illustrate how this feature works with a real-world example.

Listing 7-19. Work Sessions Table Definition and Sample Data for QuickMart Corp

```
CREATE TABLE work_sessions (
    id          NUMBER PRIMARY KEY,
    start_time  TIMESTAMP,
    end_time    TIMESTAMP,
    duration    INTERVAL DAY TO SECOND
                GENERATED ALWAYS AS (end_time - start_time) VIRTUAL
);

INSERT INTO work_sessions (id, start_time, end_time)
VALUES (1, TIMESTAMP '2024-01-01 08:00:00', TIMESTAMP '2024-01-01 17:00:00');

INSERT INTO work_sessions (id, start_time, end_time)
```

VALUES (2, TIMESTAMP '2024-01-02 09:30:00', TIMESTAMP '2024-01-02 18:15:00');

INSERT INTO work_sessions (id, start_time, end_time)
VALUES (3, TIMESTAMP '2024-01-03 07:45:00', TIMESTAMP '2024-01-03 16:30:00');

INSERT INTO work_sessions (id, start_time, end_time)
VALUES (4, TIMESTAMP '2024-01-04 08:15:00', TIMESTAMP '2024-01-04 17:45:00');

COMMIT;

Querying the table returns the work session durations as shown in Listing 7-20.

Listing 7-20. Sample Work Sessions with Calculated Durations at QuickMart Corp

```
SELECT * FROM work_sessions;
ID   START_TIME            END_TIME              DURATION
------------------------------------------------------------
1    2024-01-01T08:00:00Z  2024-01-01T17:00:00Z  +0 9:0:0
2    2024-01-02T09:30:00Z  2024-01-02T18:15:00Z  +0 8:45:0
3    2024-01-03T07:45:00Z  2024-01-03T16:30:00Z  +0 8:45:0
4    2024-01-04T08:15:00Z  2024-01-04T17:45:00Z  +0 9:30:0
```

With Oracle 23AI, QuickMart's analysts can now use SUM and AVG directly on the INTERVAL durations, eliminating the need for complex conversions. Listing 7-21 demonstrates how to compute total and average durations seamlessly.

Listing 7-21. Calculating Total and Average Work Durations at QuickMart

```
SELECT SUM(duration) AS total_duration,
       AVG(duration) AS average_duration
FROM work_sessions;
```

The results, shown in Table 7-10, provide accurate total and average work durations.

CHAPTER 7　SQL, PLSQL ENHANCEMENTS AND NEW FUNCTIONS

Table 7-10. *Aggregated Total and Average Work Durations*

TOTAL_DURATION	AVERAGE_DURATION
+1 12:0:0	+0 9:0:0

Moreover, Oracle 23AI enables SUM and AVG as analytic window functions on INTERVAL data, supporting advanced reporting such as cumulative duration calculations. Listing 7-22 illustrates a query computing cumulative sums and averages ordered by session start time.

Listing 7-22. Cumulative SUM and AVG of Work Durations Using Analytic Functions

```
SELECT
    id,
    start_time,
    end_time,
    duration,
    SUM(duration) OVER (ORDER BY start_time) AS cumulative_sum_duration,
    AVG(duration) OVER (ORDER BY start_time) AS cumulative_avg_duration
FROM work_sessions;
```

The output, displayed in Table 7-11, offers valuable insights for workforce management by showing running totals and averages without any additional data manipulation.

Table 7-11. *Cumulative Duration Aggregates for Work Sessions*

ID	START_TIME	END_TIME	DURATION	TOTAL_DURATION	AVERAGE_DURATION
1	2024-01-01T08:00:00Z	2024-01-01T17:00:00Z	+0 9:0:0	+0 9:0:0	+0 9:0:0
2	2024-01-02T09:30:00Z	2024-01-02T18:15:00Z	+0 8:45:0	+0 17:45:0	+0 8:52:30
3	2024-01-03T07:45:00Z	2024-01-03T16:30:00Z	+0 8:45:0	+1 2:30:0	+0 8:50:0
4	2024-01-04T08:15:00Z	2024-01-04T17:45:00Z	+0 9:30:0	+1 12:0:0	+0 9:0:0

This enhancement dramatically simplifies interval data handling, enabling organizations like QuickMart to perform complex temporal analytics directly within SQL. By removing previous constraints, Oracle 23AI streamlines development and improves query efficiency.

Internal Mechanism of INTERVAL Aggregation in Oracle 23AI

Oracle 23AI introduces native support for aggregating INTERVAL DAY TO SECOND data types by directly operating on these values without converting them to numeric types. The internal mechanism leverages enhanced aggregation algorithms that efficiently process INTERVAL data during SUM and AVG operations. It simplifies queries by bypassing type conversions, utilizing optimized memory management and time-series aggregation techniques, enabling seamless integration with analytic functions like windowing. This approach improves performance, especially in large datasets, while maintaining accurate handling of time-based calculations.

As illustrated in Table 7-12, the flow of operations for INTERVAL aggregation highlights the direct processing of interval data and its optimized execution within analytic queries.

Table 7-12. Operational Flow of INTERVAL DAY TO SECOND Aggregation in Oracle 23AI

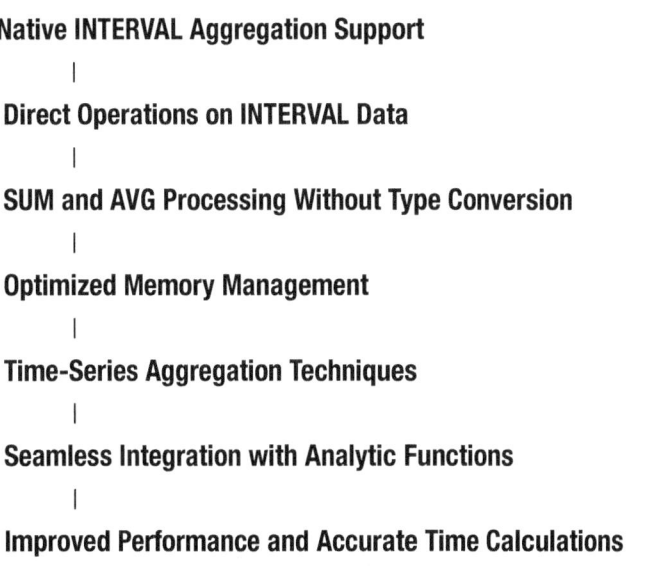

CHAPTER 7　SQL, PLSQL ENHANCEMENTS AND NEW FUNCTIONS

Aggregation over INTERVAL Data Types Differs Between Pre-23AI Versions and 23AI

Before Oracle 23AI, aggregation on INTERVAL data types was limited to only the MIN and MAX functions. Users had to convert INTERVAL values to numeric types for operations like SUM and AVG, which increased query complexity and hindered direct analytic usage. With Oracle 23AI, SUM and AVG are fully supported natively on INTERVAL data types, enabling simpler queries and enhanced functionality with analytic functions.

As shown in Table 7-13, the new capabilities provide clear improvements across key aspects of aggregation involving INTERVAL data.

Table 7-13. Comparison Between Pre-23AI and Oracle 23AI Aggregation over INTERVAL Data Types

Feature	Pre-23AI Versions	Oracle 23AI
Supported Aggregate Functions	Only MIN and MAX were supported for INTERVAL data types.	SUM and AVG are now supported for INTERVAL data types.
Usage in Aggregation	Aggregation required converting INTERVAL to numeric types, complicating queries.	Direct aggregation on INTERVAL data types is now possible.
Analytic Functions	Limited support for INTERVAL data types in analytic functions.	Enhanced support for INTERVAL data types in analytic functions.
Query Complexity	Higher complexity due to necessary data type conversions.	Simplified queries with direct support for INTERVAL data types.

This enhancement reduces query complexity and improves performance by allowing direct and efficient aggregation of INTERVAL data, making Oracle 23AI a significant upgrade for time-based data processing.

Real-Time Business Use Cases for INTERVAL Aggregation in Oracle 23AI

Oracle 23AI's enhanced support for native aggregation over INTERVAL data types unlocks valuable insights across diverse industries. By enabling direct SUM and AVG operations on time intervals, businesses can simplify complex time-based calculations and improve operational efficiency. The following table highlights key real-world scenarios where INTERVAL aggregation drives measurable benefits.

Table 7-14. *Real-Time Business Use Cases for INTERVAL Aggregation in Oracle 23AI*

Business Sector	Use Case	Benefit
HR and Payroll	Work hours and overtime tracking	Simplifies payroll and ensures compliance.
IT and Cloud Services	System downtime analysis	Enhances SLA reporting and incident resolution.
Customer Service	Support response time tracking	Improves efficiency and customer satisfaction.
Manufacturing	Process duration optimization	Identifies bottlenecks and boosts productivity.
Airlines and Logistics	Flight scheduling and delays	Enhances operational planning and efficiency.
Healthcare	Patient monitoring and stay duration	Optimizes resource allocation and patient care.

This capability empowers organizations to perform accurate, efficient time-based analytics directly within SQL, fostering better decision-making and operational excellence.

Common Questions About Aggregation over INTERVAL Datatypes in Oracle 23AI

Oracle 23AI's support for aggregation over INTERVAL datatypes introduces new capabilities but also prompts important questions regarding its behavior and limitations. One frequent concern is how the system handles edge cases such as overlapping intervals or null values during aggregation. Oracle treats overlapping intervals independently, aggregating each as distinct values, while null values are excluded from calculations unless explicitly included through functions like NVL.

CHAPTER 7   SQL, PLSQL ENHANCEMENTS AND NEW FUNCTIONS

Another key question involves the impact of this feature on query performance. By enabling direct aggregation without the need for type conversions, Oracle 23AI significantly improves performance—particularly in large datasets—although proper query optimization remains essential for best results.

When working in **mixed-version environments**—where some database nodes or applications are running versions of Oracle prior to 23AI—compatibility issues may arise. In such configurations, legacy systems may not recognize or properly handle INTERVAL aggregations, leading to syntax errors or incomplete query execution. To mitigate this, Oracle recommends either upgrading all participating database components to 23AI or using compatibility views that convert INTERVAL datatypes into supported formats for backward-compatible processing.

Finally, challenges may arise when performing INTERVAL aggregation in distributed database setups. Issues such as latency, data consistency, and time zone handling require careful data distribution and resource management to maintain performance and accuracy.

Despite these challenges, Oracle 23AI's native INTERVAL aggregation support offers a robust and efficient solution for time-based analytics within complex database environments.

Key Takeaway   Oracle 23AI significantly enhances time-based calculations by enabling direct aggregation on INTERVAL DAY TO SECOND data types. This advancement simplifies the aggregation of durations such as work hours or process times and supports cumulative and running total calculations through analytic functions. It enables more intuitive and efficient time-series analytics, improving reporting and session tracking. These capabilities make time-based reporting, duration tracking, and process optimization easier, delivering valuable benefits across diverse industries including HR, IT, customer service, manufacturing, airlines, and healthcare.

Extending this focus on performance and efficiency, the next section introduces Oracle 23AI's Automatic PL/SQL to SQL Transpiler—an innovation that eliminates costly SQL-to-PL/SQL context switches by transparently rewriting eligible function calls into native SQL. This breakthrough allows developers to retain modular PL/SQL design while still achieving high-performance SQL execution.

CHAPTER 7　SQL, PLSQL ENHANCEMENTS AND NEW FUNCTIONS

Boosting SQL Performance with Automatic PL/SQL to SQL Transpiler in 23AI

Modern database systems often strive to reduce the latency introduced by redundant engine context switches. Oracle 23AI addresses this long-standing challenge through the introduction of the Automatic PL/SQL to SQL Transpiler, a performance-oriented innovation that enables SQL queries to seamlessly incorporate previously slow-performing PL/SQL logic. By internally converting eligible PL/SQL function calls into native SQL expressions, Oracle eliminates the overhead caused by SQL-to-PL/SQL context switching. This transparent optimization integrates deeply with the SQL optimizer and requires no changes to existing application code, making it ideal for both legacy modernization and high-performance enterprise workloads.

Understanding the Internal Optimization Flow

The transformation occurs entirely during the query parsing and optimization phases. When a query includes a call to a simple PL/SQL function, Oracle inspects the function logic and determines if it can be inlined as a SQL expression. If eligible, the function call is replaced internally with its SQL-equivalent form. This bypasses the procedural engine altogether and allows the SQL executor to process the query as a pure set-based operation, improving efficiency.

This mechanism is especially impactful in WHERE clauses, which often serve as the filtering backbone for high-volume queries. As a result, overall query performance improves significantly, especially in analytics and reporting scenarios where such functions are frequently used.

CASE STUDY: REVENUE ANALYSIS AT QUICKMART

QuickMart, a retail enterprise with a rapidly expanding transaction volume, encountered performance issues during revenue analysis on its large SALES table. The company uses a PL/SQL function `calculate_revenue` to determine total revenue per transaction, computed as the product of `unit_price` and `quantity`. However, invoking this function within SQL queries led to notable performance degradation due to the SQL-to-PL/SQL context switching overhead.

To resolve this, QuickMart adopted Oracle 23AI's Automatic SQL Transpiler.

Creating the Sales Dataset

QuickMart's database team first initialized the sales dataset by creating a transactional table and populating it with a large volume of sales records. This setup is shown in Listing 7-23.

Listing 7-23. Creation and Population of the SALES Table

```
DROP TABLE sales PURGE;

CREATE TABLE sales (
    sale_id NUMBER PRIMARY KEY,
    product_id NUMBER NOT NULL,
    unit_price NUMBER(10,2),
    quantity NUMBER
);

Insert Sample Data:
BEGIN
    FOR i IN 1..100000 LOOP
        INSERT INTO sales VALUES (
            i,
            MOD(i, 1000) + 1,   -- Simulating 1000 products
            ROUND(DBMS_RANDOM.VALUE(10, 1000), 2), -- Random price between
            10 and 1000
            TRUNC(DBMS_RANDOM.VALUE(1, 10))   -- Random quantity between
            1 and 10
        );
    END LOOP;
    COMMIT;
END;
/
```

Encapsulating Revenue Logic in PL/SQL

To modularize their business logic, QuickMart created a function named `calculate_revenue`, as shown in Listing 7-24. This function multiplies the unit price and quantity to yield total transaction revenue.

Listing 7-24. Definition of the `calculate_revenue` PL/SQL Function

```
CREATE OR REPLACE FUNCTION calculate_revenue(p_price NUMBER, p_qty NUMBER)
RETURN NUMBER AS
BEGIN
    RETURN p_price * p_qty;
END;
/
```

Measuring Baseline Performance Without Transpilation

In the baseline scenario, the function is used in a SQL query to filter transactions with revenue above $5000. This results in individual calls to the PL/SQL engine for each row, as reflected in the execution plan. The plan confirms the use of `calculate_revenue` in the filter condition, as shown in Listing 7-25.

Listing 7-25. Baseline Query Without Transpiler

```
EXPLAIN PLAN SET STATEMENT_ID = 'sales_revenue_function' FOR
SELECT sale_id, product_id, unit_price, quantity
FROM sales
WHERE calculate_revenue(unit_price, quantity) > 5000;

SELECT * FROM DBMS_XPLAN.DISPLAY;
```

Enabling SQL Transpiler and Optimizing the Query

After enabling the SQL Transpiler feature at the session level, QuickMart reruns the same query. Oracle now internally replaces the function call with its SQL equivalent, simplifying the execution path and removing context switch overhead. This updated behavior is shown in Listing 7-26.

Listing 7-26. Optimized Query with Transpiler Enabled

```
ALTER SESSION SET sql_transpiler = 'on';

EXPLAIN PLAN SET STATEMENT_ID = 'sales_revenue_transpiled' FOR
SELECT sale_id, product_id, unit_price, quantity
FROM sales
WHERE calculate_revenue(unit_price, quantity) > 5000;

SELECT * FROM DBMS_XPLAN.DISPLAY;
```

The execution plan now shows a filter condition of unit_price * quantity > 5000, indicating successful transpilation and inlining of the function logic.

Key Business Benefits

For QuickMart, this enhancement translated into faster reporting and more scalable analytics without rewriting any existing business logic. The Automatic PL/SQL to SQL Transpiler not only improved execution time but also simplified SQL tuning, reduced CPU utilization, and eliminated the need to refactor modular PL/SQL code into native SQL manually.

Oracle 23AI's Automatic SQL Transpiler addresses a longstanding bottleneck in database systems: the cost of context switching between SQL and PL/SQL. As demonstrated by QuickMart's revenue analysis scenario, this feature significantly enhances query performance while preserving code modularity. This innovation exemplifies Oracle's continued investment in intelligent automation, bridging performance with developer productivity.

Internal Mechanism of Automatic SQL Transpiler in Oracle 23AI

Oracle 23AI's Automatic SQL Transpiler dynamically analyzes SQL queries in real-time, detecting eligible PL/SQL function calls. It then converts these functions into equivalent SQL expressions, eliminating SQL-to-PL/SQL context switching. This transformation seamlessly integrates with the query optimizer, ensuring efficient execution while maintaining query accuracy.

CHAPTER 7 SQL, PLSQL ENHANCEMENTS AND NEW FUNCTIONS

The internal transformation workflow is illustrated in the diagram below.

Table 7-15. *Internal Flow of Automatic SQL Transpiler in Oracle 23AI*

Automatic SQL Transpiler in Oracle 23AI
|
Real-Time Analysis of SQL Queries
|
Detection of Eligible PL/SQL Function Calls
|
Conversion to Equivalent SQL Expressions
|
Elimination of SQL-to-PL/SQL Context Switching
|
Seamless Integration with Query Optimizer
|
Efficient Execution and Maintained Query Accuracy

By enabling native execution of PL/SQL logic within SQL, Oracle 23AI dramatically reduces the latency associated with hybrid SQL-PL/SQL workloads and simplifies the path to performance optimization—particularly in data-intensive enterprise environments.

Comparison of the Automatic SQL Transpiler in Oracle 23AI with Previous Versions

In previous Oracle versions, developers frequently faced performance issues when embedding PL/SQL function calls within SQL queries—particularly in filter predicates or aggregations. These function calls triggered SQL-to-PL/SQL context switching, resulting in slower execution, higher CPU usage, and increased complexity during query tuning. Developers were often forced to manually rewrite logic directly in SQL or restructure queries to avoid performance penalties.

Oracle 23AI introduces the **Automatic SQL Transpiler**, a game-changing feature that eliminates these inefficiencies by dynamically converting eligible PL/SQL function calls into equivalent SQL expressions. This allows Oracle to process the logic natively within the SQL engine, reducing context switching and boosting execution speed. As shown in Table 3-4, this enhancement delivers significant advantages over earlier releases.

Table 7-16. Comparison Between Pre-23AI and Oracle 23AI SQL Transpiler Behavior

Aspect	Pre-23AI Behavior	Oracle 23AI Behavior
Function Execution in SQL	PL/SQL functions executed separately, incurring context-switching overhead.	Functions are automatically transpiled into native SQL expressions.
Performance Impact	Queries suffered from latency and CPU overhead due to repeated function calls.	Improved performance through set-based SQL execution and reduced switching.
Manual Optimization	Developers had to manually rewrite or inline logic to achieve better performance.	Optimization occurs automatically during parsing—no code changes required.
Packaged Functions	All PL/SQL functions, including those in packages, executed with context switching.	Initially only standalone functions were transpiled; latest tests show support for some packaged functions.

This automatic optimization empowers developers to retain the modularity of PL/SQL while benefiting from SQL's performance advantages—striking the ideal balance between maintainability and execution efficiency.

Sample Real-Time Business Use Cases for the Automatic PL/SQL to SQL Transpiler in Oracle 23AI

While the internal mechanism of Oracle 23AI's Automatic SQL Transpiler reveals its technical efficiency, its full impact is best understood through real-world applications. In industries where performance, scale, and responsiveness are critical, this feature plays a key role in accelerating insights and reducing overhead. The following business scenarios illustrate how different sectors can benefit from this native optimization capability.

Table 7-17. Business Use Cases and Benefits of the Automatic SQL Transpiler in Oracle 23AI

Use Case	Description	Benefit
Ecommerce Orders	Speeds up total order value calculations.	Faster processing.
Fraud Detection	Eliminates function overhead in transaction checks.	Real-time alerts.
Retail Analytics	Optimizes revenue and discount queries.	Quick insights.
Banking Risk Assessment	Transpiles financial risk functions to SQL.	Faster evaluations.
Healthcare Billing	Enhances insurance claim calculations.	Efficient billing.
Inventory Tracking	Speeds up stock-level analysis.	Real-time tracking.

By automatically rewriting PL/SQL logic into native SQL, Oracle 23AI reduces latency and simplifies query execution paths—making it easier for organizations to deliver timely, data-driven services across critical applications.

Common Questions About Automatic PL/SQL to SQL Transpiler in Oracle 23AI

As with any behind-the-scenes optimization, Oracle 23AI's Automatic SQL Transpiler raises important questions about its selection logic, impact on performance, and safety in execution. This section addresses the most common concerns to provide clarity and confidence in its practical application.

A key question is how Oracle determines which functions to transpile. The system analyzes SQL in real time and only transpiles deterministic, stateless, and computationally simple PL/SQL functions—excluding those that involve side effects or access global state.

Another frequent inquiry is the performance benefit. By avoiding SQL-to-PL/SQL context switching, Oracle can improve query performance by 30–50%, reducing CPU overhead and enhancing throughput for analytic and transactional workloads.

Some developers ask if the feature can be toggled for specific scenarios. Oracle offers session-level control via `ALTER SESSION SET sql_transpiler = 'on'`, allowing fine-grained enablement without global changes to application logic.

Accuracy is also a concern. Oracle enforces strict type checks and validates execution plans during transpilation to ensure that query semantics are preserved. The result is a seamless blend of transparency and efficiency—critical for modern enterprise workloads.

Key Takeaway By eliminating SQL-to-PL/SQL context switching and automatically transforming eligible function calls into native SQL, Oracle 23AI's Automatic SQL Transpiler streamlines query execution and enhances performance without requiring any code changes. This hands-off optimization enables businesses to accelerate analytics, reduce processing overhead, and improve scalability across a wide range of applications.

As organizations seek greater transparency and control over data operations, performance alone is not enough. The next chapter explores Oracle 23AI's advancements in database annotations and auditing—features that strengthen accountability, traceability, and governance across modern data ecosystems.

CHAPTER 8

Database Annotations and Auditing Enhancements

Introduction

This chapter explores powerful enhancements introduced in Oracle 23AI around **database annotations** and **auditing capabilities**. These features are designed to improve data governance, traceability, and operational accountability across modern enterprise environments. Each section provides a clear explanation of the feature, supported by practical case studies that demonstrate their application in real-world scenarios.

You will find step-by-step guidance for implementation, along with comparative insights highlighting the evolution from earlier Oracle versions. Under-the-hood technical details are included to help readers understand the internal workings of these features. Business use cases across sectors such as finance, healthcare, and ecommerce illustrate the tangible value of these enhancements. The chapter also addresses frequently asked questions to clarify usage boundaries and best practices.

Every section concludes with a brief summary to reinforce key takeaways.

Annotations in Oracle Database 23AI

Modern enterprise databases require more than just efficient data storage and retrieval; they also demand robust, dynamic metadata management. In Oracle 23AI, the introduction of annotations marks a significant evolution in how metadata can be embedded directly within schema definitions. Unlike static SQL comments, annotations offer structured name-value metadata pairs that can be queried, modified, or dropped without altering base object definitions. This chapter explores how annotations enhance clarity, documentation, and governance of database objects, and demonstrates their practical application with a real-world case study from QuickMart.

> **CASE STUDY: IMPROVING SCHEMA DOCUMENTATION FOR QUICKMART'S HR SYSTEM**
>
> QuickMart, a rapidly growing retail chain, needed a more efficient way to document its employee management tables. Traditional database comments were insufficient for large development teams and dynamic environments. Oracle 23AI's annotations provided the solution by embedding structured metadata directly into table and column definitions, thereby streamlining internal documentation and governance.

Creating Annotated Database Objects

QuickMart begins by defining an `employees` table where each column is enhanced with relevant annotations. These annotations describe UI display names, classification groupings, and ownership metadata. As shown in Listing 8-1, annotations are embedded alongside data types and offer immediate context to both developers and analysts.

Listing 8-1. Creating a Table with Annotations in Oracle 23AI

```
CREATE TABLE employees (
    emp_id          NUMBER          ANNOTATIONS (PrimaryKey, UI_Display
                                    'Employee ID', Classification
                                    'Employee Info'),
    emp_name        VARCHAR2(100)   ANNOTATIONS (UI_Display 'Employee Name',
                                    Classification 'Employee Info'),
    department      VARCHAR2(50)    ANNOTATIONS (UI_Display 'Department',
                                    Classification 'Employee Info'),
    hire_date       DATE            ANNOTATIONS (UI_Display 'Hire Date',
                                    Classification 'Employment Info'),
    salary          NUMBER(10, 2)   ANNOTATIONS (UI_Display 'Salary',
                                    Classification 'Employment Info')
) ANNOTATIONS (Classification 'Employee Management Table', Owner
'HR Team');
```

CHAPTER 8   DATABASE ANNOTATIONS AND AUDITING ENHANCEMENTS

Data is then inserted into the employees table to simulate production records.

Listing 8-2. Inserting into Employee Table

```
INSERT INTO employees (emp_id, emp_name, department, hire_date, salary)
VALUES (1, 'John Doe', 'IT', DATE '2020-01-15', 80000.00);

INSERT INTO employees (emp_id, emp_name, department, hire_date, salary)
VALUES (2, 'Jane Smith', 'HR', DATE '2019-11-30', 65000.00);

INSERT INTO employees (emp_id, emp_name, department, hire_date, salary)
VALUES (3, 'Alice Johnson', 'Finance', DATE '2021-03-10', 70000.00);

COMMIT;
```

Managing and Modifying Annotations Dynamically

To address evolving security policies, QuickMart's HR team later decides to limit the visibility of salary data and internalize certain table-level details. Instead of altering the base schema, they simply update the annotation values using DDL, as shown in Listing 8-3.

Listing 8-3. Updating and Dropping Annotations

```
ALTER TABLE employees ANNOTATIONS (Visibility 'Internal Use Only');

-- Add a visibility annotation to the salary column
ALTER TABLE employees MODIFY (salary ANNOTATIONS (Visibility
'Confidential'));

-- Drop an existing annotation
ALTER TABLE employees MODIFY (salary ANNOTATIONS (DROP Visibility));
```

These changes reflect immediately and are nonintrusive, meaning they do not require recompilation or affect dependent applications.

CHAPTER 8   DATABASE ANNOTATIONS AND AUDITING ENHANCEMENTS

Querying Annotations for Governance and Reporting

Oracle 23AI includes a system view called USER_ANNOTATIONS_USAGE, which provides a unified way to retrieve and audit annotations across all schema objects. QuickMart uses this to generate metadata documentation for internal reviews, as shown in Listing 8-4.

Listing 8-4. Querying Annotation Metadata

```
SELECT object_name,
       object_type,
       column_name,
       annotation_name,
       annotation_value
FROM   user_annotations_usage
ORDER BY object_name, column_name, annotation_name;
```
Sample Output:

Table 8-1. *Internal Flow of Annotations Management in Oracle 23AI*

OBJECT_NAME	OBJECT_TYPE	COLUMN_NAME	ANNOTATION_NAME	ANNOTATION_VALUE
EMPLOYEES	TABLE		Classification	Employee Management Table
EMPLOYEES	TABLE		Owner	HR Team
EMPLOYEES	COLUMN	EMP_ID	PrimaryKey	
EMPLOYEES	COLUMN	EMP_ID	UI_Display	Employee ID
EMPLOYEES	COLUMN	EMP_NAME	UI_Display	Employee Name
EMPLOYEES	COLUMN	DEPARTMENT	UI_Display	Department
EMPLOYEES	COLUMN	HIRE_DATE	UI_Display	Hire Date
EMPLOYEES	COLUMN	SALARY	UI_Display	Salary

Business Impact of Annotations

The annotations feature significantly enhances metadata visibility and schema clarity for QuickMart. Developers no longer rely solely on external documentation, which improves onboarding and reduces query misinterpretation. The flexibility to modify annotations dynamically allows DBAs to enforce internal data policies and audit compliance effortlessly. For cross-functional teams managing complex data environments, annotations become a central element of self-documenting design.

Annotations in Oracle 23AI represent a shift toward more transparent, maintainable, and adaptive database design. By embedding metadata directly within database objects, organizations like QuickMart can manage evolving requirements with minimal disruption. In the following section, we will explore the new auditing enhancements that complement annotations by strengthening compliance and traceability.

Internal Mechanism of Annotations in Oracle 23AI

Annotations in Oracle 23AI are stored as structured metadata in system catalog views rather than being embedded directly within table definitions. When queried, Oracle retrieves annotations from metadata views like USER_ANNOTATIONS_USAGE, ensuring minimal performance overhead. Modifications (add, update, delete) are dynamically applied to these metadata structures without altering the underlying schema, enabling flexible and efficient metadata management.

This internal process is depicted in the flow diagram below.

Table 8-2. Internal Flow of Annotations Management in Oracle 23AI

Annotations in Oracle 23AI
|
Stored As Structured Metadata in System Catalog Views
|
Not Embedded Directly in Table Definitions
|
Retrieved from Metadata Views (e.g., USER_ANNOTATIONS_USAGE)
|
Ensures Minimal Performance Overhead
|
Modifications Dynamically Applied (Add, Update, Delete)
|
No Alteration to Underlying Schema
|
Enables Flexible and Efficient Metadata Management

By separating metadata from schema definitions and enabling runtime flexibility, Oracle 23AI empowers users to document, audit, and classify their data assets in a structured yet adaptable way—paving the path for better governance and self-describing schemas.

Difference Between Annotation and Comments

While traditional comments have long served as a basic documentation tool within Oracle databases, Oracle 23c introduces annotations as a more structured and flexible alternative. The key distinctions between these two approaches lie in their purpose, structure, and applicability across database objects. Table 8-3 summarizes the major differences between traditional comments and the new annotation framework introduced in Oracle 23c.

Table 8-3. *Comparison Between Traditional Comments and Annotations in Oracle*

Feature	Pre-23c (Comments)	Oracle 23c (Annotations)
Purpose	Free-text descriptions	Structured name-value metadata
Flexibility	Static, plain text	Dynamic key-value pairs, multiple annotations per object
Programmatic Access	Limited to comment views	Detailed, queryable annotation views
Supported Objects	Limited (tables, columns, etc.)	Extensive (tables, columns, indexes, etc.)
Modification	Replace entire comment	Add, modify, or drop specific annotations
Application Integration	Minimal	High, with semantic and structured metadata

By enabling granular and semantically meaningful metadata tagging, annotations provide a richer, more manageable way to document and interact with schema elements. This makes them especially useful for dynamic application environments, automated tooling, and robust metadata governance strategies.

Sample Real-Time Business Use Cases for Oracle 23AI Annotations

Understanding the internal mechanism of Oracle 23AI annotations is just the beginning. Their real value emerges when applied to practical business scenarios. This section outlines how organizations can leverage annotations to improve metadata clarity, ensure data security, and streamline data governance. From HR analytics to audit trails, annotations offer a structured way to enrich database semantics without altering underlying schemas.

Table 8-4. Real-World Applications and Benefits of Annotations in Oracle 23AI

Use Case	Description	Benefit
Employee Analysis	Tag salary data to analyze pay gaps.	Enhances query clarity.
Data Security	Mark sensitive columns as "Confidential" or "PII."	Strengthens compliance.
Data Governance	Assign metadata like "Owner" and "Retention Policy."	Simplifies audits.
BI Report Labels	Use annotations for user-friendly column names.	Improves reporting.
Data Lineage	Track "Source System" and "Last Updated By."	Aids auditing.

By embedding rich metadata directly into the database layer, annotations help teams across analytics, governance, compliance, and reporting operate more efficiently—with fewer dependencies on external documentation or manual tracking systems.

Common Questions About Annotations in Oracle Database 23AI

As Oracle 23AI introduces a more structured approach to metadata through annotations, several questions naturally arise regarding their governance, performance, and integration. This section addresses the most common considerations.

A key advantage of annotations is their ability to improve data governance. Unlike traditional comments, annotations support name-value pairs that are queryable, helping organizations assign ownership, define retention policies, and classify sensitive information directly within the database structure. This enhances auditability and regulatory compliance.

Another frequent concern is whether annotations affect query performance. Fortunately, annotations are stored in dedicated metadata views and accessed only when explicitly queried. This separation ensures that normal query execution remains unaffected and that storage overhead is negligible.

Annotations also align well with AI and cloud-native ecosystems. By supporting dynamic tagging and structured semantics, they improve schema discovery, automate data pipeline behavior, and facilitate AI-driven classification across distributed environments.

From a security perspective, annotations should be governed carefully. Best practices include restricting modification access, avoiding sensitive content within annotations, and integrating them with Oracle's existing security frameworks such as Virtual Private Database (VPD) and Data Masking.

Together, these capabilities make annotations a robust tool for modern data governance, offering a significant upgrade over legacy documentation methods.

Key Takeaway   Annotations in Oracle 23AI represent a significant advancement in how metadata is managed within the database. By introducing a structured and dynamic approach to tagging database objects with name-value pairs, Oracle enables developers and administrators to enhance schema clarity, improve governance, and streamline documentation—all without altering the underlying schema. These enhancements elevate the developer experience and support more intelligent, self-descriptive database environments.

As organizations place increasing emphasis on data transparency and accountability, metadata alone is not enough. Auditing becomes essential—not only for compliance but also for security and operational oversight. In the next section, we explore the auditing enhancements in Oracle 23AI, with a focus on Unified Auditing and its new ability to track activity at the column level.

Auditing Enhancements in Oracle 23AI

In an era of growing data privacy regulations and heightened compliance demands, database auditing has become a core component of enterprise data governance. Oracle 23AI marks a pivotal evolution in this space by fully transitioning to **Unified Auditing**, simultaneously deprecating the older, traditional auditing model. Among its most powerful new capabilities is **column-level auditing**, which allows administrators to selectively audit access to specific columns rather than entire tables. This focused approach not only improves auditing precision but also minimizes performance overhead and unnecessary log entries—critical for organizations that manage sensitive data at scale.

> **CASE STUDY: FINE-GRAINED AUDITING FOR PII IN QUICKMART'S ORDER SYSTEM**
>
> QuickMart, a rapidly expanding retail chain, manages millions of transactions in its **Customer Orders** system. As part of its compliance with privacy regulations such as GDPR and CCPA, the company must carefully audit all interactions involving personally identifiable information (PII). This includes tracking updates and queries related to sensitive fields like customer names and transaction amounts.
>
> Rather than enabling full-table auditing, which generates excessive logs and adds unnecessary processing cost, QuickMart implements Oracle 23AI's **column-level auditing** to precisely monitor these high-risk data points.

Creating the Audit-Enabled Table

The first step involves creating customer orders in testuser1 schema, including the sensitive columns. As shown in Listing 8-5, the `customer_orders` table includes customer names, order amounts, and metadata like order dates.

Listing 8-5. Creating and Populating the Customer Orders Table

```
-- Drop the table if it exists.
drop table if exists customer_orders purge;

-- Create the Customer Orders table.
create table customer_orders (
    order_id        number generated always as identity,
    customer_name   varchar2(50),
    order_amount    number(10, 2),
    order_date      date default sysdate
);
```

```
-- Insert test data.
insert into customer_orders (customer_name, order_amount)
values ('Alice', 100.50);

insert into customer_orders (customer_name, order_amount)
values ('Bob', 200.75);

commit;
```

Defining the Audit Policy

Next, an administrator connects to the database and creates a fine-grained audit policy, targeting only the columns that require monitoring. The policy, shown in Listing 8-6, tracks any updates to the customer_name and order_amount columns, as well as any SELECT activity on order_amount.

Listing 8-6. Creating and Enabling a Column-Level Audit Policy

```
create audit policy sensitive_data_audit
  actions update(customer_name, order_amount) on testuser1.customer_orders,
          select(order_amount) on testuser1.customer_orders
  container = current;

-- Enable the audit policy.
audit policy sensitive_data_audit;
```

This policy ensures that QuickMart has visibility into every attempt to read or change sensitive transaction data—without bloating the audit trail with irrelevant actions.

Executing Operations to Trigger Auditing

After the policy is in place, routine operations continue as usual. QuickMart's application and staff perform a mix of read and write operations, some of which are designed to be audited while others are intentionally excluded. The queries and updates are shown in Listing 8-7.

Connect back as the testuser1 and perform some actions.

Listing 8-7. Example User Operations on the Customer Orders Table

```sql
-- Not audited: Insert operation.
insert into customer_orders (customer_name, order_amount)
values ('Charlie', 300.00);

commit;

-- Not audited: Querying non-audited columns.
select order_id, order_date from customer_orders;

-- Audited: Updating the customer_name column.
update customer_orders
set    customer_name = 'Alice Cooper'
where  customer_name = 'Alice';

-- Audited: Updating the order_amount column.
update customer_orders
set    order_amount = 150.00
where  order_amount = 100.50;

-- Audited: Querying the order_amount column.
select order_amount from customer_orders;
```

Only operations that involve the explicitly audited columns (customer_name and order_amount) trigger entries in the Unified Audit Trail.

Reviewing the Audit Results

To validate the effectiveness of the audit policy, QuickMart's database administrators run a query against the UNIFIED_AUDIT_TRAIL view. This displays every logged operation involving the sensitive columns, as shown in Table 8-5.

Listing 8-8. Audit Trail Query

```sql
select event_timestamp,
       dbusername,
       action_name,
       object_schema,
       object_name,
```

```
        sql_text
from    unified_audit_trail
where   object_name = 'CUSTOMER_ORDERS'
order BY event_timestamp;
```

Expected Audit Trail Output:

Table 8-5. *Audit Trail Results for Sensitive Column Access*

EVENT_TIMESTAMP	DBUSERNAME	ACTION_NAME	OBJECT_SCHEMA	OBJECT_NAME	SQL_TEXT
26-JAN-25 10:45:21.123 PM	TESTUSER1	UPDATE	TESTUSER1	CUSTOMER_ORDERS	update customer_orders set customer_name...
26-JAN-25 10:46:01.456 PM	TESTUSER1	UPDATE	TESTUSER1	CUSTOMER_ORDERS	update customer_orders set order_amount...
26-JAN-25 10:46:30.789 PM	TESTUSER1	**SELECT**	TESTUSER1	CUSTOMER_ORDERS	select order_amount from customer_orders...

This focused audit output confirms that only the relevant interactions were captured, helping QuickMart stay compliant without the burden of excessive audit logs.

Business Implications and Takeaways

Column-level auditing in Oracle 23AI represents a major leap in precision and efficiency for enterprise audit strategies. By limiting the scope of auditing to sensitive data only, organizations like QuickMart can significantly reduce log volume, improve database performance, and gain deeper visibility into how critical information is accessed and modified.

This capability is particularly valuable in industries subject to strict compliance standards, where audit trails must be both detailed and efficient. Combined with Unified Auditing's centralized management model, column-level control provides the foundation for scalable, policy-driven governance in modern data environments.

Internal Mechanism of Column-Level Auditing in Oracle 23AI

Oracle 23AI's Unified Auditing leverages optimized internal logging mechanisms that selectively capture audit events at the column level, reducing unnecessary entries. It integrates with the policy-based audit framework, where audit conditions are efficiently evaluated in-memory to minimize performance overhead. The audit records are then securely stored in the unified audit trail, ensuring fast retrieval and compliance with minimal impact on database operations.

This internal mechanism is visually represented in the flow diagram below.

Table 8-6. Internal Flow of Column-Level Auditing in Oracle 23AI

Runtime Operation
|
In-Memory Evaluation of Audit Policies
|
Column-Level Matching Logic
|
Selective Audit Logging
|
Secure Storage in Unified Audit Trail
|
Optimized Retrieval for Compliance

This flow demonstrates how Oracle efficiently intercepts and records only relevant audit events, achieving a fine balance between compliance, performance, and scalability.

Oracle Database 23c (23AI) Auditing Features Differ from Previous Versions

Prior to Oracle 23AI, database auditing relied on a dual model that supported both Traditional and Unified Auditing, often creating inconsistencies and administrative overhead. Granularity was limited, and any action triggered a full table-level audit, generating excessive entries even when only specific columns were of interest. Oracle 23AI simplifies and strengthens the auditing model by fully adopting Unified Auditing and introducing column-level auditing, making the process more targeted and efficient. As shown in Table 8-7, these enhancements significantly improve both performance and compliance alignment.

Table 8-7. Comparison Between Pre-23c and Oracle 23AI Auditing Features

Feature	Pre-23c (Traditional Auditing)	Oracle 23c (23AI Unified Auditing)
Auditing Type	Supported both Traditional Auditing and Unified Auditing.	Traditional Auditing desupported, only Unified Auditing is allowed.
Column-Level Auditing	No support for column-level auditing.	Allows auditing specific columns in tables and views.
Granularity of Auditing	Audited actions applied to the entire table or view.	Actions can be scoped to specific columns, reducing unnecessary entries.
Performance Optimization	Higher audit trail overhead due to broader scope.	Reduced overhead by ignoring irrelevant actions on nonaudited columns.
Ease of Transition	Transition to Unified Auditing required manual changes.	Unified Auditing is the default; enforced transition simplifies setup.

By consolidating and refining its auditing framework, Oracle 23AI enables organizations to enforce more precise data governance policies while maintaining optimal system performance—ensuring readiness for modern regulatory requirements.

CHAPTER 8　DATABASE ANNOTATIONS AND AUDITING ENHANCEMENTS

Business Use Cases for Oracle 23AI Column-Level Auditing

While the internal mechanics of column-level auditing in Oracle 23AI reflect its advanced technical design, the true impact is seen in real-world applications across highly regulated and data-sensitive industries. By narrowing the scope of audits to specific columns, organizations gain tighter control over sensitive data access and modification while reducing the volume of unnecessary audit entries. This section explores common business scenarios where column-level auditing improves compliance, fraud detection, and operational transparency.

Table 8-8. *Business Use Cases and Benefits of Column-Level Auditing in Oracle 23AI*

Use Case	Industry	Scenario	Key Benefits
1. Fraud Detection	Banking	Audit transaction updates and balance queries.	Prevents unauthorized changes, ensures compliance (SOX, PCI DSS regulators).
2. Patient Data Security	Healthcare	Track edits to diagnoses and billing access.	Ensures HIPAA compliance, protects PII, reduces audit noise.
3. Price Integrity	Ecommerce	Monitor price and discount changes.	Detects fraud, ensures accurate financials, prevents manipulation.
4. Tax Compliance	Government	Audit income data changes and access.	Ensures GDPR/CCPA compliance, supports legal audits.
5. Salary Protection	HR and Payroll	Track salary edits and compensation queries.	Prevents payroll fraud, protects employee privacy.

Column-level auditing empowers organizations to align their data governance practices with modern regulatory standards while enhancing system performance and audit clarity.

Common Questions About Auditing Enhancements in Oracle 23c

As organizations move toward more fine-grained and compliance-focused auditing, Oracle 23AI's enhancements naturally prompt questions about their practical benefits and impact on system performance. This section addresses key concerns to help readers understand the value of these improvements.

A frequent question is how column-level auditing improves performance. By capturing audit data only for specific columns—rather than the entire table—Oracle reduces unnecessary logging, resulting in lower storage usage, faster queries, and less audit noise during high-throughput operations.

Many also ask how Oracle 23AI supports evolving data privacy regulations like GDPR and CCPA. The answer lies in its ability to audit only sensitive fields such as PII, allowing for precise tracking and minimized data exposure, which is critical for privacy compliance and audit readiness.

In high-volume environments, performance bottlenecks are a concern. Oracle 23AI mitigates this by using selective and optimized logging. It integrates seamlessly with Oracle Analytics, enabling real-time anomaly detection without taxing system resources.

Lastly, Unified Auditing greatly simplifies security administration. As the default model in 23AI, it removes the need for legacy transitions, centralizes audit management, and streamlines policy definition—making it easier for administrators to enforce and monitor security controls at scale.

Key Takeaway   Oracle Database 23c (23AI) marks a pivotal evolution in auditing by fully adopting Unified Auditing and retiring Traditional Auditing. The introduction of column-level auditing allows organizations to capture only the most relevant data interactions, significantly improving audit precision and system performance. By reducing storage overhead, filtering unnecessary events, and aligning with regulatory standards such as GDPR and CCPA, this enhancement strengthens both security posture and compliance readiness.

CHAPTER 8 DATABASE ANNOTATIONS AND AUDITING ENHANCEMENTS

Building on this foundation of secure and intelligent auditing, the next chapter explores broader advancements in database security and access control. From simplified privilege management to the SQL Firewall, Oracle 23AI introduces a suite of features designed to safeguard data, empower developers, and enforce access policies with greater efficiency.

CHAPTER 9

Security, Data Masking and Privilege Management

Introduction

This chapter explores key security and access control enhancements in Oracle 23AI that simplify privilege management, improve data protection, and support regulatory compliance. It introduces features such as schema-level privileges, the DB_DEVELOPER_ROLE, SQL Firewall, enhanced data redaction and masking, and read-only users—all aimed at streamlining administration and securing sensitive information. Real-world case studies illustrate practical implementation in diverse business contexts, while internal mechanisms are briefly explained to clarify how these features operate efficiently behind the scenes. Comparisons with previous Oracle versions highlight improvements, and each section concludes with a summary to reinforce key insights and facilitate informed adoption.

Simplifying Privilege Management with Schema Privileges in 23AI

Managing database access efficiently is a cornerstone of secure and scalable enterprise systems. In Oracle Database 23AI, a major leap forward in this area comes in the form of **Schema Privileges**—a feature designed to reduce administrative complexity by allowing privilege assignments at the schema level, rather than at the individual object level. This simplifies permission management and ensures that users automatically gain access to both existing and newly created objects within a schema, eliminating the need for continuous privilege updates.

In earlier versions of Oracle, administrators had to grant privileges for every table, view, and procedure individually. This not only increased operational overhead but also introduced the risk of misconfigured access due to inconsistent grants. Schema Privileges solve this by enabling consistent, centralized control that scales as the schema evolves.

CASE STUDY: QUICKMART UNIFIES ACCESS ACROSS DEPARTMENTS

QuickMart, a growing retail enterprise, manages its operations through dedicated schemas for **Sales**, **Inventory**, and **Payments**. Previously, the company relied on object-level privilege management, which proved to be a time-consuming and error-prone process. Each new table, such as one tracking promotional sales or updated pricing models, required manual grants to analysts and team leads. This approach led to frequent delays, security gaps, and the use of overly broad privileges like `SELECT ANY TABLE`, which exposed more data than necessary.

With the introduction of Schema Privileges in Oracle 23AI, QuickMart found a cleaner, more secure way to manage access.

As shown in Listing 9-1, privileges such as SELECT, INSERT, UPDATE, and DELETE can now be granted at the schema level. These permissions automatically apply to all current and future objects within the schema, ensuring that users like SALES_ANALYST can perform their tasks without repeated administrative intervention.

Listing 9-1. Granting Schema-Level Privileges for the Sales Schema

```
grant select any table on schema sales_user to sales_analyst;
grant insert any table on schema sales_user to sales_analyst;
grant update any table on schema sales_user to sales_analyst;
grant delete any table on schema sales_user to sales_analyst;
```

This approach provides a secure and consistent privilege model that improves governance and reduces maintenance burden.

Monitoring and Managing Schema Privileges

Another valuable addition in Oracle 23AI is the introduction of dedicated data dictionary views for monitoring schema-level privileges. Administrators at QuickMart can now easily audit access rights and enforce least-privilege principles.

To review granted privileges, administrators use DBA_SCHEMA_PRIVS, which shows all schema-level grants for a specific user or role. ROLE_SCHEMA_PRIVS and SESSION_SCHEMA_PRIVS offer similar visibility for role-based and session-specific grants respectively, as shown in Listing 9-2.

Listing 9-2. Querying Schema Privileges Across Views

```
--Checking Schema-Level Privileges
SELECT * FROM DBA_SCHEMA_PRIVS WHERE GRANTEE = 'SALES_ANALYST';
--Checking Role-Based Schema Privileges
SELECT * FROM ROLE_SCHEMA_PRIVS;
--Checking Current Session's Schema Privileges
SELECT * FROM SESSION_SCHEMA_PRIVS;
```

With these tools, QuickMart's database team gains actionable insights into access control across environments, further enhancing both security and transparency.

Schema Privileges in Oracle 23AI offer a modern and scalable approach to access management that aligns with the dynamic needs of enterprise systems. For organizations like QuickMart, this feature reduces administrative complexity, enhances data protection, and enables rapid onboarding of users without compromising governance. By eliminating repetitive grants and supporting dynamic schema growth, Oracle has equipped administrators with a tool that promotes both efficiency and security.

Internal Mechanism of Schema Privileges in Oracle 23AI

Schema Privileges in Oracle 23AI operate by associating granted permissions at the schema level, maintaining metadata in system views like DBA_SCHEMA_PRIVS. Instead of storing privileges for individual objects, the database dynamically applies schema-level grants to all existing and newly created objects within the schema. This mechanism ensures real-time privilege enforcement and eliminates the need for object-level privilege updates, improving security and scalability.

The internal structure of this mechanism is outlined in Table 9-1.

Table 9-1. *Internal Structure of Schema Privileges in Oracle 23AI*

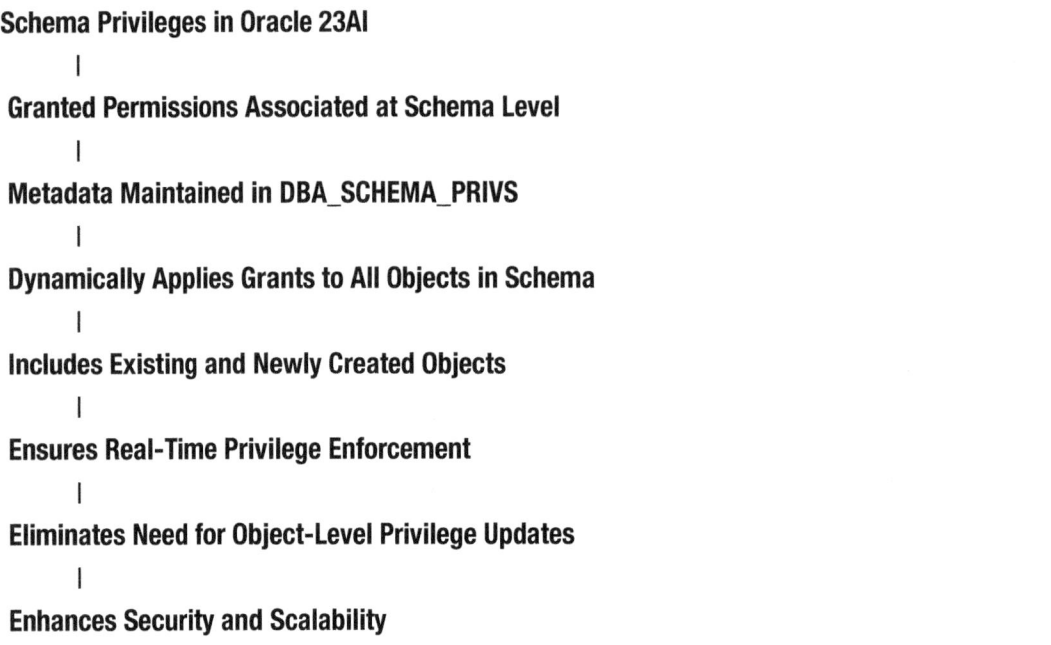

This internal model reflects Oracle's continued evolution toward declarative and policy-driven access control. By treating the schema as a unit of privilege enforcement, Oracle 23AI simplifies permission tracking, improves governance, and supports large-scale environments like those seen at QuickMart with ease and precision.

Real-Time Business Use Cases for Schema Privileges in Oracle 23AI

Oracle 23AI's Schema Privileges introduce a more scalable, declarative model for access control by allowing permissions to be granted at the schema level rather than individually across database objects. This capability proves especially useful in real-time enterprise environments where object creation is dynamic and access needs are role-driven. The following examples illustrate how various industries—including retail, finance, healthcare, and logistics—benefit from this enhancement in Oracle 23AI.

Table 9-2. *Real-Time Business Use Cases for Schema Privileges in Oracle 23AI*

Use Case	Description	Benefit
Retail Chain Access	Grant schema privileges to Sales, Inventory, and Payments teams.	Automates access to new tables, reducing manual updates.
Finance System	Assign schema privileges to roles like Account Managers and Auditors.	Simplifies role-based access with tight security.
RBAC for Enterprise	Grant schema privileges to developers, testers, and analysts.	Reduces admin workload and ensures seamless updates.
Healthcare Data	Provide SELECT to doctors and UPDATE to medical staff for patient records.	Enhances security and ensures real-time data access.
Supply Chain Operations	Assign schema privileges to suppliers (READ), warehouse managers (UPDATE), and logistics teams (INSERT).	Automates access control across supply chain data.

These use cases highlight the flexibility and efficiency Oracle 23AI offers for organizations like QuickMart that manage growing datasets across specialized teams. By aligning privileges with schemas, rather than objects, administrators can enforce consistent policies, enhance compliance, and respond quickly to changing business needs.

Common Questions About Schema Privileges in Oracle 23AI

Schema Privileges in Oracle 23AI offer a simpler and more secure way to manage access across database objects. Naturally, this raises key questions among DBAs and developers working in dynamic environments.

A common question is how Schema Privileges differ from traditional role-based access. Unlike RBAC, which requires manual grants for each object, Schema Privileges apply automatically to all current and future objects within a schema—reducing overhead and simplifying management.

Security is also a frequent concern. Schema Privileges limit access to a specific schema, avoiding broad grants like SELECT ANY TABLE and minimizing cross-schema exposure.

Another question involves naming conflicts across schemas. Since privileges are schema-scoped, users can only access objects in the schema they've been explicitly granted access to—even if other schemas contain objects with the same name.

Finally, when privileges are revoked at the schema level, access to all objects in that schema is removed immediately. This allows QuickMart and similar organizations to quickly respond to role changes or security needs.

In short, Schema Privileges bring clarity, efficiency, and stronger governance to database access control in Oracle 23AI.

Key Takeaway With the introduction of Schema Privileges in Oracle 23AI, QuickMart has redefined how it manages access control—shifting from manual, object-level grants to a more streamlined and scalable schema-level approach. This not only reduces administrative complexity but also reinforces secure and compliant privilege enforcement across development and production environments.

Building upon this momentum, the next section explores another innovation designed to support modern development teams: the **DB_DEVELOPER_ROLE**. This new role simplifies access for developers by bundling essential privileges into a single, secure profile—ensuring efficient development workflows without compromising security principles.

Streamlining Application Development with DB_DEVELOPER_ROLE in 23AI

Oracle 23AI introduces a new role—**DB_DEVELOPER_ROLE**—that redefines how development privileges are provisioned in modern application environments. This consolidated role is tailored specifically for developers, eliminating the traditional need to assign a combination of CONNECT, RESOURCE, and other object-level grants. By adopting the principle of least privilege, Oracle ensures that developers receive only the essential access required to build, modify, and query database objects—nothing more, nothing less. This simplifies role management, enhances security posture, and accelerates developer onboarding, especially in agile and DevOps-driven teams.

CHAPTER 9   SECURITY, DATA MASKING AND PRIVILEGE MANAGEMENT

CASE STUDY: QUICKMART'S DEVELOPER ACCESS MODERNIZATION

At QuickMart, a large retail organization with multiple in-house applications for sales, inventory, and analytics, the database team had historically granted developers the CONNECT and RESOURCE roles by default. While this ensured smooth development, it also introduced challenges. Developers often ended up with more privileges than necessary, creating security concerns and making it harder to track actual access needs over time. With growing compliance requirements and expanding development teams, QuickMart sought a more controlled and auditable way to assign development privileges.

Oracle 23AI's DB_DEVELOPER_ROLE provided the ideal solution. This unified role encapsulated the exact privileges developers needed—such as creating tables, views, procedures, and running basic queries—without the overhead of broader or legacy role grants. As a result, the database administrators could centrally manage developer access while enforcing tighter privilege boundaries across development environments.

Granting the DB_DEVELOPER_ROLE to Developers

Using the GRANT statement, QuickMart's administrators could assign the new role to developers in a single, streamlined step. For example, to grant access to a developer named testuser1, the following command was used.

Listing 9-3. Granting DB_DEVELOPER_ROLE to a developer in Oracle 23AI

```
grant db_developer_role to testuser1;
```

This eliminated the need to grant multiple roles like CONNECT, RESOURCE, and CREATE individually, reducing both administrative effort and the potential for misconfigured permissions.

Revoking and Verifying Developer Privileges

Should a developer switch teams or no longer require database access, administrators could simply revoke the role.

Listing 9-4. Revoking Developer Access Via DB_DEVELOPER_ROLE

```
revoke db_developer_role from testuser1;
```

To confirm that the role was assigned or removed, QuickMart's administrators used the following query against the role privilege view.

Listing 9-5. Verifying Assigned Roles for a User

```
SELECT GRANTED_ROLE FROM DBA_ROLE_PRIVS WHERE GRANTEE = 'TESTUSER1';
```

This approach allowed for centralized auditability and quick checks during periodic reviews or compliance audits.

Real-World Impact and Operational Gains

QuickMart reported measurable improvements in both security governance and operational efficiency. Developers could be onboarded faster, with appropriate access that aligned with their job functions. Administrators no longer had to create customized scripts or track dozens of object-level privileges manually. The DB_DEVELOPER_ROLE became a foundational tool in QuickMart's move toward secure, policy-driven DevSecOps practices.

Internal Mechanism of DB_DEVELOPER_ROLE in Oracle 23AI

The DB_DEVELOPER_ROLE in Oracle 23AI is a predefined role that consolidates essential development privileges, reducing the need for multiple role grants. Internally, it maps to a curated set of system privileges stored in DBA_SYS_PRIVS, ensuring controlled access while enforcing the principle of least privilege. When assigned, the role dynamically provides necessary permissions without exposing excessive administrative rights, streamlining privilege management and enhancing security.

The internal structure of the DB_DEVELOPER_ROLE is illustrated in Table 9-3.

Table 9-3. *Internal Structure of DB_DEVELOPER_ROLE in Oracle 23AI*

DB_DEVELOPER_ROLE in Oracle 23AI
|
Predefined Role for Development Privileges
|
Consolidates Essential Privileges
|
Mapped to System Privileges in DBA_SYS_PRIVS
|
Ensures Controlled Access and Least Privilege
|
Dynamically Grants Required Permissions
|
Avoids Excessive Administrative Rights
|
Enhances Security and Streamlines Privilege Management

This design enables organizations to onboard and manage developers quickly, ensuring they can perform necessary tasks without granting overly broad access, thereby reinforcing secure and efficient development workflows in Oracle 23AI.

Real-Time Business Use Cases for the DB_DEVELOPER_ROLE Feature in Oracle 23AI

Oracle 23AI's DB_DEVELOPER_ROLE introduces a streamlined approach to privilege management tailored for application developers. By consolidating essential permissions into a single role, it aligns with security best practices while reducing the administrative burden of managing separate roles and granular grants. This design not only supports faster development cycles but also enforces the principle of least privilege—critical for secure application delivery in enterprise environments. The table below highlights real-world scenarios where organizations benefit from adopting this feature for agility, governance, and operational efficiency.

Table 9-4. Real-Time Business Use Cases for DB_DEVELOPER_ROLE in Oracle 23AI

Use Case	Description	Benefit
Software Development Teams	Grant **DB_DEVELOPER_ROLE** to developers for access management.	Simplifies privilege management and reduces overhead.
DevOps in CI/CD Pipelines	Provide **DB_DEVELOPER_ROLE** for smooth deployment and testing.	Ensures correct access with minimized security risks.
Cloud-Based SaaS Development	Assign **DB_DEVELOPER_ROLE** to cloud software development teams.	Streamlines access control and limits excess permissions.
Database Migration Projects	Use **DB_DEVELOPER_ROLE** for developers during database migrations.	Simplifies access and enhances security during migration.
Agile Development	Grant **DB_DEVELOPER_ROLE** to agile teams for quick iteration.	Speeds up development and simplifies privilege management.

By incorporating this role into their access management strategy, organizations like QuickMart can support secure, agile, and scalable development workflows while reducing the administrative burden on DBAs and platform engineers.

Common Questions About DB_DEVELOPER_ROLE in Oracle 23AI

Oracle 23AI's DB_DEVELOPER_ROLE is a streamlined, security-aware role that simplifies privilege management for developers. As organizations adopt this role to modernize access control, a few key questions frequently arise regarding its scope, benefits, and operational use.

A common question is how DB_DEVELOPER_ROLE differs from traditional roles like CONNECT and RESOURCE. Unlike these older roles, which often grant excessive privileges, DB_DEVELOPER_ROLE provides only the essential permissions needed for application development—ensuring adherence to the principle of least privilege and reducing security risk.

Another concern is its fit within CI/CD pipelines and agile workflows. Because it includes just enough access for tasks such as schema design, object creation, and query execution, it integrates seamlessly into automated deployment environments without requiring additional access grants.

Flexibility is also addressed through role composition. While DB_DEVELOPER_ROLE itself is fixed, administrators can create composite roles that include it alongside other schema- or project-specific privileges, allowing tailored access control without compromising security.

In sum, Oracle 23AI's DB_DEVELOPER_ROLE simplifies developer onboarding, minimizes administrative overhead, and enforces a cleaner, more secure access model suited to modern application lifecycles.

Key Takeaway   By adopting the DB_DEVELOPER_ROLE, QuickMart has successfully streamlined developer privilege management while maintaining a strong security posture. This role-based approach minimizes administrative effort, enforces the principle of least privilege, and supports agile development practices without compromising database integrity. As a result, the company can focus on rapid innovation and efficient application delivery with confidence in its access controls.

Building on the theme of enhanced database security, the next section explores another key feature in Oracle 23AI—**the SQL Firewall**. This capability introduces robust protections by actively monitoring and restricting SQL activity in real time, offering a critical layer of defense against unauthorized access and data misuse.

Securing Data Access with SQL Firewall in 23AI

Oracle 23AI introduces the SQL Firewall, an advanced security enhancement that empowers administrators to monitor, restrict, and log SQL queries in real time. This feature is instrumental in protecting enterprise data from unauthorized access, SQL injection attacks, and compliance violations. By providing an automated way to define approved SQL behavior and identify deviations, SQL Firewall enhances both proactive and reactive security postures.

CHAPTER 9   SECURITY, DATA MASKING AND PRIVILEGE MANAGEMENT

CASE STUDY: PROTECTING FINANCIAL DATA ACCESS AT QUICKMART

QuickMart, a retail and logistics enterprise, stores its financial transactions in a sensitive schema known as `finance_data`. With multiple users accessing this schema for reporting and analytics, unauthorized or unintended queries posed a significant risk to data confidentiality and integrity. The company needed a solution to audit and enforce query access, particularly for users like `TESTUSER1`, who accessed critical financial data.

To secure this access, QuickMart implemented Oracle 23AI's SQL Firewall. The security team began by granting the required administrative privileges to the designated database administrator.

As shown in Listing 9-6, the `sql_firewall_admin` privilege was granted to the ADMIN user from the SYS account.

Listing 9-6. Granting SQL Firewall Administration Privileges

```
grant sql_firewall_admin to ADMIN;
```

Once privileges were in place, the ADMIN user enabled the SQL Firewall using the DBMS package.

Listing 9-7. Enabling SQL Firewall

```
exec dbms_sql_firewall.enable;
```

Firewall status was verified with the following query.

Listing 9-8. Checking SQL Firewall Status

```
select status from dba_sql_firewall_status;
```

With the firewall active, QuickMart began capturing SQL queries issued by TESTUSER1. This was initiated via the `DBMS_SQL_FIREWALL.CREATE_CAPTURE` procedure.

CHAPTER 9 SECURITY, DATA MASKING AND PRIVILEGE MANAGEMENT

Listing 9-9. Capturing SQL Activity for a User

```
begin
  dbms_sql_firewall.create_capture (
    username        => 'TESTUSER1',
    top_level_only => true,
    start_capture  => true);
end;
/
```

After enabling capture, the TESTUSER1 account executed typical queries such as this:

```
select * from ADMIN.finance_data where status = 'Approved';
select sum(amount) from ADMIN.finance_data;
```

These queries were automatically logged by the SQL Firewall. QuickMart's security team retrieved this activity by querying the capture logs, as shown in Listing 9-10.

Listing 9-10. Retrieving Captured SQL Logs

```
select command_type,
       current_user,
       --client_program,
       --os_user,
       --ip_address,
       sql_text
from   dba_sql_firewall_capture_logs
where  username = 'TESTUSER1';
```

Sample output included structured logging of both queries, with complete SQL text and the originating user:

COMMAND_TYPE	CURRENT_USER	SQL_TEXT
SELECT	TESTUSER1	SELECT * FROM ... FROM ADMIN.finance_data ...
SELECT	TESTUSER1	SELECT SUM(amount) FROM ADMIN.finance_data

Based on this activity, QuickMart generated a whitelist to define acceptable queries for the user. As shown in Listing 9-11, an allow-list was created for TESTUSER2 to demonstrate the general process.

Listing 9-11. Generating SQL Firewall Allow-List

exec dbms_sql_firewall.generate_allow_list ('TESTUSER2');

This allow-list ensures that any future queries deviating from the approved patterns are automatically blocked or flagged, enforcing strict data access control.

Oracle 23AI's SQL Firewall provides a structured approach to safeguarding data access through real-time SQL monitoring, logging, and enforcement. By integrating it into their security strategy, QuickMart effectively protected sensitive finance data from unauthorized use, improved regulatory compliance, and minimized risk from insider threats. This feature reflects a broader trend toward proactive, policy-driven security in modern database environments. The next section explores how Oracle 23AI enhances data masking and redaction for even deeper protection at the data layer.

Internal Mechanism of SQL Firewall in Oracle 23AI

SQL Firewall in Oracle 23AI operates by intercepting and logging SQL queries in real time, utilizing a built-in capture framework to monitor database interactions. It dynamically generates allow-lists by analyzing executed queries, enforcing strict access controls to prevent unauthorized operations. The system integrates with session tracking, capturing metadata like user context, IP addresses, and OS details, ensuring robust security against SQL injection and privilege misuse.

As illustrated in Table 9-5, the SQL Firewall mechanism forms a comprehensive defense system that tightly controls SQL execution paths through layered monitoring, validation, and enforcement.

Table 9-5. *Internal Workflow of SQL Firewall Enforcement in Oracle 23AI*

SQL Firewall in Oracle 23AI
|
Real-Time SQL Query Interception
|
Built-in Capture Framework for Monitoring
|
Dynamic Allow-List Generation
|
Enforces Strict Access Controls
|
Integrates with Session Tracking
|
Captures User Context, IP, and OS Details
|
Protects Against SQL Injection and Privilege Misuse

Differences Between Pre-23AI and Oracle 23AI SQL Firewall

Oracle 23AI introduces the SQL Firewall, a built-in security mechanism that significantly enhances the monitoring and control of SQL queries at runtime. Unlike earlier versions that relied on manual logging or third-party tools, Oracle 23AI provides native capabilities for capturing and enforcing SQL activity using dynamic allow-lists. This improvement elevates database security by preventing unauthorized access and offering detailed context for every SQL interaction. The comparison below outlines how the SQL Firewall in Oracle 23AI differs from earlier versions.

CHAPTER 9 SECURITY, DATA MASKING AND PRIVILEGE MANAGEMENT

Table 9-6. *Comparison of SQL Firewall Capabilities: Pre-23AI vs. Oracle 23AI*

Feature	Pre-23AI	Oracle 23AI (New Feature)
SQL Firewall Availability	No built-in SQL Firewall feature	Introduces SQL Firewall for enhanced security
SQL Query Monitoring	Manual logging or third-party tools required	Native SQL capture and logging mechanism
Access Control	Relies on traditional roles and privileges	Uses allow-list enforcement for approved queries
Session Context Tracking	Limited session context logging	Logs session attributes like IP, OS user, etc.

By embedding SQL query governance directly into the database engine, Oracle 23AI provides administrators with real-time visibility and control over database activity—strengthening compliance, reducing exposure to threats, and simplifying security management across enterprise environments.

Real-Time Business Use Cases for the SQL Firewall Feature in Oracle Database 23AI

Oracle 23AI's SQL Firewall introduces a powerful, policy-driven layer of security that monitors, logs, and restricts SQL queries in real time. By enforcing approved query patterns and capturing session context, it helps protect sensitive data from unauthorized access and misuse. The following table outlines key business scenarios where SQL Firewall delivers strategic value across different industries.

Table 9-7. Real-Time Business Use Cases for SQL Firewall in Oracle 23AI

Use Case	Description	Benefit
1. Protecting Financial Data	Monitor/block unauthorized queries on financial data.	Ensures security, compliance, and data integrity.
2. Securing Healthcare Databases	Track/block unauthorized access to healthcare data.	Protects patient privacy and ensures compliance.
3. Preventing Data Exfiltration	Monitor queries to block unauthorized data extraction from customer databases.	Safeguards customer data and prevents breaches.
4. Securing Financial Reporting	Restrict SQL access to financial reporting systems.	Ensures accurate, untampered financial reports.
5. Blocking SQL Injection in Ecommerce	Detect/block SQL injection attempts on ecommerce platforms.	Protects customer data and platform integrity.

By embedding intelligent SQL control directly within the database engine, Oracle 23AI enables organizations to enforce data governance at the query level, reducing risk and strengthening compliance across mission-critical applications.

Common Questions About SQL Firewall in Oracle 23AI

Oracle 23AI's SQL Firewall introduces real-time query monitoring and enforcement, offering a modern approach to securing database activity. As organizations adopt this feature, several practical questions arise around its behavior, performance, and integration.

A frequent question is how SQL Firewall enhances security beyond traditional methods. Unlike static Role-Based Access Control (RBAC), the firewall dynamically captures and blocks unauthorized SQL queries by enforcing allow-lists and detecting abnormal patterns—providing proactive protection against SQL injection and data breaches.

Another concern involves performance in high-transaction environments. Oracle 23AI minimizes overhead by capturing only relevant queries, compiling allow-lists efficiently, and using asynchronous processing to ensure fast throughput without slowing down core operations.

CHAPTER 9   SECURITY, DATA MASKING AND PRIVILEGE MANAGEMENT

When it comes to advanced threats, SQL Firewall is built to detect sophisticated SQL injection techniques by analyzing query behavior in real time. It not only logs suspicious activity but also prevents unauthorized execution before it can impact data.

Administrators also ask how this integrates with Oracle's broader security ecosystem. SQL Firewall complements tools like Database Vault by adding runtime SQL enforcement, and strengthens Audit Vault by filtering and blocking malicious queries before they reach audit logs.

In short, SQL Firewall in Oracle 23AI offers dynamic, low-overhead protection for sensitive databases—making it a key component of modern data security strategies.

Key Takeaway   Oracle Database 23AI's SQL Firewall marks a significant advancement in proactive database security. By enabling real-time SQL monitoring, automated allow-list enforcement, and detailed session tracking, it offers robust defence against unauthorized access, SQL injection, and privilege misuse. Enterprises benefit from improved visibility, reduced risk, and streamlined compliance, making SQL Firewall a foundational component of modern security architecture.

As organizations continue to strengthen data protection strategies, Oracle 23AI further empowers them with enhanced redaction and masking capabilities. The next section explores how these features, driven by AI optimization and policy precision, elevate enterprise data security to meet evolving compliance and privacy demands.

Enhanced Redaction/Data Masking in Oracle 23AI

Oracle Database 23AI introduces powerful advancements in Data Redaction and Masking, redefining enterprise-grade data protection. Building on foundational security principles, Oracle 23AI extends redaction capabilities to seamlessly support complex SQL constructs, optimize performance through AI, and eliminate long-standing limitations present in earlier versions like Oracle 19c. These enhancements ensure compliance, maintain query fidelity, and minimize administrative burden—a critical requirement for modern enterprises.

CHAPTER 9 SECURITY, DATA MASKING AND PRIVILEGE MANAGEMENT

> **CASE STUDY: QUICKMART STRENGTHENS COMPLIANCE AND PERFORMANCE**
>
> QuickMart, a global financial services firm, faced escalating challenges in maintaining compliance while preserving analytical workflows. Using Oracle 19c, they struggled with redaction inconsistencies across views, aggregation functions, and sorting clauses. Complex queries involving redacted data often failed, impairing both security and usability.
>
> Upon adopting Oracle 23AI, QuickMart successfully implemented redaction across a broad spectrum of SQL scenarios. Sensitive data in financial transaction tables was protected without compromising business insights. For example, redaction policies now apply seamlessly to views, GROUP BY clauses, DISTINCT selections, and set operators. Additionally, query performance improved significantly due to optimized evaluation paths. This transition not only ensured full regulatory compliance but also enhanced operational efficiency.

Implementing Redaction Policies with Seamless Compatibility

To demonstrate Oracle 23AI's capabilities, consider the following implementation. A user named TESTUSER1 creates a table `my_pay_txn` containing payment data. Using the DBMS_REDACT package, the ADMIN user applies a redaction policy that nullifies the payment column under all conditions. As shown in Listing 9-12, this step protects sensitive data for all downstream queries by default.

Listing 9-12. Creating Table and Applying Redaction Policy in Oracle 23AI

```
create table my_pay_txn (
  id       number generated always as identity,
  payment number
);

insert into my_pay_txn (payment) values (100.10);
insert into my_pay_txn (payment) values (100.00);
insert into my_pay_txn (payment) values (300.30);
insert into my_pay_txn (payment) values (400.40);
insert into my_pay_txn (payment) values (1000.10);
commit;
```

```
begin
  dbms_redact.add_policy(
    object_schema  => 'testuser1',
    object_name    => 'my_pay_txn',
    column_name    => 'payment',
    policy_name    => 'redact_payment',
    function_type  => dbms_redact.nullify,
    expression     => '1=1' -- Always redact
  );
end;
/
```

When TESTUSER1 queries the data, all payment values appear as NULL, as expected. This confirms successful policy enforcement.

Expanding Redaction to Views and Aggregations

One of the key breakthroughs in Oracle 23AI is support for redacted columns in views and aggregate expressions. Previously, such operations would result in runtime errors. In Oracle 23AI, these limitations are lifted. As shown in Listing 9-13, a view summarizing redacted data executes without issue.

Listing 9-13. Creating a View with Redacted Columns

```
-- Create a view using the redacted column
create or replace view my_pay_txn_v as
select sum(payment) sum_payment
from my_pay_txn;

select * from my_pay_txn_v;
```

This query returns SUM_PAYMENT = 0, confirming that redacted values are processed smoothly, even in complex expressions.

Grouping and Expression Support with Redacted Data

Oracle 23AI allows the use of redacted columns in GROUP BY clauses—a long-awaited enhancement. As illustrated in Listing 9-14, QuickMart analysts can group transaction records using rounded payment values without encountering errors.

Listing 9-14. Grouping on Redacted Columns in Oracle 23AI

```
select round(payment) as round_payment, count(*) as amount
from my_pay_txn
group by round(payment);
```

The result includes grouped NULL values, ensuring compatibility while preserving redaction.

DISTINCT and ORDER BY Support for Redacted Columns

Another major improvement is the ability to use DISTINCT and ORDER BY clauses on redacted fields. These operations previously failed in Oracle 19c due to unsupported expressions. Oracle 23AI overcomes this as demonstrated in Listing 9-15.

Listing 9-15. Using DISTINCT and ORDER BY with Redacted Columns

```
-- Use DISTINCT and ORDER BY on redacted columns
select distinct payment
from my_pay_txn
order by payment;

-- Use DISTINCT and ORDER BY with truncation
select distinct trunc(payment)
from my_pay_txn
order by trunc(payment);
```

These queries execute successfully, returning expected redacted outputs such as (null) or zero-equivalent results.

CHAPTER 9 SECURITY, DATA MASKING AND PRIVILEGE MANAGEMENT

Using Set Operators on Redacted Columns

Set operators such as UNION, INTERSECT, and MINUS now operate flawlessly over redacted columns in Oracle 23AI. This significantly improves compatibility in multisource reporting scenarios. Listing 9-16 illustrates this functionality.

Listing 9-16. Using Set Operators with Redacted Columns in Oracle 23AI

```
-- Using UNION with redacted columns
select payment from my_pay_txn
union all
select level from dual connect by level <= 5;
```

All redacted values appear as NULL, while nonredacted data from the DUAL table is returned alongside, demonstrating error-free execution.

Performance Boost via Function-Based Indexes

Oracle 23AI also supports function-based indexes and extended statistics on redacted columns. This provides significant performance gains without compromising security. In Listing 9-17, an index is created on the rounded payment value.

Listing 9-17. Creating Function-Based Index on Redacted Column

```
-- Create function-based index on redacted column
create index idx_payment_round on my_pay_txn (round(payment));
```

This index can now be leveraged by the optimizer to speed up grouped and filtered queries.

Oracle 23AI delivers comprehensive advancements in data redaction and masking, enabling organizations like QuickMart to achieve both high compliance and operational agility. By eliminating limitations tied to views, aggregations, set operators, and expressions, redaction policies now integrate seamlessly into modern analytics and reporting pipelines. These capabilities elevate Oracle 23AI beyond prior versions, offering robust, AI-optimized security without sacrificing performance.

Differences in Data Redaction Features Between Oracle Database Pre-23AI (e.g., 19c) and 23AI

Oracle 23AI introduces major advancements in Data Redaction capabilities, significantly improving how sensitive data is protected in enterprise environments. These enhancements eliminate long-standing limitations in earlier releases like Oracle 19c, offering full SQL compatibility, performance optimization, and broader coverage across SQL constructs. Organizations adopting Oracle 23AI benefit from seamless integration of redaction policies into complex queries, enhanced analytics support, and no additional cost in Autonomous Database environments. The following comparison outlines the functional improvements delivered by Oracle 23AI over previous versions.

Table 9-8. Functional Comparison of Data Redaction Features: Pre-23AI vs. Oracle 23AI

Feature	Pre-Oracle 23AI (e.g., 19c)	Oracle 23AI
View Support	Redaction not supported in views	Fully supported in views and inline views
Virtual Columns	Not supported	Fully supported
GROUP BY Support	Causes ORA-00979 errors	Fully supported
DISTINCT and ORDER BY	Causes ORA-01791 errors	Fully supported without errors
Set Operators	Causes ORA-28094 errors	Fully supported with UNION, INTERSECT, MINUS
SQL Expressions	Redaction fails on expressions	Fully supported across expressions
Policy Optimization	Redaction policy applied unnecessarily	Optimized to reduce redundant evaluations
Function-Based Indexes	Not supported on redacted columns	Fully supported for indexing and statistics
Autonomous DB Cost	Extra license required for redaction	Included by default, no additional cost

CHAPTER 9   SECURITY, DATA MASKING AND PRIVILEGE MANAGEMENT

With these upgrades, Oracle 23AI delivers a robust, intelligent redaction framework that helps enterprises like QuickMart maintain data confidentiality without compromising query functionality or performance—bringing both compliance and operational efficiency to the forefront of database security.

Internal Mechanism of Enhanced Redaction in Oracle 23AI

Oracle 23AI optimizes redaction by integrating AI-driven anomaly detection, minimizing redundant policy evaluations, and ensuring SQL compatibility across views and expressions. It processes redaction at query execution, applying function-based indexing and extended statistics for performance efficiency. Unlike previous versions, it seamlessly masks data while allowing analytical operations like GROUP BY, DISTINCT, and ORDER BY without errors.

The internal redaction workflow is outlined in Table 9-9 and reflects how Oracle 23AI brings together performance, compatibility, and intelligent automation into a unified data security framework.

Table 9-9. *Internal Workflow of Enhanced Redaction in Oracle 23AI*

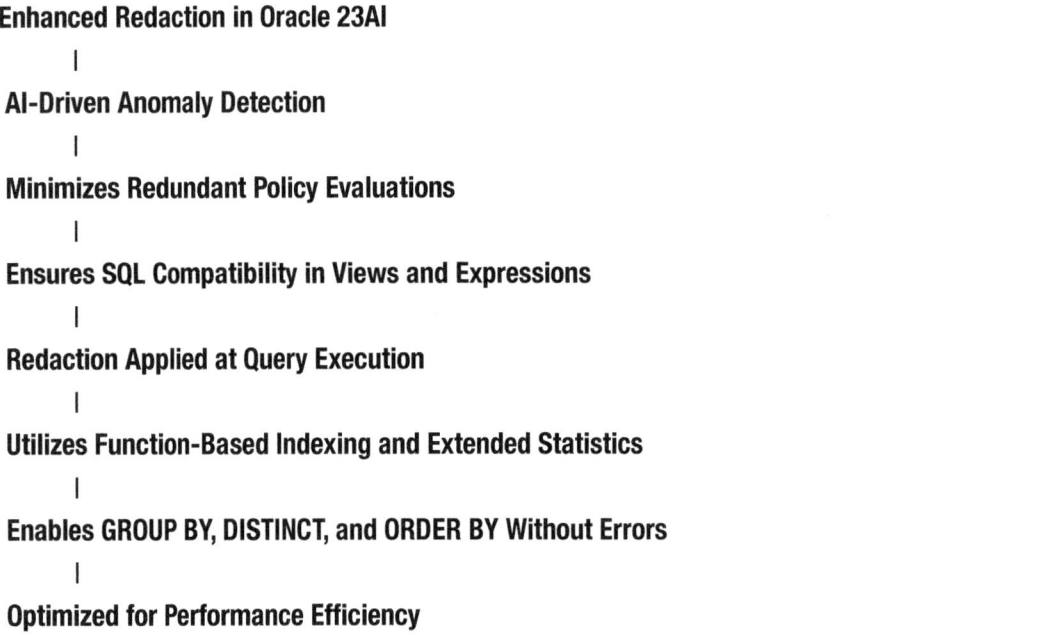

This architecture enables Oracle 23AI to provide robust, policy-driven redaction that meets modern compliance requirements while supporting dynamic analytics and enterprise-scale performance.

Real-Time Business Use Cases for Oracle 23AI Enhanced Data Redaction

The enhancements in Oracle 23AI Data Redaction introduce a new era of secure, compliant, and performance-optimized data masking. By supporting SQL compatibility across complex expressions and enabling AI-driven redaction logic, Oracle empowers organizations to protect sensitive data without sacrificing analytics or system responsiveness. These capabilities directly benefit a wide range of industries where data privacy and real-time insights must coexist.

The following table outlines real-world scenarios where Oracle 23AI's advanced redaction delivers measurable business impact.

Table 9-10. Real-Time Business Use Cases for Enhanced Data Redaction in Oracle 23AI

Use Case	Benefit
Protecting Financial Data	Secures sensitive banking and payment details while enabling seamless analytics, ensuring compliance with regulations like PCI DSS.
Healthcare Data Privacy	Redacts patient identifiers during clinical queries, preserving confidentiality and enabling HIPAA-compliant medical research.
Fraud Detection in Ecommerce	Masks sensitive payment and user data while allowing fraud pattern analysis in real time, supporting secure yet agile response systems.
Government Data Security	Protects citizen identifiers while enabling census or policy analytics, combining security with effective governance.
Telecom Customer Protection	Secures subscriber billing data while allowing trend analysis for revenue optimization and service personalization.

By incorporating these features into their architectures, enterprises can align operational agility with robust security frameworks—delivering trusted data access for users while maintaining compliance across industries.

CHAPTER 9   SECURITY, DATA MASKING AND PRIVILEGE MANAGEMENT

Common Questions About Oracle 23AI Redaction Enhancements

Oracle 23AI brings significant improvements to data redaction, allowing enterprises to better protect sensitive data while maintaining full compatibility with analytical queries. These advancements naturally raise several questions around performance, security, and compliance.

One frequent question is how Oracle 23AI optimizes redaction performance over previous versions. The answer lies in the system's ability to minimize redundant policy evaluations and support function-based indexes on redacted columns. This results in faster query execution and more efficient filtering, sorting, and aggregation of masked data.

Another common query relates to the security implications of allowing SQL expressions on redacted columns. Oracle 23AI ensures that all operations—such as GROUP BY, ORDER BY, and expression-based queries—are executed on redacted (masked) values, not the original data. Security is further enforced through robust role-based access controls and database auditing.

Developers and DBAs also ask about the benefits of function-based indexes on redacted columns. These indexes improve performance when accessing masked data by optimizing query plans and reducing unnecessary table scans, especially in high-transaction or analytics-heavy environments.

Finally, organizations often want to know how these enhancements support compliance with regulations like GDPR, PCI-DSS, and HIPAA. Oracle 23AI enables seamless, policy-driven redaction across complex SQL constructs, making it easier to meet data protection standards without compromising query flexibility or incurring additional cost in Autonomous Database deployments.

Together, these features make Oracle 23AI's redaction framework more secure, performant, and compliant—empowering businesses to scale securely while preserving analytical capabilities.

Key Takeaway   Oracle Database 23AI sets a new benchmark in data protection by removing longstanding redaction limitations. Enterprises now benefit from full SQL compatibility, allowing operations such as GROUP BY, DISTINCT, ORDER BY, and set operators on redacted columns without errors. Performance is further optimized by eliminating redundant policy evaluations, while compliance with key regulations like GDPR, CCPA, and PCI-DSS is achieved without compromising analytical capabilities. Most notably, data redaction is now included at no extra cost in Autonomous Database, delivering both enhanced security and significant cost savings.

Building on this foundation of secure and efficient data access, Oracle 23AI also introduces enhanced user access controls through the **Read-Only User** feature. This capability enables administrators to enforce strict read-only access for specific users, ensuring data integrity by preventing unintended changes while still supporting safe query execution and controlled PL/SQL activity. The following section explores how this feature helps organizations like QuickMart manage access throughout the user lifecycle with precision and confidence.

Read-Only User in 23AI

As organizations seek to balance access control with operational agility, the Read-Only User feature in Oracle Database 23AI introduces a new level of precision in privilege management. Designed to grant visibility into data without permitting modifications, this capability proves especially effective in environments where temporary, audit-driven, or observational access is needed. It allows administrators to restrict users from performing DML and DDL operations while still enabling them to query data and execute nonmutative PL/SQL procedures.

> **CASE STUDY: MANAGING SECURE ACCESS IN QUICKMART'S TRAINING AND EVALUATION ENVIRONMENT**
>
> QuickMart, a rapidly expanding retail enterprise, frequently engages new analysts, interns, and third-party vendors who need access to transaction data for evaluation and insights. Prior to Oracle 23AI, QuickMart relied on a complex matrix of roles and privileges to manage this access, which often resulted in configuration errors and administrative burden. By adopting the Read-Only User feature, QuickMart was able to streamline access control while minimizing security risks.

Provisioning a Read-Only User

To initiate secure access, QuickMart provisioned a user named readonly_user, granting only the necessary privileges for data exploration. This user was created using the new READ ONLY clause, ensuring that any attempt to perform DML or DDL operations would be automatically blocked by the system.

As shown in Listing 9-18, the readonly_user was created with query privileges and unrestricted tablespace quota for read operations.

Listing 9-18. Creating a Read-Only User in Oracle 23AI

```
DROP USER IF EXISTS readonly_user CASCADE;

CREATE USER readonly_user IDENTIFIED BY readonly_Pass1# QUOTA UNLIMITED ON users READ ONLY;

GRANT CONNECT, SELECT ANY TABLE TO readonly_user;
```

Querying vs. Modifying Data

Once provisioned, readonly_user successfully queried tables like employees, as expected. However, attempts to modify schema objects or data, such as creating a table, triggered an error.

Listing 9-19. Attempt to Perform a Write Operation with Read-Only User

```
-- Successful query operation
SELECT * FROM employees;

-- Attempt to create a table
CREATE TABLE test_table (id NUMBER);
-- ORA-28194: Can perform read operations only
```

This restriction is enforced at the system level and cannot be bypassed through direct privilege grants. Even if a DBA grants CREATE TABLE to readonly_user, the user's read-only status renders it inert, maintaining policy enforcement and consistency.

Upgrading Read-Only Access for Development Stages

In some scenarios, users at QuickMart begin with observational access but eventually transition into development or analytics roles. Oracle 23AI supports seamless privilege escalation through a single statement that modifies the user's access level.

Listing 9-20. Upgrading a Read-Only User to Read-Write Mode

```
ALTER USER readonly_user READ WRITE;
```

Following this change, the user is immediately able to perform write operations, as illustrated in Listing 9-21.

Listing 9-21. Validating Read-Write Behavior After Privilege Change

```
CREATE TABLE test_table (id NUMBER);
INSERT INTO test_table VALUES (1);
COMMIT;
SELECT * FROM test_table;
```

This approach allows QuickMart to stage access over time—from passive analysis to active participation—without recreating accounts or duplicating schema configurations.

Strategic Use and Best Practices

QuickMart realized significant advantages from using Read-Only Users in audit reviews, analyst onboarding, and vendor assessments. The feature offered a reliable way to limit exposure without obstructing insight-driven activities. Nevertheless, in production systems, care must be taken to avoid accidental escalation to read-write status.

Best practices include coupling Read-Only User provisioning with database auditing and governance controls to track changes and ensure policy compliance.

Strategic Implications

The Read-Only User feature in Oracle 23AI enables a secure and adaptable access model, ideal for nonproduction and analytic environments. By combining strict enforcement with administrative flexibility, it reduces operational risk while supporting a structured user lifecycle. For companies like QuickMart, this capability translates into simplified access control, enhanced governance, and a smoother path from data review to responsible development.

Internal Mechanism of Read-Only User in Oracle 23c

Oracle 23c enforces the **READ ONLY** mode at the user level by restricting execution of DML and DDL operations while allowing SELECT queries and nonwrite PL/SQL executions. Internally, the database kernel validates user privileges at the session level, ensuring commands violating read-only constraints trigger **ORA-28194** errors. The **ALTER USER READ WRITE** command dynamically updates the user metadata, enabling full write access without recreating the user.

The internal flow of privilege enforcement is shown in Table 9-11.

Table 9-11. Internal Privilege Enforcement Workflow for Read-Only Users in Oracle 23AI

User Session
|
Privilege Validation
|
Read-Only Mode Enforcement
|
Restriction on DML and DDL Execution
|
ORA-28194 Error (if violation occurs)
|
ALTER USER READ WRITE (to enable write access)

How Oracle 23AI Differs from Earlier Versions

Prior to Oracle 23AI, controlling user access to prevent DDL and DML operations required indirect workarounds—such as using roles with limited privileges or database triggers. Oracle 23AI eliminates these complexities with native support for read-only user creation and dynamic access switching. As shown in Table 9-12, this feature introduces capabilities that were not available in previous releases.

Table 9-12. Comparison Between Pre-23c and Oracle 23AI Read-Only Access Control

Aspect	Pre-23c Behavior	Oracle 23c Behavior
Read-Only User Creation	Users could not be explicitly set as read-only at creation.	Users can now be explicitly created as read-only with READ ONLY.
DDL/DML Restriction	No built-in mechanism to restrict users from performing DDL/DML.	Read-only users cannot perform DDL/DML operations (ORA-28194).
PL/SQL Execution	PL/SQL execution was unrestricted for users.	Read-only users can only execute PL/SQL without write operations.
Dynamic Read-Write Switching	No capability to dynamically switch users between read-only and read-write.	Users can be dynamically switched using ALTER USER commands.

This native capability ensures more robust, standardized enforcement of access policies across all environments.

Sample Real-Time Business Use Cases for the Read-Only User Feature in Oracle 23c

While the technical mechanisms of the Read-Only User feature ensure strict separation of query and write capabilities, its practical relevance shines in environments where data integrity and controlled access are essential. The scenarios outlined in Table 9-13 demonstrate how different sectors benefit from granting temporary, view-only access without compromising data protection.

Table 9-13. Business Use Cases and Benefits of the Read-Only User Feature

Use Case	How the Read-Only Feature Adds Value
Financial Reporting (Banking)	Reduces risk of accidental DML during sensitive month-end or year-end reviews.
Product Analytics (Retail)	Allows data analysts to query sales trends without risking inventory changes.
Regulatory Audits (Healthcare)	Enables external auditors to access records without altering patient data.
Internal Controls (Finance)	Supports segregation of duties by restricting update access during audits.
Vendor Collaboration (Consulting)	Grants partners visibility into shared datasets without exposing write paths.
Onboarding and Training (Tech)	Offers safe access to realistic datasets for new hires or trainees.

These examples are not made possible *because* of the feature, but are made *more secure and operationally efficient* by leveraging it.

These examples reflect real-world practices where controlled data visibility plays a critical role in maintaining system reliability, reducing risk, and ensuring compliance. By assigning read-only access in such scenarios, administrators can tailor permissions to business needs—offering flexibility without sacrificing control.

Common Questions About Read-Only Users in Oracle 23c

As with any feature designed for enhanced control and security, the Read-Only User capability in Oracle 23c invites important questions regarding its behavior, enforcement, and practical utility. This section explores some of the most frequently asked questions, offering clarity and expert insight into how this feature operates in real-world environments.

One common question concerns how Oracle 23c ensures secure transitions between read-only and read-write access. The answer lies in its use of the ALTER USER command, which allows authorized administrators to change a user's access mode dynamically.

This transition respects the database's access policies and ensures only approved users can modify their access rights, maintaining strict governance over write capabilities.

Another point of interest is whether read-only users can execute PL/SQL procedures that involve write operations. Oracle strictly enforces the read-only restriction by preventing any execution of procedures that include DDL or DML statements such as INSERT, UPDATE, or DELETE. If such an operation is attempted, the system triggers an ORA-28194 error, indicating the user's read-only status prohibits the action.

In production environments, organizations often need to grant query access to sensitive data without risking accidental modifications. Scenarios such as financial reporting, internal audits, regulatory reviews, and controlled training environments typically rely on robust access controls to maintain data integrity. While these controls have traditionally been implemented through custom roles and permissions, the **Read-Only User** feature in Oracle 23c offers a standardized, built-in mechanism to enforce this restriction more reliably.

What sets this feature apart is not the ability to *enable* these scenarios—since they could already be managed through careful privilege design—but rather its ability to **simplify and enforce read-only access declaratively**. By defining a user as READ ONLY at the time of creation, administrators eliminate the complexity of manually configuring and maintaining granular object-level privileges.

This is especially valuable in compliance-driven industries like healthcare and finance, where regulatory requirements mandate strict control over who can view versus modify sensitive data. By preventing DML and DDL at the session level, the Read-Only User feature strengthens auditability and minimizes the risk of policy violations, supporting better governance and accountability across the enterprise.

Key Takeaway   The Read-Only User feature in Oracle 23c provides a robust mechanism for controlling database access in sensitive or structured environments. By supporting dynamic switching between read-only and read-write modes, organizations can gradually enable full access while protecting critical data assets. This approach not only improves security and operational flexibility but also aligns well with industry compliance needs. As Oracle continues to evolve its security and access control capabilities, features like this pave the way for more resilient and responsibly managed database systems.

CHAPTER 9 SECURITY, DATA MASKING AND PRIVILEGE MANAGEMENT

With foundational access controls in place, we now turn our attention to the powerful innovations in data processing and integrity introduced in Oracle 23AI. The next chapter explores advanced capabilities such as SQL Property Graphs, domain-based constraints, concurrent materialized view refreshes, and other features that collectively empower organizations to extract deeper insights, enforce stricter data rules, and manage large-scale data workloads with greater efficiency.

CHAPTER 10

Advanced Data Processing and Integrity Features

Introduction

This chapter introduces advanced data processing and integrity features in Oracle Database 23AI that significantly enhance how modern applications manage, analyze, and ensure the quality of their data. It explores five key innovations: SQL Property Graphs for deep relationship analytics, Domain-Based Constraints for centralized data validation, the ability to rename LOB segments, concurrent materialized view refreshes, and Logical Partition Change Tracking (LPCT) for efficient incremental processing. Each section includes practical case studies—such as those from QuickMart—to illustrate business impact, along with clear implementation steps and architectural insights. Comparisons with earlier Oracle versions help contextualize improvements, while internal mechanism explanations deepen understanding. Real-world scenarios demonstrate how these capabilities support high-performance, scalable, and compliant systems across industries. Summaries at the end of each section reinforce key takeaways, ensuring clarity and practical readiness.

CHAPTER 10 ADVANCED DATA PROCESSING AND INTEGRITY FEATURES

Unlocking Advanced Data Insights with SQL Property Graphs in 23AI

Oracle Database 23AI brings a significant advancement in data analysis through SQL Property Graphs (SQL/PGQ), enabling users to model and analyze interconnected data directly within the database using standard SQL. This capability integrates graph analytics with relational data, empowering developers and analysts to uncover complex relationships and patterns that are difficult to detect with traditional relational queries. The feature is particularly powerful for enterprise applications involving social networks, fraud detection, recommendation engines, and dynamic relationship mapping.

To illustrate this capability, consider the case of **QuickMart**, a digital-first retail enterprise aiming to enhance its customer engagement strategy by analyzing social connections among users of its online platform. The company sought a way to uncover mutual relationships to better understand influence networks and personalize outreach efforts.

> **CASE STUDY: ANALYZING SOCIAL CONNECTIONS WITH SQL PROPERTY GRAPHS AT QUICKMART**
>
> QuickMart wanted to analyze its user base to identify mutual connections between customers—particularly focusing on identifying mutual friends of a specific user, John Doe. With Oracle 23AI's SQL Property Graphs, the company could model these social relationships efficiently and perform sophisticated graph queries directly within the database.

Setting Up User and Relationship Data

To begin, QuickMart defined two relational tables: one to store user information and another to store relationships between users. These two tables formed the foundation of the property graph structure.

As shown in Listing 10-1, the `app_users` table holds user-specific data, including first and last names, email addresses, and signup dates.

Listing 10-1. Table Definition and Sample Inserts for Users

```
drop table app_users;

CREATE TABLE app_users (
    user_id NUMBER PRIMARY KEY,
    first_name VARCHAR2(50),
    last_name VARCHAR2(50),
    email VARCHAR2(100),
    signup_date DATE
);

-- Insert sample users
INSERT INTO app_users (user_id, first_name, last_name, email, signup_date)
VALUES (1, 'John', 'Doe', 'john.doe@example.com', SYSDATE);

INSERT INTO app_users (user_id, first_name, last_name, email, signup_date)
VALUES (2, 'Jane', 'Smith', 'jane.smith@example.com', SYSDATE);

INSERT INTO app_users (user_id, first_name, last_name, email, signup_date)
VALUES (3, 'Jim', 'Brown', 'jim.brown@example.com', SYSDATE);

COMMIT;
```

To complement this, the user_relationships table captures directional relationships between users such as friendship, as seen in Listing 10-2.

Listing 10-2. Table Definition and Sample Inserts for Relationships

```
drop table user_relationships;

CREATE TABLE user_relationships (
    relationship_id NUMBER PRIMARY KEY,
    source_id NUMBER,
    target_id NUMBER,
    relationship_type VARCHAR2(50)
);
```

Chapter 10 Advanced Data Processing and Integrity Features

```
-- Insert sample relationships
INSERT INTO user_relationships (relationship_id, source_id, target_id,
relationship_type)
VALUES (1, 1, 2, 'Friend');  -- John and Jane are friends

INSERT INTO user_relationships (relationship_id, source_id, target_id,
relationship_type)
VALUES (2, 1, 3, 'Friend');  -- John and Jim are friends

INSERT INTO user_relationships (relationship_id, source_id, target_id,
relationship_type)
VALUES (3, 2, 3, 'Friend');  -- Jane and Jim are friends

COMMIT;
```

Modeling the Property Graph

With the relational structures in place, QuickMart used Oracle 23AI's CREATE PROPERTY GRAPH syntax to define a property graph that treats users as vertices and their relationships as edges. This is illustrated in Listing 10-3.

Listing 10-3. Creating the SQL Property Graph

```
-- Drop the existing property graph if any
DROP PROPERTY GRAPH IF EXISTS social_network_pg;

-- Create the property graph
CREATE PROPERTY GRAPH social_network_pg
    VERTEX TABLES (
        app_users   -- Table representing the user vertices
        KEY(user_id)  -- Primary key of the user table
        LABEL app_user  -- Label for the vertices
        PROPERTIES (user_id, first_name, last_name)   -- Properties
        associated with vertices
    )
```

```
  EDGE TABLES (
      user_relationships AS related   -- Edge table representing the
      relationships
      KEY(relationship_id)   -- Primary key of the relationship table
      SOURCE KEY(source_id) REFERENCES app_users(user_id)  -- Source user
      reference
      DESTINATION KEY(target_id) REFERENCES app_users(user_id)  -- Target
      user reference
      PROPERTIES (relationship_id, relationship_type)  -- Properties
      associated with edges
  );
```

This graph structure enables intuitive pattern-matching queries and traversal using SQL/PGQ syntax, unlocking new analytical possibilities.

Querying for Mutual Friends

Once the graph was created, QuickMart's analysts wanted to find all mutual friends of John Doe—users who are directly or indirectly connected to him through "Friend" relationships. The query in Listing 10-4 accomplishes this by navigating the graph and aggregating results.

Listing 10-4. SQL/PGQ Query to Find Mutual Friends of John Doe

```
-- Query mutual friends of John Doe (first_name = 'John', last_name
= 'Doe')
SELECT DISTINCT
    full_names,
    user_ids
FROM graph_table(social_network_pg
    MATCH
    (v1 IS app_user)   -- Start at the app_user vertex label
    (-[e IS related WHERE e.relationship_type = 'Friend']-> (v2 IS app_
    user WHERE v2.first_name != 'John')) {1,2}  -- Traverse friends with
    1-2 hops
    WHERE v1.first_name = 'John' AND v1.last_name = 'Doe'  -- Filter for
    John Doe
```

```
    COLUMNS (
        LISTAGG(v2.first_name || ' ' || v2.last_name, ', ') AS full_names,
        -- Aggregate the names of mutual friends
        LISTAGG(v2.user_id, ', ') AS user_ids  -- Aggregate the user IDs of
        mutual friends
    )
);
```

Explanation of the Query:

- **MATCH Clause**: The query begins at a vertex v1 representing a user (John Doe). It follows edges (represented by e) of the relationship type 'Friend' to another user v2. Starts at **John Doe** and follows **'Friend' relationships** up to **2 hops**.

- **WHERE Clause**: We specify the user John Doe as the starting point (v1.first_name = 'John' AND v1.last_name = 'Doe').

- **LISTAGG Aggregation**: Returns a **comma-separated list** of mutual friends' names and IDs.

This query navigates from John Doe's vertex and follows "Friend" relationships up to two hops, identifying mutual friends and aggregating their names and IDs into comma-separated strings. The results appear in tabular format, such as the following.

Table 10-1. Output of SQL/PGQ Query

FULL_NAMES	USER_IDS
Jane Smith, Jim Brown	2, 3
Jim Brown	3
Jane Smith	2

Evolving the Social Network Graph

To demonstrate the extensibility of this model, QuickMart added a new user and created a new friendship connection with John Doe. This addition was straightforward, as shown in Listing 10-5.

CHAPTER 10 ADVANCED DATA PROCESSING AND INTEGRITY FEATURES

Listing 10-5. Inserting a New User and Relationship

```
-- Add a new user (Sarah Johnson)
INSERT INTO app_users (user_id, first_name, last_name, email, signup_date)
VALUES (4, 'Sarah', 'Johnson', 'sarah.johnson@example.com', SYSDATE);

-- Add a new relationship (Sarah and John are friends)
INSERT INTO user_relationships (relationship_id, source_id, target_id,
relationship_type)
VALUES (4, 1, 4, 'Friend');

COMMIT;
```

With these updates, running the mutual friend query(Listing 10-4) again now includes Sarah Johnson in the result set.

Table 10-2. *Output of **SQL/PGQ** Query*

FULL_NAMES	USER_IDS
Jane Smith, Jim Brown	2, 3
Jim Brown	3
Jane Smith	2
Sarah Johnson	4

This case study illustrates how QuickMart effectively used Oracle Database 23AI's SQL Property Graphs to unlock rich, connected insights from social data using familiar SQL constructs. By mapping relationships as vertices and edges and querying them with graph-aware syntax, the company could derive deeper understanding of user communities and social ties. These capabilities bridge the gap between relational modeling and graph analysis—positioning Oracle 23AI as a powerful platform for modern, interconnected data workloads.

Internal Mechanism of SQL Property Graphs in Oracle 23AI

SQL Property Graphs in Oracle 23AI leverage an internal adjacency list model, mapping vertices and edges efficiently using index-optimized storage. Graph traversal and pattern matching are executed via SQL/PGQ, utilizing Oracle's parallel query engine and in-memory processing for performance. This integration eliminates self-joins, enabling seamless deep-link analysis within relational structures.

As shown in Table 10-3, the operational flow of SQL Property Graphs highlights how Oracle 23AI enables scalable and efficient graph analytics through intelligent data structures and parallel execution.

Table 10-3. Operational Flow of SQL Property Graphs in Oracle 23AI

Define Graph on Relational Tables
|
Use Adjacency List Model for Vertex and Edge Mapping
|
Leverage Index-Optimized Storage for Fast Access
|
Execute Queries Using SQL/PGQ Syntax
|
Utilize Parallel Query Engine and In-Memory Processing
|
Eliminate Self-Joins for Faster Deep-Link Analysis

Real-Time Business Use Cases for Oracle Database 23AI's SQL Property Graphs

Oracle Database 23AI's SQL Property Graphs enable enterprises to model and analyze interconnected data efficiently using graph-based querying within SQL. By leveraging graph traversal, pattern detection, and relationship analysis directly on relational data, businesses can unlock deep insights in real-time. The use of index-optimized graph structures and SQL/PGQ syntax supports advanced analytics at scale. The table below highlights real-world scenarios where SQL Property Graphs drive measurable business outcomes.

Table 10-4. Real-Time Use Cases of SQL Property Graphs in Oracle Database 23AI

Business Sector	Use Case	Benefit
Financial Services	Fraud detection through account link analysis	Enhances security, prevents financial fraud, and supports compliance.
Social Media and Marketing	Analyzing user connections and fake profile detection	Improves user engagement, ad targeting, and trust.
Manufacturing and Supply Chain	Optimizing logistics by mapping supplier dependencies	Reduces costs, avoids bottlenecks, and increases operational efficiency.
Retail and ECommerce	Product recommendations based on shared preferences	Boosts sales, enhances customer experience, and improves retention.
Cybersecurity and IT Ops	Network threat detection via graph-based topology	Strengthens threat detection, minimizes breaches, and ensures compliance.

Common Questions About SQL Property Graph in Oracle Database 23AI

Oracle SQL Property Graphs in 23AI introduce a compelling way to model and query connected data directly within a relational database. However, as with any powerful feature, it prompts several key questions about its capabilities and how it compares with purpose-built graph systems.

One frequent comparison is with Neo4j—a native graph database. While Neo4j focuses exclusively on graph-based operations, Oracle SQL Property Graphs offer the unique advantage of integrating graph analysis into a relational environment using standard SQL syntax through SQL/PGQ. This eliminates the need to manage separate systems and provides seamless access to graph functionality with full ACID compliance and Oracle's enterprise-grade scalability.

Scalability is another common concern, especially for datasets involving billions of relationships. Oracle 23AI addresses this through advanced features like parallel graph traversal, adjacency list indexing, and in-memory acceleration. The platform also benefits from Exadata enhancements and table partitioning, ensuring performance even with massive graphs.

CHAPTER 10 ADVANCED DATA PROCESSING AND INTEGRITY FEATURES

Security is a critical area as well. Oracle SQL Property Graphs inherit robust relational security mechanisms, including row-level access control, encryption, and auditing. Advanced features such as Virtual Private Database (VPD) and Oracle Audit Vault help ensure data governance and secure multitenant deployments.

A final question often revolves around performance relative to traditional SQL joins. Unlike standard joins that require complex self-joins for relationship resolution, SQL/PGQ leverages graph-specific traversal algorithms. These not only reduce query complexity but also provide significantly faster execution, especially for deep or recursive link analysis.

Overall, Oracle SQL Property Graphs bring graph analytics into the core of the Oracle database engine—offering developers the ability to analyze highly connected data without sacrificing performance, security, or compatibility with existing SQL-based systems.

Key Takeaway Oracle Database 23AI's SQL Property Graphs offer a powerful and scalable solution for analyzing complex, interconnected data using familiar SQL syntax. Through the QuickMart case study, we explored how social networks can be modeled and queried efficiently without relying on an external graph database. By using SQL/PGQ, organizations gain the ability to do the following:

Analyze intricate relationships through straightforward SQL queries.

Uncover meaningful insights directly within the relational environment.

Drive use cases like fraud detection, recommendation systems, and supply chain optimization with high performance and minimal overhead.

Seamlessly integrated into Oracle ADB-S, SQL Property Graphs transform relational data into a rich source of intelligence, empowering enterprises to discover, connect, and analyze their information like never before.

Building on this foundation of intelligent data modeling, Oracle 23AI further enhances data integrity and consistency through the introduction of **Domain-Based Constraints**—a feature designed to centralize and streamline the enforcement of business rules across schemas. Let's explore how this capability simplifies constraint management and strengthens data quality in the next section.

Enhanced Data Integrity with Domain-Based Constraints in 23AI

Modern enterprise systems require a scalable and reliable way to enforce data integrity across complex relational schemas. Oracle Database 23AI introduces the Domains feature, allowing developers to define reusable, named constraints that can be applied consistently across multiple tables. This approach centralizes data validation logic, simplifies schema management, and improves maintainability. Rather than repeating check constraints across various columns and tables, developers can define and reuse domains, reducing code duplication and enhancing data governance. This feature represents a major step forward in enforcing consistent business logic at the data layer.

> **CASE STUDY: ENFORCING DATA CONSISTENCY IN QUICKMART'S ONLINE ORDER SYSTEM**
>
> QuickMart, a growing ecommerce retailer, needed to ensure robust data validation for its order processing system. Common issues, such as invalid pricing or inconsistent order statuses, had led to reporting inaccuracies and system errors. To address these concerns and scale efficiently, QuickMart adopted Oracle 23AI's Domains feature to enforce standardized business rules for product prices and order statuses across its database.

Defining Reusable Domains for Business Rules

To implement this approach, QuickMart first created a domain named price to guarantee that all product prices remain positive. As shown in Listing 10-6, the domain includes a check constraint that disallows zero or negative values.

Listing 10-6. Creating a Domain for Positive Product Prices

```
-- Drop the domain if it already exists
DROP DOMAIN IF EXISTS price FORCE;

-- Create a domain for product prices
CREATE DOMAIN price AS NUMBER
CONSTRAINT price CHECK (VALUE > 0);
```

Next, a domain named order_status_domain was defined using the ENUM data type, which restricts order status entries to the valid values: pending, processed, shipped, and delivered. This ensures consistency and prevents erroneous or misspelled status entries from being stored in the database.

Listing 10-7. Creating a Domain for Valid Order Statuses

```
-- Drop the domain if it already exists
DROP DOMAIN IF EXISTS order_status_domain;

-- Create a domain for order statuses
CREATE DOMAIN order_status_domain AS ENUM (
    pending,
    processed,
    shipped,
    delivered
);
```

Creating the Orders Table with Domain Constraints

With both domains defined, QuickMart proceeded to create its orders table. As shown in Listing 10-8, the table uses the price domain for the price column and the order_status_domain for the status column. This structure ensures that all inserted data adheres to the predefined business rules.

Listing 10-8. Creating the Orders Table Using Domain Constraints

```
-- Drop the table if it already exists
DROP TABLE IF EXISTS orders PURGE;

-- Create the orders table
CREATE TABLE orders (
    order_id       NUMBER GENERATED ALWAYS AS IDENTITY PRIMARY KEY,
    customer_name  VARCHAR2(100),
    product_name   VARCHAR2(100),
    price          price, -- Using the price domain
    status         order_status_domain -- Using the order status domain
);
```

Inserting Data and Validating Constraints

To verify the effectiveness of the domain constraints, QuickMart inserted a set of valid and invalid data entries. As shown in Listing 10-9, valid entries inserted without error, while attempts to insert a negative price failed due to the constraint defined in the price domain.

Listing 10-9. Inserting and Validating Order Data

```
-- Insert valid data into the orders table
INSERT INTO orders (customer_name, product_name, price, status)
VALUES ('Alice', 'Laptop', 999.99, order_status_domain.pending);

-- Insert invalid data: this will fail because the price is negative
INSERT INTO orders (customer_name, product_name, price, status)
VALUES ('Bob', 'Smartphone', -199.99, order_status_domain.pending);
-- This will fail

-- Insert another valid order with a different status
INSERT INTO orders (customer_name, product_name, price, status)
VALUES ('Charlie', 'Headphones', 150.00, order_status_domain.shipped);

commit;
```

Retrieving Validated Order Data

With valid records in place, a simple query can retrieve order details. Listing 10-10 uses the DOMAIN_DISPLAY function to render human-readable status labels for display.

Listing 10-10. Sample Output from Orders Table with Enforced Constraints

```
-- Query to view the orders table with order details
SELECT order_id, customer_name, product_name, price, DOMAIN_DISPLAY(status)
AS status
FROM orders;
```

Output:

ORDER_ID	CUSTOMER_NAME	PRODUCT_NAME	PRICE	STATUS
1	Alice	Laptop	999.99	PENDING
3	Charlie	Headphones	150	SHIPPED

By leveraging domain-based constraints in Oracle 23AI, QuickMart successfully enforced key business rules at the database layer. This led to fewer data quality issues, improved reporting accuracy, and streamlined development by reusing domain definitions. The feature's flexibility ensures that as business needs grow—such as adding tax validation or shipping limits—new domains can be created and applied consistently without altering table definitions. As enterprises continue to emphasize data quality, features like domain-based constraints play a vital role in building scalable and reliable systems.

Internal Mechanism of Domains in Oracle 23AI

Oracle 23AI's Domains feature streamlines data validation by introducing centralized, reusable constraint logic at the schema level. Rather than repeating similar constraints across multiple tables, developers define domain rules once and apply them consistently wherever needed. Internally, each domain functions as a named constraint object, tightly integrated into Oracle's query optimization and storage engine. During DML operations, Oracle applies these domain constraints automatically, eliminating the need for application-layer validation and minimizing the risk of inconsistency. This architecture enhances data integrity and simplifies schema maintenance while improving performance in high-volume transactional environments.

This mechanism is visually represented in the flow diagram below.

Table 10-5. Internal Flow of Domain-Based Constraint Enforcement in Oracle 23AI

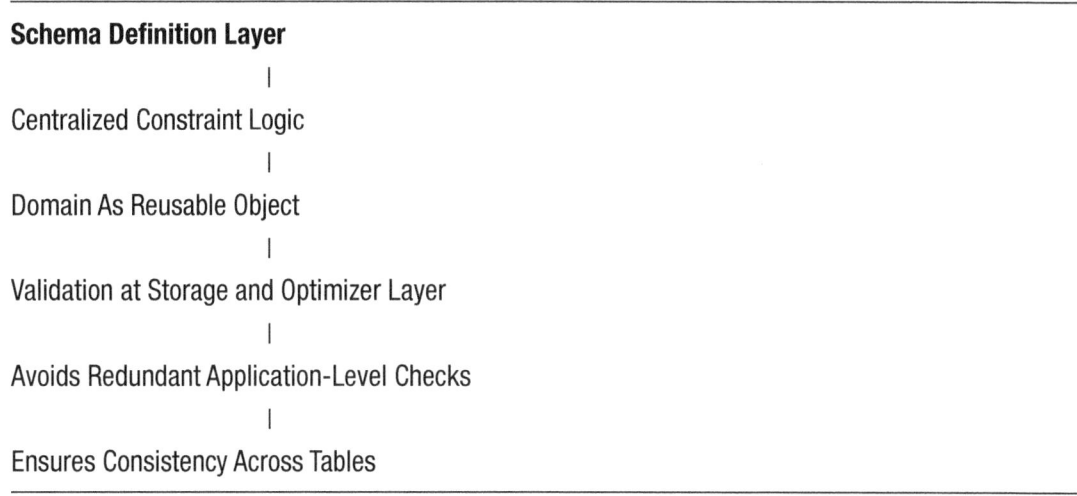

Top Differences Between the Current Solution and the Pre-23AI Version

Before Oracle 23AI, enforcing consistent business rules like price validation or order status control required duplicating constraints across multiple tables or relying on application logic. These approaches were error-prone and hard to maintain at scale. Oracle 23AI addresses this challenge by introducing Domains—a powerful feature that allows centralized, reusable constraint definitions enforced natively at the schema level. As shown in Table 10-6, this feature brings structural improvements that simplify schema design and strengthen data integrity across the database.

Table 10-6. Comparison Between Pre-23AI and Oracle 23AI Constraint Enforcement Mechanisms

Aspect	Pre-23AI Behavior	Oracle 23AI Behavior
Domain Enforcement	Constraints had to be repeated manually in each table	Centralized domains enforce constraints consistently across multiple tables.
Order Status Validation	Order status was stored as free text, leading to potential inconsistency.	ENUM-based domains ensure valid, consistent order statuses.
Data Integrity	Application logic was often used to validate inputs.	Data validation is enforced directly in the database through domain constraints.

This native domain capability in Oracle 23AI not only enhances data quality and developer productivity but also simplifies long-term schema maintenance by encapsulating business logic directly within the database layer.

Real-time Business Use Cases for the Oracle Database 23AI Domains Feature

While Oracle 23AI's Domains feature offers significant technical advantages through centralized constraint logic and reusable validation rules, its real-world impact becomes evident across varied enterprise scenarios. By embedding business logic directly into the database schema, domains help enforce data quality, reduce errors, and ensure regulatory compliance—regardless of the industry.

Table 10-7. Real-Time Business Use Cases for Oracle 23AI Domains Feature

Use Case	Benefit
Ecommerce Pricing	Ensures all product prices are positive, reducing pricing anomalies.
Order Status Validation	Standardizes order lifecycle tracking using predefined status values.
Employee Benefits	Validates employee attributes like age, department, and salary range.
Financial Transactions	Prevents erroneous or suspicious entries with numeric validations.
Healthcare Records	Enforces accuracy in patient data for compliance and better decisions.

CHAPTER 10 ADVANCED DATA PROCESSING AND INTEGRITY FEATURES

From digital commerce to critical healthcare systems, domains offer a unified, scalable approach to safeguarding data integrity where it matters most.

Common Questions About Domains in Oracle 23AI

As Oracle 23AI introduces domain-based constraints to centralize data validation, users naturally raise questions about its performance benefits, flexibility, and compatibility with existing practices. This section addresses the most common concerns to help practitioners understand the practical value of the Domains feature.

A frequent question centers on how domains improve database performance. By centralizing constraint logic at the schema level, domains eliminate the need to replicate CHECK constraints across multiple tables. This reduces metadata clutter and enforces validation at the storage layer, streamlining query execution and minimizing application-side checks.

Another key point of discussion is whether domains can be modified dynamically. Oracle 23AI allows domain definitions to be altered—such as expanding ENUM values—without affecting backward compatibility. However, more restrictive changes may trigger a revalidation of existing data to ensure integrity is maintained across all referencing tables.

Developers also ask how domains compare to traditional CHECK constraints or ENUM workarounds. Domains stand out by offering reusable, centralized rules that enhance maintainability and reduce errors across large schemas. Unlike CHECK constraints, which must be defined individually for each table, domains ensure uniform enforcement with a single definition.

Finally, in distributed database environments, domains simplify the enforcement of business rules across nodes. They promote consistency in data validation logic, reduce replication complexity, and help ensure that evolving schemas remain aligned enterprise-wide. For global systems like retail or healthcare, domains enable scalable integrity enforcement without sacrificing flexibility.

In summary, Oracle 23AI's Domains feature offers a powerful, maintainable, and performance-friendly way to enforce structured data integrity at scale.

CHAPTER 10   ADVANCED DATA PROCESSING AND INTEGRITY FEATURES

Key Takeaway   Oracle Database 23AI's Domains feature delivers a powerful shift in how data integrity is enforced, enabling reusable, centralized constraints directly at the schema level. By embedding business logic such as positive pricing and controlled order statuses within the database itself, organizations reduce redundancy, minimize manual errors, and streamline schema management. As seen in the QuickMart case study, domains not only enhance data consistency but also simplify development and maintenance across enterprise applications.

Building upon this focus on manageability and performance, the next section explores another valuable enhancement introduced in Oracle 23AI: the ability to **rename LOB segments**. This new capability addresses longstanding challenges in handling large objects by allowing metadata-level changes without data movement—resulting in faster operations, reduced downtime, and greater flexibility for DBAs managing complex partitioned environments.

Rename LOBSEGMENT in 23AI

Oracle Database 23AI introduces a highly practical enhancement for DBAs and developers managing large object (LOB) data: the ability to rename LOB segments without needing to move or rebuild them. This feature significantly reduces operational overhead and provides added flexibility in organizing and maintaining LOB storage. By treating the rename as a metadata-only operation, Oracle eliminates the resource-intensive processes that previously accompanied segment renaming. It also supports partitioned and subpartitioned tables, which makes it well-suited for enterprise-scale workloads.

> **CASE STUDY: STREAMLINING DOCUMENT MANAGEMENT AT QUICKMART**
>
> QuickMart, a retail company operating across multiple countries, manages thousands of customer transactions per day. As part of its order tracking system, QuickMart stores digital receipts, invoices, and attached documents using BLOBs in a table named `customer_orders`. Over time, database administrators sought to optimize and organize LOB segment

naming conventions to align with storage policies and improve traceability. Previously, such renaming would require rebuilding the LOB segments—a process that was disruptive, time-consuming, and expensive in terms of I/O and storage resources.

With Oracle 23AI, QuickMart's administrators were able to efficiently rename the LOB segments without moving data. The metadata-only approach allowed seamless updates to naming conventions while preserving uninterrupted access to customer documents.

Creating the Table and Viewing the Original Segment

QuickMart begins by creating the base table to store order-related BLOBs, as shown in Listing 10-11.

Listing 10-11. Creating a LOB Table for Storing Receipts

```
CREATE TABLE customer_orders (
  order_id NUMBER GENERATED ALWAYS AS IDENTITY PRIMARY KEY,
  customer_id NUMBER,
  order_date DATE,
  receipt_data BLOB
);
```

After inserting sample data, administrators query the USER_LOBS view to retrieve the system-generated LOB segment name, as seen in Listing 10-12.

Listing 10-12. Query to Retrieve the Original LOB Segment Name

```
SELECT table_name,
       column_name,
       segment_name,
       tablespace_name
FROM user_lobs
WHERE table_name = 'CUSTOMER_ORDERS';
```

Chapter 10 Advanced Data Processing and Integrity Features

Output:
```
TABLE_NAME COLUMN_NAME SEGMENT_NAME TABLESPACE_NAME
----- ---------------- -------------------------------- ----------------
CUSTOMER_ORDERS RECEIPT_DATA SYS_LOB00000123456789$$ DATA
```

The result returns a name like SYS_LOB00000123456789$$, which may not be intuitive for ongoing management.

Renaming the LOB Segment in a Regular Table

Using the new capability in Oracle 23AI, the LOB segment is renamed directly without needing to rebuild, as shown in Listing 10-13.

Listing 10-13. Renaming a LOB Segment via Metadata-Only Operation

```
ALTER TABLE customer_orders RENAME LOB(receipt_data)
SYS_LOB00000123456789$$ TO customer_receipt_segment;
```

This efficient rename operation ensures that all references remain intact while making the segment name more meaningful.

Working with Partitioned LOB Tables

QuickMart later modifies the data model to partition orders by month. Listing 10-14 shows the DDL for creating a range-partitioned table.

Listing 10-14. Creating a Partitioned LOB Table

```
DROP TABLE IF EXISTS customer_orders PURGE;
CREATE TABLE customer_orders (
  order_id NUMBER GENERATED ALWAYS AS IDENTITY PRIMARY KEY,
  customer_id NUMBER,
  order_date DATE,
  receipt_data BLOB
)
```

```
PARTITION BY RANGE (order_date) (
  PARTITION p_2023_01 VALUES LESS THAN (TO_DATE('2023-02-01', 'YYYY-
  MM-DD')),
  PARTITION p_2023_02 VALUES LESS THAN (TO_DATE('2023-03-01', 'YYYY-
  MM-DD')),
  PARTITION p_2023_03 VALUES LESS THAN (TO_DATE('2023-04-01',
  'YYYY-MM-DD'))
);
```

After data is populated, the existing LOB segments can be renamed using a similar approach. Listing 10-15 demonstrates how administrators identify and rename a specific segment.

Listing 10-15. Renaming a LOB Segment in a Partitioned Table

```
SELECT segment_name
FROM user_lobs
WHERE table_name = 'CUSTOMER_ORDERS';

Output:
SYS_LOB0000106035C00004$$

ALTER TABLE customer_orders
RENAME LOB (receipt_data) SYS_LOB0000106035C00004$$ TO T1_RECEIPT_DATA_NEW_
SEGMENT;
```

To confirm the new structure, administrators use the DBA_LOB_PARTITIONS view as shown in Listing 10-16.

Listing 10-16. Verifying Renamed LOB Segment Across Partitions

```
SELECT table_name, column_name, LOB_NAME, lob_partition_name,
tablespace_name
FROM dba_lob_partitions
WHERE table_name = 'CUSTOMER_ORDERS';
TABLE_NAME column_name LOB_NAME LOB_PARTITION_NAME TABLESPACE_NAME
```

CHAPTER 10   ADVANCED DATA PROCESSING AND INTEGRITY FEATURES

```
CUSTOMER_ORDERS RECEIPT_DATA      T1_RECEIPT_DATA_NEW_SEGMENT SYS_LOB_
P2315    DATA
CUSTOMER_ORDERS RECEIPT_DATA      T1_RECEIPT_DATA_NEW_SEGMENT SYS_LOB_
P2316    DATA
CUSTOMER_ORDERS RECEIPT_DATA      T1_RECEIPT_DATA_NEW_SEGMENT SYS_LOB_
P2317    DATA
```

If needed, segments within individual partitions can also be renamed. For example:

Listing 10-17. Renamed LOB Segment

```
ALTER TABLE customer_orders
RENAME LOB (receipt_data) PARTITION SYS_LOB_P2315 TO SYS_LOB_P2315_NEW;
```

Business Impact and Operational Benefits

This enhancement provided QuickMart with several key benefits. First, it enabled efficient LOB segment renaming without requiring LOB movement, which drastically reduced time and system load. Second, it improved manageability by allowing naming standardization of segments, which is critical for monitoring and auditing in enterprise environments. Finally, since the rename is handled at the metadata level, customer access to order data remained uninterrupted—ensuring business continuity.

In conclusion, the LOB Segment Rename feature in Oracle 23AI is a valuable addition for enterprises managing large-scale unstructured data. It simplifies administrative operations while delivering significant time and resource savings.

Internal Mechanism of LOB Segment Rename in Oracle 23AI

Oracle 23AI renames LOB segments by updating internal metadata references instead of physically moving or rebuilding LOB data. This lightweight operation modifies dictionary tables to reflect the new segment name while preserving existing storage structures. As a result, the rename process is instantaneous, minimizes downtime, and ensures uninterrupted data access.

The internal flow of this process is visualized in Table 10-8.

Table 10-8. Internal Workflow of LOB Segment Rename in Oracle 23AI

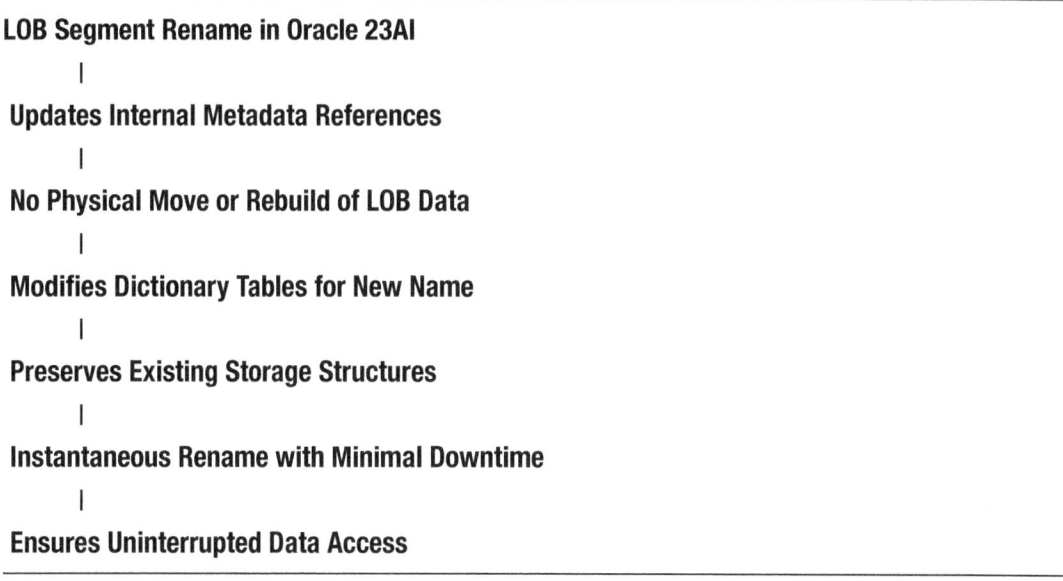

This lightweight, high-performance operation provides DBAs and developers with greater flexibility and control in managing large object storage, streamlining administrative tasks, and minimizing downtime during schema changes.

Real-Time Business Use Cases for the LOB Segment Rename Feature in Oracle 23AI

While the internal mechanism of Oracle 23AI's LOB Segment Rename feature ensures fast, metadata-only renaming of large object segments, its true business value becomes clear in operational contexts. Enterprises that manage extensive volumes of document, image, or binary data often need flexible, nondisruptive LOB management. This section illustrates how different industries use this feature to boost efficiency, minimize downtime, and reduce administrative costs.

Table 10-9. Real-Time Use Cases of LOB Segment Rename in Oracle 23AI

Use Case	Description	Business Impact
Invoice Management	Renaming LOB segments for customer invoices.	**Efficiency:** Saves time and resources.
Healthcare Data Management	Renaming LOB segments for patient records and medical images.	**Minimal Downtime:** Continuous data access.
Ecommerce Data	Renaming LOB segments for product images and receipts.	**Flexibility:** Easy data management.
Legal Documents	Renaming LOB segments for legal contracts and documents.	**Cost Savings:** Reduces rebuilding needs.
Financial Systems	Renaming LOB segments for financial reports and statements.	**Improved Efficiency:** Optimizes large data sets.

By simplifying the renaming of LOB segments without physical data movement, Oracle 23AI enables businesses to meet operational demands with minimal overhead—ensuring agility, scalability, and continuity in data-intensive environments.

Common Questions About LOB Segment Rename in Oracle 23AI

Oracle 23AI's LOB Segment Rename feature introduces a lightweight, metadata-only approach to renaming large object segments, prompting practical questions from DBAs and developers. One frequent question is how it avoids physical data movement. Oracle achieves this by simply updating internal metadata references, eliminating the need to rebuild or relocate LOB data—ensuring quick execution and minimal downtime.

The feature fully supports partitioned and subpartitioned tables, enabling LOB segments to be renamed independently across partitions. This improves flexibility in managing large, segmented datasets, particularly in enterprise-scale systems.

In contrast to other LOB-related optimizations like SecureFiles or online redefinition, which target compression or transformation, LOB segment rename focuses purely on management efficiency—delivering immediate, noninvasive results.

With reduced resource overhead and uninterrupted data access, LOB Segment Rename serves as a practical tool for modern businesses managing high volumes of binary or document data, particularly in sectors like retail, finance, and healthcare.

Key Takeaway The LOB Segment Rename feature in Oracle 23AI represents a notable leap forward in managing large object (LOB) storage. By enabling renaming through metadata updates rather than physical data movement, it significantly reduces administrative overhead, downtime, and resource usage. This streamlined process offers immense value to organizations like QuickMart that manage high volumes of LOBs—such as invoices, contracts, or medical records—allowing for better organization and improved performance without business disruption. Its flexibility and efficiency make it a vital tool for modern database operations in enterprise environments.

Building on this theme of enhanced efficiency and concurrency, the next section explores another critical enhancement in Oracle 23AI: **Materialized View Concurrent Refreshes**. This feature addresses a long-standing performance challenge in real-time analytics by enabling parallel session updates to materialized views, dramatically improving refresh performance in high-load scenarios.

Materialized View Concurrent Refreshes in 23AI

Oracle Database 23AI introduces a major enhancement in materialized view processing through the **Concurrent Refreshes** feature. Previously, even fast refreshes on materialized views—especially those using ON COMMIT—were performed serially, limiting performance and scalability in high-throughput environments. With the new **ENABLE CONCURRENT REFRESH** clause, Oracle allows multiple sessions to refresh a materialized view in parallel, eliminating contention and reducing refresh latency. This advancement is particularly valuable for real-time analytics systems that depend on fast-updating summaries derived from constantly changing data.

CHAPTER 10 ADVANCED DATA PROCESSING AND INTEGRITY FEATURES

CASE STUDY: QUICKMART'S INVENTORY AND SALES REPORTING

QuickMart, a rapidly growing retail chain, relies on two core transactional tables: inventory and sales. These tables capture product availability and purchase activity in real time. To enable fast, on-the-fly reporting for business dashboards, the IT team created a materialized view summarizing sales performance alongside current stock levels. However, due to high-frequency inserts into the sales table, the traditional refresh model led to blocking and delays, negatively affecting dashboard latency.

To resolve this, QuickMart adopted Oracle 23AI's concurrent refresh feature, which allowed multiple sessions to update the materialized view without serialization.

Creating and Populating the Base Tables

To simulate this setup, two base tables were defined: one for inventory and another for sales, as shown in Listing 10-18.

Listing 10-18. Definition and Population of inventory and sales Tables

```
DROP TABLE sales PURGE;
DROP TABLE inventory PURGE;

-- Create Inventory Table
CREATE TABLE inventory (
  product_id    NUMBER(10),
  product_name  VARCHAR2(100),
  stock_qty     NUMBER(10),
  last_updated  DATE,
  CONSTRAINT inventory_pk PRIMARY KEY (product_id)
);

-- Insert sample inventory data
INSERT INTO inventory VALUES (1, 'Laptop', 100, SYSDATE);
INSERT INTO inventory VALUES (2, 'Mobile Phone', 200, SYSDATE);
INSERT INTO inventory VALUES (3, 'Headphones', 150, SYSDATE);
COMMIT;
```

```
-- Create Sales Table
CREATE TABLE sales (
  sale_id       NUMBER(10),
  product_id    NUMBER(10),
  sale_qty      NUMBER(10),
  sale_amount   NUMBER(10,2),
  sale_date     DATE,
  CONSTRAINT sales_pk PRIMARY KEY (sale_id),
  CONSTRAINT sales_inventory_fk FOREIGN KEY (product_id) REFERENCES
  inventory(product_id)
);

-- Insert sample sales data
INSERT INTO sales VALUES (1, 1, 2, 2000.00, SYSDATE);
INSERT INTO sales VALUES (2, 2, 1, 800.00, SYSDATE);
INSERT INTO sales VALUES (3, 3, 3, 300.00, SYSDATE);
COMMIT;

-- Gather Statistics
EXEC DBMS_STATS.GATHER_TABLE_STATS(NULL, 'INVENTORY');
EXEC DBMS_STATS.GATHER_TABLE_STATS(NULL, 'SALES');
```

Enabling Fast Refresh Support with Materialized View Logs

Materialized view logs must be created on both source tables to support fast refresh operations. Listing 10-19 shows this setup.

Listing 10-19. Creating Materialized View Logs

```
DROP MATERIALIZED VIEW LOG ON inventory;

CREATE MATERIALIZED VIEW LOG ON inventory
WITH ROWID, SEQUENCE (product_id, product_name, stock_qty)
INCLUDING NEW VALUES;

DROP MATERIALIZED VIEW LOG ON sales;
```

```
CREATE MATERIALIZED VIEW LOG ON sales
WITH ROWID, SEQUENCE(product_id, sale_qty, sale_amount)
INCLUDING NEW VALUES;
```

Creating the Concurrently Refreshable Materialized View

With view logs in place, QuickMart creates the summary materialized view using the new ENABLE CONCURRENT REFRESH clause. This is shown in Listing 10-20.

Listing 10-20. Creating a Concurrently Refreshable Materialized View

```
DROP MATERIALIZED VIEW IF EXISTS inventory_sales_summary;

CREATE MATERIALIZED VIEW inventory_sales_summary
REFRESH FAST ON COMMIT
ENABLE CONCURRENT REFRESH   -- new in 23ai
AS
SELECT s.product_id,
       i.product_name,
       SUM(s.sale_qty) AS total_sales,
       SUM(s.sale_amount) AS total_revenue,
       i.stock_qty
FROM sales s
JOIN inventory i ON s.product_id = i.product_id
GROUP BY s.product_id, i.product_name, i.stock_qty;

-- Gather Statistics on Materialized View
EXEC DBMS_STATS.GATHER_TABLE_STATS(NULL, 'INVENTORY_SALES_SUMMARY');
```

Verifying Concurrent Refresh Configuration

To verify that the concurrent refresh capability is enabled, the following query can be used.

Listing 10-21. Querying Materialized View Configuration

```
SELECT mview_name, concurrent_refresh_enabled
FROM user_mviews;

Output:
MVIEW_NAME                    CONCURRENT_REFRESH_ENABLED
--  ---------------------------   ------------------------------ --
INVENTORY_SALES_SUMMARY Y
```

Business Impact of Concurrent Refreshes at QuickMart

By adopting concurrent refreshes, QuickMart eliminated serialization bottlenecks in their materialized view processing. The real-time sales dashboard is now consistently updated without causing contention, allowing the sales team to make timely decisions. The scalability of refresh operations supports the company's rapid growth, even as daily sales transactions increase.

Additionally, refresh latency has dropped significantly, enhancing reporting responsiveness and reducing system load.

Oracle 23AI's concurrent refreshes mark a significant advancement in real-time analytics enablement. This feature ensures scalability, eliminates blocking, and delivers faster updates for materialized views used in dashboards and reports. Organizations like QuickMart can now scale without performance tradeoffs.

Internal Mechanism of Concurrent Refresh in Oracle 23AI

Oracle 23AI achieves concurrent refreshes by leveraging **MV logs with ROWID tracking and SEQUENCE ordering**, ensuring transactionally consistent updates. Each refresh session processes committed changes in parallel, using **row-level locking and commit-order application** to prevent conflicts. This mechanism optimizes resource utilization, reducing refresh latency while maintaining data integrity.

The internal execution workflow of this process is illustrated in Table 10-10.

CHAPTER 10　ADVANCED DATA PROCESSING AND INTEGRITY FEATURES

Table 10-10. *Internal Workflow of Concurrent Materialized View Refresh in Oracle 23AI*

Concurrent Refresh in Oracle 23AI
|
Utilizes MV Logs with ROWID Tracking and SEQUENCE Ordering
|
Ensures Transactionally Consistent Updates
|
Processes Committed Changes in Parallel
|
Uses Row-Level Locking and Commit-Order Application
|
Prevents Conflicts and Optimizes Resource Utilization
|
Reduces Refresh Latency While Maintaining Data Integrity

Real-Time Business Use Cases for Materialized View Concurrent Refreshes in Oracle 23AI

The following business scenarios illustrate how organizations benefit from this feature in day-to-day operations.

Table 10-11. *Real-Time Use Cases of Concurrent MV Refresh in Oracle 23AI*

Use Case	Benefit
Real-Time Sales Reports	Delivers timely insights by eliminating refresh delays.
Ecommerce Tracking	Supports parallel updates for inventory and order data, improving customer experience.
Banking Fraud Detection	Ensures rapid detection of fraudulent patterns with near-instant data refresh.
Retail Inventory	Maintains accurate stock levels by enabling simultaneous updates from multiple sources.
Telecom Monitoring	Provides real-time network health metrics, supporting fast incident resolution.

By parallelizing MV refresh workloads, Oracle 23AI empowers enterprises to meet the rising demand for low-latency analytics and responsive operational dashboards—ensuring better service delivery, proactive decision-making, and optimal system performance.

Common Questions About Concurrent Refreshes of Materialized Views in Oracle 23AI

As with any performance-focused enhancement, the Concurrent Refresh feature in Oracle 23AI prompts important questions regarding consistency, behavior, and implementation. This section answers common queries to help architects and DBAs adopt the feature confidently in real-time analytics workloads.

A key concern is how Oracle maintains data consistency during concurrent refreshes. The engine uses materialized view logs with ROWID tracking and SEQUENCE ordering to ensure only committed changes are applied. This guarantees transactional integrity while allowing parallel refresh sessions.

Another common question involves conflict resolution when two transactions modify the same data. Oracle processes updates using row-level locking in commit order, eliminating contention without compromising correctness.

There are also questions around system impact. While concurrent refreshes increase CPU and memory use, they significantly reduce refresh latency—especially in high-throughput environments. Monitoring and tuning parallel execution settings can help balance this trade-off.

Organizations also ask if the feature can be enabled on existing MVs. The answer is yes—provided the MV supports FAST REFRESH ON COMMIT and has the appropriate MV logs. If not, a full rebuild may be necessary.

In summary, concurrent materialized view refreshes in Oracle 23AI offer a scalable, high-performance solution for real-time reporting. With proper configuration, they reduce blocking, accelerate analytics, and optimize resource use across dynamic enterprise systems.

CHAPTER 10　ADVANCED DATA PROCESSING AND INTEGRITY FEATURES

Key Takeaway　Oracle 23AI's Materialized View Concurrent Refreshes deliver a substantial leap in refresh efficiency for high-throughput transactional systems. By enabling the ENABLE CONCURRENT REFRESH option, organizations can eliminate serialization delays during fast on-commit refreshes, allowing multiple sessions to update materialized views concurrently. This enhancement is especially beneficial for real-time reporting in environments with frequent data changes, offering improved scalability, reduced contention, and consistent performance.

Building on these gains in refresh optimization, Oracle 23AI introduces another advanced capability—**Logical Partition Change Tracking (LPCT)**. LPCT further refines refresh behavior by identifying and updating only the affected logical partitions, minimizing resource consumption and accelerating refresh operations across large, partitioned datasets.

Logical Partition Change Tracking (LPCT) in 23AI

In large-scale transactional systems, traditional materialized view refresh methods often result in excessive overhead, particularly when only portions of the data have changed. Oracle 23AI introduces Logical Partition Change Tracking (LPCT), a performance-driven enhancement that enables more granular and efficient materialized view refreshes. Instead of requiring a full-table refresh, LPCT identifies and refreshes only the modified logical partitions. This innovation allows businesses to maintain near-real-time reporting performance without incurring the cost of full recomputation.

CASE STUDY: QUICKMART OPTIMIZES ANALYTICS WITH LPCT

QuickMart, a growing ecommerce company, handles millions of order transactions across diverse customer segments. Their BI team aggregates data on sales trends segmented by customer age and order date. Previously, refreshing the materialized view used for reporting led to high compute costs and delayed availability due to full-table scans. With Oracle 23AI, QuickMart leveraged LPCT to address these bottlenecks and achieve faster, partition-aware refreshes.

Initial Setup and Table Creation

Before implementing LPCT, the database administrator grants necessary privileges to the reporting schema as shown in Listing 10-22.

Listing 10-22. Granting Privileges to Reporting User

```
GRANT CONNECT, RESOURCE TO testuser1;
GRANT SELECT_CATALOG_ROLE TO testuser1;
GRANT CREATE MATERIALIZED VIEW TO testuser1;
```

QuickMart stores customer demographics and order details in two core business tables, customers and orders, which are created and Sample data is populated into the tables in Listing 10-23.

Listing 10-23. Creating Customers and Orders Tables

```
DROP TABLE customers PURGE;
DROP TABLE orders PURGE;

CREATE TABLE customers (
  customer_id NUMBER PRIMARY KEY,
  name        VARCHAR2(50),
  age         NUMBER,
  city        VARCHAR2(50)
);
INSERT INTO customers (customer_id, name, age, city) VALUES
(1, 'Alice', 28, 'New York'),
(2, 'Bob', 40, 'Los Angeles'),
(3, 'Charlie', 22, 'Chicago'),
(4, 'David', 55, 'Houston');
COMMIT;

CREATE TABLE orders (
  order_id    NUMBER GENERATED ALWAYS AS IDENTITY PRIMARY KEY,
  order_date  DATE,
  customer_id NUMBER,
```

CHAPTER 10 ADVANCED DATA PROCESSING AND INTEGRITY FEATURES

```
  amount          NUMBER(10,2),
  CONSTRAINT orders_cust_fk FOREIGN KEY (customer_id) REFERENCES
  customers(customer_id)
);

CREATE INDEX orders_cust_fk_i ON orders(customer_id);

INSERT INTO orders (order_date, customer_id, amount)
SELECT TO_DATE('2022', 'YYYY'),
       TRUNC(DBMS_RANDOM.VALUE(1,5)),
       ROUND(DBMS_RANDOM.VALUE(10,500),2)
FROM DUAL
CONNECT BY LEVEL < 1001;

COMMIT;
```

Enabling Logical Partition Change Tracking

LPCT requires defining logical partitions based on a chosen column such as age or order date. These partitions do not affect the physical structure of the table but provide Oracle with the metadata needed to track changes efficiently. Listing 10-24 defines logical partitions for the customers and orders tables.

Listing 10-24. Defining Logical Partitions for LPCT

```
CREATE LOGICAL PARTITION TRACKING ON testuser1.customers
PARTITION BY RANGE (age) INTERVAL (15) (
  PARTITION young VALUES LESS THAN (30)
);

-- Enable Logical Partition Change Tracking on Orders (by order date)
CREATE LOGICAL PARTITION TRACKING ON testuser1.orders
PARTITION BY RANGE (order_date)
INTERVAL(NUMTOYMINTERVAL(1, 'year')) (
  PARTITION old_orders VALUES LESS THAN (TO_DATE('01-01-2023', 'DD-MM-YYYY')),
  PARTITION recent_orders VALUES LESS THAN (TO_DATE('01-01-2024',
  'DD-MM-YYYY'))
);
```

Creating a Materialized View with LPCT Awareness

QuickMart's analytics team defines a materialized view to summarize order amounts by customer age and order date. This view is configured for fast refresh and query rewrite as shown in Listing 10-25.

Listing 10-25. Creating the Summary Materialized View

```
DROP MATERIALIZED VIEW IF EXISTS order_summary_mv;

CREATE MATERIALIZED VIEW order_summary_mv
REFRESH FAST
ENABLE QUERY REWRITE
AS
SELECT SUM(o.amount) AS total_sales,
       c.age,
       o.order_date
FROM orders o, customers c
WHERE o.customer_id = c.customer_id
GROUP BY c.age, o.order_date;

EXEC DBMS_STATS.GATHER_SCHEMA_STATS(NULL);
```

Tracking Partition Freshness

Oracle automatically tracks the freshness of each logical partition in the materialized view. As shown in Listing 10-26, the system records which partitions are fresh and which require refresh.

Listing 10-26. LPCT Partition Freshness Tracking

```
SELECT mview_name, detailobj_owner, detailobj_name,
       detail_logical_partition_name AS partition_name,
       freshness, last_refresh_time
FROM user_mview_detail_logical_partition
ORDER BY detail_logical_partition_number;
```

MVIEW_NAME	DETAILOBJ_OWNER	DETAILOBJ_NAME	PARTITION_NAME	FRESHNESS	LAST_REFRESH_TIME
ORDER_SUMMARY_MV	TESTUSER1	ORDERS	OLD_ORDERS	FRESH	10-JAN-26
ORDER_SUMMARY_MV	TESTUSER1	CUSTOMERS	YOUNG	FRESH	10-JAN-25
ORDER_SUMMARY_MV	TESTUSER1	ORDERS	RECENT_ORDERS	FRESH	10-JAN-25

CHAPTER 10 ADVANCED DATA PROCESSING AND INTEGRITY FEATURES

Simulating Data Changes and Stale Partitions

When QuickMart adds a new customer and order, only the affected partitions become stale. The rest remain fresh and continue to serve queries efficiently. This selective invalidation, verified using partition metadata views, reduces the scope and cost of refresh operations.

Listing 10-27. Inserting New Data and Triggering Stale Partitions

```
INSERT INTO customers (customer_id, name, age, city)
VALUES (5, 'Eve', 32, 'Seattle');

INSERT INTO orders (order_date, customer_id, amount)
VALUES (TO_DATE('2023-05-15','YYYY-MM-DD'), 5, 150);

COMMIT;
```

Querying Fresh Data During Staleness

Even if some partitions are stale, Oracle automatically rewrites queries to use the available fresh partitions. As shown in Listing 10-28, queries targeting a fresh age group return results from the materialized view.

Listing 10-28. Query Rewrites Leveraging Fresh Partitions

```
SELECT SUM(o.amount) total_sales,
       c.age,
       o.order_date
FROM orders o, customers c
WHERE o.customer_id = c.customer_id
AND age = 28
GROUP BY c.age, o.order_date;
```

Performing Targeted Partition Refreshes

QuickMart's DBA initiates a refresh of only the stale logical partitions using the LPCT-aware refresh mode. This is executed via the DBMS_MVIEW package with the 'L' option, as shown in Listing 10-29.

Listing 10-29. Refreshing Only Stale Logical Partitions

```
EXEC DBMS_MVIEW.REFRESH('ORDER_SUMMARY_MV', 'L');
```

The 'L' option indicates that only the **stale logical partitions** should be refreshed, rather than performing a full refresh of the materialized view.

After the refresh, the partitions are marked as fresh, and the system continues to use the optimized materialized view for faster performance.

Logical Partition Change Tracking in Oracle 23AI marks a significant leap in refresh performance and manageability. QuickMart's implementation showcases how LPCT enables precision targeting of only modified partitions, reducing system load and improving data freshness. As organizations scale their analytical workloads, LPCT offers a robust tool for ensuring timely insights without sacrificing performance or efficiency.

Internal Mechanism of Logical Partition Change Tracking (LPCT) in Oracle 23AI

Logical Partition Change Tracking (LPCT) in Oracle 23AI introduces a metadata-driven mechanism to optimize materialized view refreshes by segmenting tables into logical partitions. These partitions are not physical divisions but are defined by user-specified rules based on columns such as age or date. Oracle continuously monitors these partitions for changes.

When data is modified, only the affected logical partitions are marked as stale, while the rest remain fresh and queryable. This enables highly granular refresh behavior—during a materialized view refresh, Oracle updates only the stale partitions rather than processing the entire dataset. This incremental refresh approach reduces I/O, lowers CPU usage, and preserves query performance even for large volumes of data.

The internal flow of LPCT's metadata-driven partition tracking and refresh optimization is illustrated in Table 10-12.

Table 10-12. Internal Flow of Logical Partition Change Tracking in Oracle 23AI

Logical Partition Change Tracking Mechanism
|
Assigns Logical Partitions Based on Metadata Rules
|
Tracks Modifications at Partition Level (No Full-Table Scans)
|
Marks Only Affected Partitions As Stale on Data Change
|
Maintains Freshness for All Unmodified Partitions
|
Incremental Refresh of Only Stale Logical Partitions
|
Boosts Materialized View Efficiency with Minimal Overhead

By isolating refreshes to specific logical partitions, Oracle 23AI empowers organizations to scale materialized views without incurring the performance penalties of full-table processing. This design aligns with modern analytics workloads, especially in data-intensive domains such as ecommerce, finance, and healthcare.

Real-Time Business Use Cases for Logical Partition Change Tracking (LPCT) in 23AI

Oracle 23AI's Logical Partition Change Tracking (LPCT) enhances performance and efficiency for high-volume, dynamic workloads by refreshing only the modified portions of materialized views. This capability is especially valuable in real-time business scenarios where agility, responsiveness, and accuracy are critical. The following table outlines real-world applications of LPCT and the tangible benefits delivered to modern enterprises.

Table 10-13. Real-Time Business Use Cases for Logical Partition Change Tracking in Oracle 23AI

Use Case	Benefit
Real-Time Sales Reports	Provides up-to-the-minute updates to dashboards, enabling faster insights and agile decision-making.
Inventory Management	Enables real-time tracking of stock levels and movement, reducing stockouts and improving supply chain efficiency.
Fraud Detection	Facilitates real-time analysis of transaction data to identify anomalies, minimizing financial losses and enhancing trust.
Customer Support Optimization	Supports instant monitoring of service activity, ensuring faster resolution and improved customer satisfaction.
Dynamic Pricing	Allows price adjustments based on real-time demand and inventory changes, boosting revenue and competitiveness.

Through selective refreshes of data partitions, LPCT empowers organizations to streamline operations, optimize performance, and deliver responsive, real-time user experiences—without the overhead of full-table processing.

Common Questions About Logical Partition Change Tracking (LPCT) in Oracle 23AI

Oracle 23AI introduces Logical Partition Change Tracking (LPCT) as a strategic enhancement to materialized view refresh processes, particularly for systems managing large and evolving datasets. This feature has generated significant interest among architects and developers aiming to optimize query performance and reduce system overhead.

A key question concerns how LPCT reduces refresh costs. Rather than scanning or refreshing the entire table, LPCT tracks changes at a logical partition level—based on metadata rules—and marks only the impacted partitions as stale. During a refresh operation, only those stale segments are updated, drastically minimizing computation time.

Another common inquiry is its role in real-time analytics. LPCT maintains query performance by allowing fresh partitions to be queried while deferring refresh operations on stale ones. This selective consistency ensures uninterrupted access to up-to-date insights without sacrificing speed.

In high-volume environments like ecommerce or finance, LPCT enables faster reporting by avoiding full refresh cycles. Logical tracking also improves agility, letting businesses act on the latest data without compromising performance or operational stability.

In summary, Oracle 23AI's LPCT feature empowers enterprises to optimize materialized view refreshes efficiently, improving responsiveness and scalability in data-intensive environments.

Key Takeaway   This case study illustrates how Logical Partition Change Tracking (LPCT) in Oracle 23AI revolutionizes the way large-scale enterprises like QuickMart manage data refreshes. By focusing on changes at the logical partition level, LPCT enables incremental refreshes that avoid unnecessary full-table operations, significantly reducing system overhead. The result is faster query execution, improved resource utilization, and near real-time data synchronization—key advantages for businesses dealing with high-volume, frequently updated datasets.

As we move forward, the focus shifts to broader **Partitioning and Storage Optimization** strategies introduced in Oracle 23AI and 23c. The next chapter explores advanced partitioning capabilities and enhancements in SQL operations—such as improved DML handling and multirow inserts—that together enable more efficient data management and operational agility performance, and streamline storage usage across complex workloads.

CHAPTER 11

Partitioning and Storage Optimization

Introduction

This chapter explores the key enhancements in Oracle 23AI and 23c that streamline partitioning and storage optimization. It introduces improved metadata management using HIGH_VALUE_CLOB and HIGH_VALUE_JSON, replacing the legacy LONG datatype. These features simplify administration, improve scalability, and support efficient refreshes in large, dynamic datasets. The chapter also covers SQL improvements like enhanced DML RETURNING and multirow INSERTs that reduce complexity and boost performance. Practical examples, implementation steps, internal insights, and real-world case studies are provided throughout, with summaries and FAQs to reinforce key takeaways.

Enhanced Partitioning in 23AI

Partitioning plays a crucial role in managing large datasets efficiently, especially in systems with dynamic data growth and diverse query patterns. Oracle 23AI builds upon previous capabilities by introducing refined features that improve usability, performance, and programmability. One major improvement is the replacement of the legacy LONG datatype used for partition boundaries in Oracle 19c with modern and more accessible formats in Oracle 23c: `HIGH_VALUE_CLOB` and `HIGH_VALUE_JSON`. This evolution reflects Oracle's commitment to supporting modern data practices while maintaining compatibility and high performance.

CHAPTER 11   PARTITIONING AND STORAGE OPTIMIZATION

CASE STUDY: QUICKMART'S SALES PARTITIONING STRATEGY

QuickMart, a national retail chain, manages a rapidly growing volume of transactional sales data. The company seeks a partitioning strategy that ensures high query performance and efficient data organization. Their goal is to automatically manage sales records by year and region while simplifying data maintenance and improving report performance.

To meet this goal, QuickMart creates a partitioned sales table using a combination of range partitioning (on sale_date) and list subpartitioning (on region), as shown in Listing 11-1.

Listing 11-1. Creating a Sales Table with Interval and Subpartitioning

```
DROP TABLE IF EXISTS sales PURGE;

CREATE TABLE sales (
    sale_id     NUMBER,
    region      VARCHAR2(50),
    sale_date   DATE,
    amount      NUMBER
)
PARTITION BY RANGE (sale_date)
INTERVAL (NUMTOYMINTERVAL(1, 'YEAR'))
SUBPARTITION BY LIST (region)
SUBPARTITION TEMPLATE (
    SUBPARTITION region_northwest VALUES ('Northwest'),
    SUBPARTITION region_southeast VALUES ('Southeast'),
    SUBPARTITION region_southwest VALUES ('Southwest'),
    SUBPARTITION region_northeast VALUES ('Northeast')
) (
    PARTITION sales_2021 VALUES LESS THAN (TO_DATE('2022-01-01',
    'YYYY-MM-DD')),
    PARTITION sales_2022 VALUES LESS THAN (TO_DATE('2023-01-01',
    'YYYY-MM-DD'))
);
```

This design yields several key benefits. The **range partitioning** ensures that sales data is automatically segmented by year, eliminating the need for manual partition maintenance. **List subpartitioning** further divides each yearly partition into regions, significantly enhancing performance for region-targeted queries. Unlike earlier versions such as Oracle 19c—where interval partitions only appeared with sequential data arrival—Oracle 23AI introduces smarter automation that preemptively handles future time intervals without requiring data-driven triggers.

By keeping all data internally stored within the database and eliminating the need for manual partition management, this partitioning strategy provides QuickMart with a scalable and query-efficient foundation for long-term sales analytics.

Populating the Table with Sample Data

QuickMart loads transactional records from 2021 to 2023 into the `sales` table, as shown in Listing 11-2.

Listing 11-2. Inserting Sales Records

```
INSERT INTO sales VALUES (1, 'Northwest', TO_DATE('2021-03-15',
'YYYY-MM-DD'), 1000);
INSERT INTO sales VALUES (2, 'Southeast', TO_DATE('2021-07-20',
'YYYY-MM-DD'), 1500);
INSERT INTO sales VALUES (3, 'Southwest', TO_DATE('2021-12-25',
'YYYY-MM-DD'), 2000);
INSERT INTO sales VALUES (4, 'Northeast', TO_DATE('2021-06-05',
'YYYY-MM-DD'), 1800);

INSERT INTO sales VALUES (5, 'Northwest', TO_DATE('2022-02-10',
'YYYY-MM-DD'), 1200);
INSERT INTO sales VALUES (6, 'Southwest', TO_DATE('2022-08-18',
'YYYY-MM-DD'), 2300);
INSERT INTO sales VALUES (7, 'Southeast', TO_DATE('2022-11-30',
'YYYY-MM-DD'), 1700);
```

CHAPTER 11 PARTITIONING AND STORAGE OPTIMIZATION

```
INSERT INTO sales VALUES (8, 'Northeast', TO_DATE('2023-03-10',
'YYYY-MM-DD'), 2200);
INSERT INTO sales VALUES (9, 'Southwest', TO_DATE('2023-07-15',
'YYYY-MM-DD'), 2500);
Commit;
```

QuickMart analyzes its yearly and regional sales using an aggregate query as shown in Listing 11-3.

Run a Query to Check the Total Sales for Each Year and Region

Listing 11-3. Querying Total Sales by Year and Region

```
SELECT TO_CHAR(sale_date, 'YYYY') AS year, region, SUM(amount) AS
total_sales
FROM sales
GROUP BY TO_CHAR(sale_date, 'YYYY'), region
ORDER BY year, region;

YEAR    REGION        TOTAL_SALES
-----   ----------    -----------
2021    Northeast     1800
2021    Northwest     1000
```

Monitoring Partitions and Subpartitions

QuickMart uses Oracle metadata views to monitor partition boundaries and subpartition layouts. Listing 11-4 demonstrates how to examine this structure.

Listing 11-4. Viewing Subpartitions

```
SELECT partition_name, subpartition_name, high_value
FROM user_tab_subpartitions
ORDER BY partition_name, subpartition_name;
```

PARTITION_NAME	SUBPARTITION_NAME	HIGH_VALUE
SALES_2021	SALES_2021_REGION_NORTHEAST	'Northeast'
SALES_2021	SALES_2021_REGION_NORTHWEST	'Northwest'
SYS_P4961	SYS_SUBP4957	'Northwest'
SYS_P4961	SYS_SUBP4958	'Southeast'

When data for 2024 is inserted, Oracle automatically creates a new partition.

Listing 11-5. Auto-Creating Partitions

```
INSERT INTO sales VALUES (10, 'Northwest', TO_DATE('2024-01-05',
'YYYY-MM-DD'), 3000);

SELECT partition_name
FROM user_tab_partitions
WHERE table_name = 'SALES';
```

Modern Boundary Representation with CLOB and JSON

One of the most important innovations in Oracle 23c is the introduction of HIGH_VALUE_CLOB and HIGH_VALUE_JSON. These columns provide modern, readable, and programmable access to partition boundaries.

QuickMart queries partition boundaries using HIGH_VALUE_CLOB, as illustrated in Listing 11-6.

Listing 11-6. Using HIGH_VALUE_CLOB to View Partition Boundaries

```
SELECT partition_name, high_value_clob
FROM user_tab_partitions
WHERE table_name = 'SALES'
ORDER BY partition_name;
```

PARTITION_NAME	HIGH_VALUE (as DATE)
SALES_2021	01-JAN-2022
SALES_2022	01-JAN-2023
SYS_P4961	01-JAN-2024

To enhance programmability, QuickMart also uses JSON functions with HIGH_VALUE_JSON to retrieve and manipulate boundary dates, as shown in Listing 11-7.

Listing 11-7. Using JSON Functions to Extract Boundary Values

```
select partition_name,
       json_serialize(high_value_json) as high_value_json,
       json_value(high_value_json, '$.high_value' returning date) as high_
       value_date
from   dba_tab_partitions
where  table_name = 'SALES'
order by 1;
```

output:

PARTITION_NAME	HIGH_VALUE_JSON	HIGH_VALUE_DATE
SALES_2021	{"high_value":"2022-01-01T00:00:00"}	01-JAN-2022 00:00:00
SALES_2022	{"high_value":"2023-01-01T00:00:00"}	01-JAN-2023 00:00:00
SALES_2023	{"high_value":"2024-01-01T00:00:00"}	01-JAN-2024 00:00:00
SALES_2024	{"high_value":"2025-01-01T00:00:00"}	01-JAN-2025 00:00:00

Oracle 23AI and 23c significantly modernize partitioning through enhanced metadata handling and automated boundary tracking. QuickMart's use case illustrates how interval and subpartitioning can be effectively combined with new CLOB and JSON representations to improve manageability and performance. These advancements not only simplify DBA tasks but also pave the way for better analytics and real-time insights in high-volume environments.

Internal Mechanism of Enhanced Partitioning in Oracle 23AI

Oracle 23AI replaces the LONG datatype in partition boundaries with HIGH_VALUE_CLOB and HIGH_VALUE_JSON, enabling seamless access and manipulation. Interval partitioning now autonomously manages future partitions without requiring sequential

CHAPTER 11 PARTITIONING AND STORAGE OPTIMIZATION

data arrival. JSON-based partition storage enhances query performance by allowing efficient boundary retrieval and programmatic access.

The operational workflow in Table 11-1 illustrates the internal steps driving this enhanced partitioning architecture in Oracle 23AI.

Table 11-1. *Operational Workflow of Enhanced Partitioning in Oracle 23AI*

Enhanced Partitioning in Oracle 23AI
|
Replaces LONG Datatype in Partition Boundaries
|
Uses HIGH_VALUE_CLOB and HIGH_VALUE_JSON for Seamless Access
|
Interval Partitioning Manages Future Partitions Autonomously
|
No Requirement for Sequential Data Arrival
|
JSON-Based Partition Storage Enhances Query Performance
|
Allows Efficient Boundary Retrieval and Programmatic Access

Differences in Enhanced Partitioning between Pre-23c (Pre-23 AI) and Oracle 23c (23 AI)

Oracle 23AI delivers significant enhancements in partition boundary management, offering a more accessible, performant, and developer-friendly experience. By replacing the legacy LONG datatype with CLOB and JSON-based formats, Oracle 23AI streamlines metadata access and enables programmatic querying of partition definitions. These improvements simplify database operations, boost performance, and improve compatibility with modern tools and applications, as outlined in the comparison below.

CHAPTER 11 PARTITIONING AND STORAGE OPTIMIZATION

Table 11-2. *Functional Comparison of Partitioning Capabilities: Pre-23AI vs. Oracle 23AI*

Feature	Oracle 19c (Pre-23AI)	Oracle 23c (23AI)
High Value Representation	Stored as LONG datatype in HIGH_VALUE	Stored as CLOB in HIGH_VALUE_CLOB and as JSON in HIGH_VALUE_JSON
Access to High Value	Difficult to manipulate due to LONG format	Simplified access through standard SQL and JSON APIs
Support for JSON	Not available	Full support for JSON representation of partition boundaries
Data Extraction	Requires conversion using TO_LOB() or other workarounds	Easy and programmatic access using JSON_VALUE() and JSON_SERIALIZE()
Performance	Performance overhead due to limitations of LONG datatype	Improved performance and usability with CLOB and JSON handling

With these advancements, Oracle 23AI empowers DBAs and developers to manage partitioned tables more efficiently, providing enhanced flexibility, faster metadata access, and seamless integration with modern SQL and JSON-based tools.

Real-Time Business Use Cases for Enhanced Partitioning in Oracle 23c

The partitioning enhancements introduced in Oracle 23AI—particularly the transition to CLOB and JSON-based boundary representation—empower organizations to manage time-series and categorical data with improved performance and operational agility. These capabilities support large-scale, real-time analytics, reducing query latency and simplifying partition management. The table below showcases real-world scenarios where these advancements in partitioning deliver measurable value.

Table 11-3. Real-Time Business Use Cases for Enhanced Partitioning in Oracle 23AI

Use Case	Benefit
Retail Sales	Enables faster regional and yearly sales analysis for dynamic trend insights.
Financial Transactions	Accelerates transaction reporting by organizing data by date and type.
Ecommerce Orders	Streamlines order tracking and demand forecasting through date-region partitioning.
Healthcare Records	Improves patient record retrieval by partitioning across admission date and department.
Supply Chain Management	Enhances inventory tracking by partitioning on time and product, with subpartitioning by region.

These features position Oracle 23AI as a high-performance, scalable platform for enterprises needing precise control over large and growing datasets. By aligning partition strategy with business dimensions such as geography, time, and category, organizations can unlock faster analytics, smoother operations, and data-driven decision-making at scale.

Common Questions About Enhanced Partitioning in Oracle 23c

Oracle 23c introduces critical enhancements in partitioning that simplify data access, boost performance, and modernize metadata handling. These improvements address key concerns faced in previous versions like Oracle 19c.

A common question is how partition boundary storage has evolved. Oracle 19c used the LONG datatype, which was hard to query and manipulate. Oracle 23c replaces it with HIGH_VALUE_CLOB and HIGH_VALUE_JSON, enabling easier, structured access.

Users also ask about the role of JSON in boundary queries. With HIGH_VALUE_JSON, partition boundaries can now be queried using JSON functions like JSON_VALUE, allowing direct extraction of values such as dates.

Another frequent concern is around interval partitioning behavior. Oracle 23c eliminates the need for sequential data arrival—future partitions are created automatically as needed, without manual intervention.

These changes also reduce reliance on legacy conversion functions (e.g., TO_LOB()), simplifying development and administration tasks.

By adopting modern datatypes and automation, Oracle 23c makes partitioning more efficient, scalable, and easier to integrate into real-time enterprise workloads.

Together, these enhancements make partitioning faster, more flexible, and better suited to today's data growth patterns.

Key Takeaway   Oracle 23c brings forward a robust set of enhancements in partitioning, replacing the legacy LONG datatype with modern CLOB and JSON formats. These upgrades streamline how partition boundaries are stored and accessed, allowing developers and DBAs to manage large, evolving datasets with greater efficiency and precision. By simplifying access and improving query performance, the new model empowers organizations to maintain high-performance partitioned tables while accommodating future data growth seamlessly.

Building on these improvements in data structure and access, Oracle 23c also introduces powerful enhancements to core DML operations. The next section explores how innovations like the expanded DML RETURNING clause and multirow INSERT statements further optimize data management and reduce coding complexity, making everyday database operations faster and more intuitive.

Optimizing Data Management and Efficiency with Oracle 23c Enhancements

Modern enterprise applications demand data operations that are not only fast but also intuitive and developer-friendly. Oracle 23c introduces thoughtful SQL enhancements designed to simplify everyday data manipulation tasks. This chapter explores two such advancements: enhanced support for the DML RETURNING clause and the introduction of multirow INSERT statements using a simplified VALUES syntax. These features enable real-time data auditing and reduce code complexity, especially for systems managing large volumes of transactional data. We illustrate their practical value through a use case from QuickMart, a retail company modernizing its product and order management systems.

> **CASE STUDY: SIMPLIFYING PRODUCT AND ORDER TRANSACTIONS AT QUICKMART**
>
> QuickMart, a mid-sized retail chain, faced growing complexity in managing its product catalog and customer orders. Developers had to write verbose PL/SQL blocks to capture old and new data during updates, and inserting multiple rows required repeated single-row inserts or INSERT ALL constructs, leading to code bloat and decreased performance. With the rollout of Oracle 23c, QuickMart sought to modernize these operations by leveraging the newly introduced features.

Tracking Product Updates with Enhanced DML RETURNING Clause

QuickMart's developers wanted a straightforward method to audit price and description changes to products. Oracle 23c enhances the DML RETURNING clause by allowing users to capture both old and new values during a single update operation.

Listing 11-8 shows how QuickMart uses this feature to streamline change tracking for product updates.

Listing 11-8. Create Product Table and Insert

```
-- Create the products table
DROP TABLE IF EXISTS products;

CREATE TABLE products (
  product_id NUMBER,
  product_name VARCHAR2(100),
  price NUMBER,
  description VARCHAR2(255),
  CONSTRAINT products_pk PRIMARY KEY (product_id)
);
```

```
-- Insert sample product data
INSERT INTO products (product_id, product_name, price, description)
VALUES (1, 'Laptop', 999.99, 'High-performance laptop');
INSERT INTO products (product_id, product_name, price, description)
VALUES (2, 'Smartphone', 499.99, 'Latest model smartphone');
COMMIT;
```

To track changes, the update operation uses RETURNING old ... new ... syntax, as shown in Listing 11-9.

```
-- Declare variables to hold old and new values
SET SERVEROUTPUT ON
DECLARE
  l_old_price         products.price%type;
  l_old_description   products.description%type;
  l_new_price         products.price%type;
  l_new_description   products.description%type;
BEGIN
  -- Update query with RETURNING clause
  UPDATE products
  SET price = price * 1.1,
      description = description || ' (Updated)'
  WHERE product_id = 2
  RETURNING old price, old description, new price, new description
  INTO l_old_price, l_old_description, l_new_price, l_new_description;

  -- Display the old and new values
  DBMS_OUTPUT.PUT_LINE('l_old_price        = ' || l_old_price);
  DBMS_OUTPUT.PUT_LINE('l_old_description  = ' || l_old_description);
  DBMS_OUTPUT.PUT_LINE('l_new_price        = ' || l_new_price);
  DBMS_OUTPUT.PUT_LINE('l_new_description  = ' || l_new_description);

  -- Rollback changes
  ROLLBACK;
END;
/
```

CHAPTER 11 PARTITIONING AND STORAGE OPTIMIZATION

The output confirms that Oracle accurately returns the old and new values during the update.

Listing 11-9. Using the RETURNING Clause to Capture Old and New Values

```
l_old_price        = 499.99
l_old_description  = Latest model smartphone
l_new_price        = 549.989
l_new_description  = Latest model smartphone (Updated)
```

Bulk Inserting Orders with Multirow VALUES Clause

QuickMart also needed to simplify order creation during flash sales. Prior to Oracle 23c, inserting multiple orders involved multiple statements or more complex constructs like INSERT ALL. Oracle 23c now allows multiple rows to be inserted using a single INSERT INTO ... VALUES syntax.

Listing 11-10 demonstrates this enhancement.

Listing 11-10. Creating and Inserting into the Orders Table

```
-- Create the orders table
DROP TABLE IF EXISTS orders;

CREATE TABLE orders (
  order_id NUMBER PRIMARY KEY,
  customer_name VARCHAR2(100),
  order_date DATE,
  total_amount NUMBER
);

-- Multi-row insert with the VALUES clause
INSERT INTO orders (order_id, customer_name, order_date, total_amount) VALUES
    (1, 'Alice Johnson', TO_DATE('2025-02-09', 'YYYY-MM-DD'), 250.75),
    (2, 'Bob Smith', TO_DATE('2025-02-09', 'YYYY-MM-DD'), 150.50),
    (3, 'Charlie Davis', TO_DATE('2025-02-09', 'YYYY-MM-DD'), 320.00);

COMMIT;
```

This simplified syntax improves readability, reduces parsing overhead, and enhances developer productivity—all critical for high-volume insert operations.

With Oracle 23c, QuickMart successfully modernized its data operations by adopting enhanced SQL features that reduce complexity and increase efficiency. The DML RETURNING clause now enables seamless auditing of updates, while the multirow VALUES syntax improves performance and code simplicity for inserts. These enhancements reflect Oracle's continued evolution toward developer-friendly and high-performance data management capabilities.

Internal Mechanism of Enhanced DML and Multirow Insert in Oracle 23c

Oracle 23c optimizes DML execution by leveraging in-memory structures and reduced context switches, minimizing overhead when retrieving old and new values via the RETURNING clause. The multirow INSERT with VALUES clause enhances SQL parsing efficiency by batching multiple row inserts into a single execution plan, reducing redo and undo overhead. These enhancements improve transactional efficiency by optimizing memory utilization and reducing round trips, ensuring faster data manipulation.

The operational flow of these optimizations is shown in Table 11-4.

Table 11-4. *Internal Structure of Oracle 23c Enhanced DML and Multirow Insert*

Enhanced DML and Multirow Insert in Oracle 23c
|
Optimizes DML with In-Memory Structures
|
Reduces Context Switches and Overhead
|
RETURNING Clause for Efficient Value Retrieval
|
Multirow INSERT Batches Execution
|
Minimizes Redo, Undo, and Round Trips

This architectural refinement allows Oracle 23c to significantly streamline transactional operations, especially in high-throughput scenarios where bulk updates and inserts are frequent. The result is a more scalable and efficient database system, with enhanced developer productivity and faster application response times.

Real-Time Business Use Cases for Optimizing Data Management in Oracle 23c

Oracle 23c enhances data manipulation through advanced DML capabilities such as the enhanced RETURNING clause and the multirow INSERT with VALUES syntax. These features streamline real-time data processing by reducing execution overhead and simplifying transactional workflows. The following table outlines practical business scenarios where these optimizations deliver tangible benefits across key operational areas.

Table 11-5. *Real-Time Business Use Cases for Optimizing Data Management in Oracle 23c*

Use Case	Benefit
Inventory Management	Efficient tracking of inventory changes using DML RETURNING allows real-time stock control and reduced chances of stockouts.
Customer Order Processing	Multirow INSERT accelerates order entry, ensuring faster fulfillment and improved customer satisfaction.
Financial Data Updates	Tracks both old and new values during updates, ensuring transparency and accurate financial reporting.
Employee Performance Reviews	Allows bulk updates to employee metrics with immediate feedback on changes, supporting faster HR assessments.

These enhancements empower businesses like QuickMart to streamline their operational workflows and support real-time decision-making with minimal system complexity.

CHAPTER 11   PARTITIONING AND STORAGE OPTIMIZATION

Common Questions About Oracle 23c DML RETURNING and Multirow Insert Enhancements

Oracle 23c introduces powerful enhancements to DML operations, notably the extended RETURNING clause and the streamlined multirow INSERT using the VALUES clause. These features have prompted common questions among developers working with high-volume transactional systems.

A key question concerns the impact of the enhanced RETURNING clause on performance. By reducing database round trips and enabling direct retrieval of both old and new values, it significantly boosts performance in large-scale applications, especially during updates.

Some developers wonder if the multirow INSERT can be used for UPDATE or DELETE operations. The answer is no—this enhancement applies exclusively to INSERT. For bulk updates or deletes, MERGE statements or procedural batch processing remain the standard approach.

Another consideration is memory usage during large updates with RETURNING. Since both old and new values are retained, operations on very large datasets may consume more memory. Proper resource planning is essential in such scenarios.

When it comes to constraints, the multirow INSERT adheres strictly to rules like primary keys and not-null constraints. If any row violates a constraint, that row's insert will fail unless handled explicitly using error logging or conflict resolution strategies.

In summary, Oracle 23c's DML and multirow enhancements offer significant productivity and performance benefits but also require thoughtful implementation for large or constraint-sensitive datasets.

Key Takeaway   Oracle 23c introduces transformative enhancements that significantly improve data manipulation efficiency. The extended DML RETURNING clause allows developers to capture both old and new values during updates, simplifying audit trails and state tracking. Additionally, the multirow INSERT with the VALUES clause streamlines bulk data insertion, reducing SQL complexity and improving execution speed. These capabilities are especially valuable in high-volume environments like retail, healthcare, and finance, where data integrity and operational agility are critical.

Building on these developer-centric enhancements, the next chapter explores how **Oracle 23AI** further empowers modern application development and diagnostics. We begin with JavaScript stored procedures—a leap forward in enabling multi-language programmability within the database—followed by a deep dive into the improved error messaging system designed to accelerate root cause analysis and issue resolution.

CHAPTER 12

Developer Enhancements and Troubleshooting

Introduction

This chapter explores key developer-focused enhancements in Oracle 23AI that significantly improve coding efficiency, debugging, and real-time troubleshooting. Central to this chapter are innovations such as JavaScript stored procedures, which enable developers to natively write and execute logic in JavaScript within the database, and enriched error messaging that offers deeper diagnostic insights during failures. These features are presented with practical implementation steps, real-world case studies, and comparisons to earlier versions to highlight their advantages. Internal mechanisms are also briefly discussed to shed light on how Oracle optimizes performance and diagnostics under the hood. From accelerating development cycles to enhancing operational resilience, this chapter demonstrates how Oracle 23AI empowers developers and DBAs alike with a smarter, more responsive programming and troubleshooting environment.

Enhancing Database Efficiency with JavaScript Stored Procedures in 23AI

Oracle 23AI continues to elevate developer productivity by integrating modern programming paradigms directly into the database engine. A notable advancement in this release is the introduction of JavaScript stored procedures through the Multilingual Engine (MLE). This capability allows JavaScript logic to run natively inside the Oracle database, reducing overhead, simplifying deployment, and enabling faster execution without relying on the Java Virtual Machine (JVM). This chapter examines how Oracle 23AI's JavaScript support helps streamline business logic through a practical case study from QuickMart, an online grocery company. The case study contrasts the traditional Java stored procedure approach with the new JavaScript-based mechanism, offering clear insight into the performance and maintenance benefits.

CASE STUDY: OPTIMIZING ORDER CALCULATIONS AT QUICKMART

QuickMart operates a high-traffic online grocery platform, processing thousands of customer orders daily. A core business function is calculating order totals by combining product prices with tax rates and customer-specific discounts. Prior to Oracle 23AI, QuickMart implemented this logic using Java stored procedures, which introduced considerable complexity in deployment, maintenance, and performance. Java required manual code loading via loadjava, introduced JVM overhead, and was difficult to modify or debug. The adoption of JavaScript stored procedures in Oracle 23AI offered QuickMart a modern, lightweight, and high-performance alternative.

To begin, QuickMart's developers created a basic product catalog using the grocery_items table to simulate real-world items and their prices, as shown in Listing 12-1.

Listing 12-1. Creating and Populating the Grocery Items Table

```sql
CREATE TABLE grocery_items (
    item_id NUMBER PRIMARY KEY,
    name VARCHAR2(50),
    price NUMBER
);

INSERT INTO grocery_items VALUES (1, 'Milk', 2.5);
INSERT INTO grocery_items VALUES (2, 'Bread', 1.5);
INSERT INTO grocery_items VALUES (3, 'Eggs', 3.0);
COMMIT;
```

Challenges with Java Stored Procedures Before Oracle 23AI

In their legacy implementation, QuickMart relied on a Java method to compute the final order total based on a product's price, applicable tax, and customer discount. The Java class was compiled externally and loaded into the database using `loadjava`, and a PL/SQL wrapper was needed to expose the logic for database calls. This approach added deployment complexity and introduced performance bottlenecks due to the JVM context switch. The code used for this method is shown in Listing 12-2, followed by the PL/SQL function in Listing 12-3.

Listing 12-2. Java Method to Calculate Order Totals

```java
import java.sql.*;

public class OrderProcessor {
    public static double calculateOrderTotal(double price, double taxRate,
    double discount) {
        double taxAmount = price * (taxRate / 100);
        double discountAmount = price * (discount / 100);
        return price + taxAmount - discountAmount;
    }
}
```

After Java was loaded into Oracle, the calculation was wrapped in a PL/SQL function.

Listing 12-3. PL/SQL Wrapper for the Java Method

```sql
CREATE OR REPLACE FUNCTION get_order_total(
    price NUMBER,
    tax_rate NUMBER,
    discount NUMBER
) RETURN NUMBER AS LANGUAGE JAVA
NAME 'OrderProcessor.calculateOrderTotal(double, double, double) return double';
/
```

To load the compiled class into the database, the following command was used:

```
loadjava -user system/password -resolve OrderProcessor.java
```

To execute the logic within SQL, the query was this:

```
SELECT get_order_total(10, 5, 10) AS total_price FROM dual;
TOTAL_PRICE
----------------
      9.5
```

While this solution functionally worked, its operational inefficiencies led QuickMart to explore alternatives introduced in Oracle 23AI.

Migrating to JavaScript Stored Procedures in Oracle 23AI

With Oracle 23AI's native JavaScript support via MLE, QuickMart reimplemented the same business logic using a JavaScript module. This approach required no external compilation, class loading, or PL/SQL wrapping in Java. The entire implementation resided within the database and executed efficiently without JVM invocation.

The new JavaScript module was defined in Listing 12-4.

Listing 12-4. JavaScript MLE Module for Order Total Calculation

```
CREATE OR REPLACE MLE MODULE grocery_order_module
LANGUAGE JAVASCRIPT AS
/**
 * Calculates the total order price including tax and discount.
 * @param {number} price - Base price of the item.
 * @param {number} taxRate - Tax percentage.
 * @param {number} discount - Discount percentage.
 * @returns {number} Final price after tax and discount.
 */
function calculateOrderTotal(price, taxRate, discount) {
    const taxAmount = price * (taxRate / 100);
    const discountAmount = price * (discount / 100);
    return price + taxAmount - discountAmount;
}
```

```
export { calculateOrderTotal };
/
```

To invoke this module from SQL, QuickMart created a function wrapper using the new MLE MODULE syntax, shown in Listing 12-5.

Listing 12-5. SQL Wrapper to Execute JavaScript Module

```
CREATE OR REPLACE FUNCTION get_order_total_js(
    price NUMBER,
    tax_rate NUMBER,
    discount NUMBER
) RETURN NUMBER AS
MLE MODULE grocery_order_module
SIGNATURE 'calculateOrderTotal';
/
```

To retrieve the order total, the following query was executed:

```
SELECT get_order_total_js(10, 5, 10) AS total_price FROM dual;
TOTAL_PRICE
-----------
        9.5
```

This returned the expected output, confirming the accuracy and performance of the JavaScript logic without the prior deployment overhead or JVM delays.

By embracing JavaScript stored procedures in Oracle 23AI, QuickMart simplified its order calculation process, reduced technical debt, and achieved faster execution times. The in-database execution of JavaScript logic eliminated the dependency on the JVM and made the system easier to manage and scale. This capability marks a shift toward modern, flexible programming models within the Oracle ecosystem and illustrates Oracle's commitment to meeting developers where they are.

CHAPTER 12 DEVELOPER ENHANCEMENTS AND TROUBLESHOOTING

Internal Mechanism of JavaScript Stored Procedures in Oracle 23AI

Oracle 23AI introduces a transformative enhancement to database programmability by embedding JavaScript execution natively within the database engine via the Multilingual Engine (MLE). Unlike earlier architectures that required Java stored procedures to operate within the JVM—resulting in increased setup complexity, performance overhead, and challenging maintenance—MLE in Oracle 23AI compiles and executes JavaScript functions directly in the SQL engine. This eliminates the need for JVM dependencies, enabling direct, memory-resident execution of business logic with lower latency. Developers can invoke JavaScript routines as native PL/SQL functions, seamlessly accessing and manipulating relational data. This architecture not only improves code maintainability and reduces round trips but also ensures faster response times for computational logic like pricing, tax calculations, and discount application.

This mechanism is visually represented in the flow diagram below.

Table 12-1. *Internal Flow of JavaScript Stored Procedure Execution in Oracle 23AI*

JavaScript Stored Procedures in Oracle 23AI
  |
Powered by Multilingual Engine (MLE)
  |
Executes JavaScript Natively (No JVM)
  |
Direct Integration with SQL Engine
  |
In-Memory Execution for Efficiency

This modernized approach allows enterprises like QuickMart to embed dynamic business logic using a familiar scripting language, accelerating development while enhancing runtime performance—especially for data-intensive operations such as order calculations, recommendations, and personalization workflows.

Performance and Maintainability Comparison with Pre-23AI

While understanding the internal mechanism of JavaScript stored procedures is crucial, it is equally valuable to assess how Oracle 23AI compares with pre-existing approaches in terms of real-world development and operational efficiency. The transition from traditional Java stored procedures to JavaScript via the Multilingual Engine (MLE) offers notable advantages in setup simplicity, execution speed, and ease of maintenance. This comparative overview highlights how Oracle 23AI addresses longstanding developer pain points and accelerates modernization efforts.

Table 12-2. Comparative Overview of Java vs. JavaScript Stored Procedures in Oracle

Feature	Java Stored Procedure (Pre-23AI)	JavaScript Stored Procedure (MLE—23AI)
Setup	Requires Java installation and loadjava	No additional setup needed
Execution Speed	JVM overhead, slower execution	Faster, runs natively in DB
Debugging	Complex, requires Java tools	Simple, uses SQL Actions
Maintainability	Hard to update	Easy to modify
Performance Overhead	High (JVM inside DB)	Low (Native MLE execution)

By eliminating the JVM dependency, Oracle 23AI enables a streamlined development lifecycle, empowering developers to iterate faster and deploy logic more efficiently. These improvements translate into reduced operational overhead, faster application performance, and an overall lower total cost of ownership for database-driven applications.

Real-Time Business Use Cases: Boosting Database Efficiency with JavaScript Stored Procedures in Oracle 23c

While Oracle 23AI's support for JavaScript stored procedures offers a modern, efficient development paradigm, its true value lies in how it transforms real-time operations across industries. By allowing JavaScript to execute natively within the database engine, organizations can implement lightweight business logic with immediate impact. The following table outlines practical use cases where this feature delivers measurable improvements in performance, responsiveness, and customer experience.

Table 12-3. Real-World Applications and Benefits of JavaScript Stored Procedures in Oracle 23AI

Use Case	Description	Business Impact
Real-Time Sales Reports	Instant updates to sales dashboards.	Faster insights, better decisions.
Inventory Management	Real-time tracking of stock levels and automatic updates.	Reduced stockouts, optimized inventory levels.
Customer Support Ticketing	Real-time tracking of customer issues and support tickets.	Faster issue resolution, improved customer satisfaction.
Fraud Detection	Real-time analysis of transactions to detect fraudulent activity.	Reduced losses, improved security and trust.
Dynamic Pricing	Real-time adjustment of product prices based on demand or competition.	Increased revenue, optimized pricing strategies.

These scenarios illustrate how native JavaScript execution in the Oracle engine simplifies the development of real-time, high-performance applications. By embedding logic closer to the data, businesses reduce latency, streamline operations, and gain a competitive edge through enhanced responsiveness.

Common Questions About JavaScript Stored Procedures in Oracle 23AI

JavaScript stored procedures in Oracle 23AI prompt key questions as teams adopt this new capability. A frequent query is how they improve performance over Java. The answer lies in native execution via the Multilingual Engine (MLE), which removes JVM overhead, reducing latency and resource consumption.

Many also ask why JavaScript is preferable. Unlike Java, it requires no separate installation or tools—code is easier to write, debug, and maintain directly in SQL. This simplifies development and aligns better with modern full-stack practices.

Some concerns arise around system impact. Since JavaScript runs natively, it uses fewer resources, enabling better scalability. While migrating from Java may involve some refactoring, the long-term gains in performance and maintainability are significant.

In short, JavaScript stored procedures mark a shift toward lightweight, efficient, and developer-friendly in-database logic.

Key Takeaway By leveraging JavaScript stored procedures in Oracle Database 23AI, businesses like QuickMart can modernize their database logic with faster execution, reduced overhead, and easier maintenance. The Multilingual Engine (MLE) empowers developers to embed JavaScript natively within SQL, offering a streamlined and more agile alternative to traditional Java-based solutions. This transformation simplifies order calculations, improves developer productivity, and enhances operational efficiency.

Building on these advances in developer experience, Oracle 23AI further elevates productivity through enhanced error diagnostics. In the next section, we explore how the introduction of improved error messages significantly reduces troubleshooting time by delivering clearer, context-rich insights during development and debugging.

CHAPTER 12   DEVELOPER ENHANCEMENTS AND TROUBLESHOOTING

Enhancing Troubleshooting with Improved Error Messages in 23AI

As enterprise data environments grow in complexity, the cost of resolving database errors quickly becomes a critical concern. In earlier releases of Oracle Database, error messages were often vague or generic, making it difficult for developers to pinpoint the cause of failures without additional diagnostics. Oracle Database 23AI addresses this long-standing challenge with a significant enhancement: more descriptive and actionable error messages. This improvement directly supports faster root-cause analysis and smoother debugging workflows, minimizing downtime and improving developer productivity.

By delivering precise context—such as pointing out missing columns in a query or displaying the configured system limits—Oracle now reduces the guesswork involved in troubleshooting. These upgrades not only accelerate development cycles but also help reinforce security and operational reliability across environments.

> **CASE STUDY: RESOLVING OPERATIONAL INEFFICIENCIES AT QUICKMART WITH ENHANCED ERROR FEEDBACK**
>
> QuickMart, a rapidly expanding retail chain with a strong online presence, processes thousands of customer orders each day. Its development and operations teams previously encountered delays in resolving SQL errors that emerged during order management, product updates, or system scaling activities. The root of the problem was often the generic nature of Oracle's legacy error messages. Without specific guidance, developers spent extra time isolating and correcting issues—resulting in service disruptions and reduced operational efficiency.
>
> With the rollout of Oracle Database 23AI, QuickMart's engineering team began using the newly enhanced error diagnostics. The impact was immediate: developers received contextual insights for each failure, enabling quicker fixes and cleaner code. Let's examine a few real-world examples from QuickMart's order processing system.

Creating the Customer Orders Table

To simulate the environment used by QuickMart, we begin by creating a basic table to store customer orders. This foundational structure allows us to test how enhanced error messages apply in everyday operations such as inserts, queries, and system configuration.

Listing 12-6. Creating and Populating the Customer Orders Table

```
DROP TABLE IF EXISTS customer_orders;

CREATE TABLE customer_orders (
    order_id INT PRIMARY KEY,
    customer_name VARCHAR(100),
    product_name VARCHAR(100),
    quantity INT,
    order_date DATE
);

INSERT INTO customer_orders (order_id, customer_name, product_name, quantity, order_date)
VALUES
    (1, 'Alice Brown', 'Laptop', 2, SYSDATE),
    (2, 'John Smith', 'Smartphone', 1, SYSDATE),
    (3, 'Emma Wilson', 'Tablet', 3, SYSDATE);

 commit;
```

This table serves as the basis for demonstrating Oracle's improved error output when common SQL mistakes occur.

Identifying Group By Mistakes with Enhanced Syntax Suggestions

A frequent source of confusion in SQL development is incorrect use of aggregate functions. In earlier versions, developers who misused the GROUP BY clause were shown a cryptic message. With 23AI, Oracle now specifies the exact problem—clarifying which columns are missing and how they should be addressed.

CHAPTER 12 DEVELOPER ENHANCEMENTS AND TROUBLESHOOTING

Listing 12-7. Executing a Faulty GROUP BY Query

```
SELECT order_id, customer_name, COUNT(*)
FROM customer_orders
GROUP BY order_id;
```

Before Oracle 23AI

ORA-00979: not a GROUP BY expression

After Oracle 23AI

ORA-00979: Column "CUSTOMER_NAME" must appear in the GROUP BY clause or be used in an aggregate function.

By clearly indicating the offending column and suggesting a fix, this enhancement prevents back-and-forth debugging cycles.

Understanding System Limits with Clarity on Resource Exhaustion

QuickMart's production environment occasionally experiences resource saturation during promotional campaigns. Previously, hitting the process limit in Oracle triggered a vague error, giving administrators little idea how to address it. Oracle 23AI now embeds configuration values directly in the error output.

Using a privileged account (such as **SYSDBA**), run the following to simulate the process limit breach:

Listing 12-8. Simulating a Process Limit Breach

```
ALTER SYSTEM SET processes = 5;
```

Then, attempt to open too many sessions.

Before Oracle 23AI

ORA-00020: maximum number of processes exceeded

This message lacked context, making it unclear how to resolve the issue.

After Oracle 23AI

ORA-00020: Exceeded maximum number of processes (5) specified in initialization parameter.

This small but vital change reduces diagnosis time and guides administrators toward immediate solutions.

Securing SQL Execution with Improved Identifier Validation

Accidental omission of quotes or misplacement of identifiers can sometimes cause syntax errors—or worse, open vulnerabilities. When a developer at QuickMart mistakenly ran a query without quoting a string literal, earlier Oracle versions returned a vague error. Oracle 23AI now echoes the invalid identifier, helping both with debugging and security hardening.

Listing 12-9. Invalid SQL Execution Attempt

```
SELECT * FROM customer_orders WHERE customer_name = John;
```

Before Oracle 23AI

ORA-00904: invalid identifier

After Oracle 23AI

ORA-00904: "JOHN": invalid identifier

This not only helps developers fix the problem but also increases security by preventing potential SQL injection vulnerabilities.

Oracle 23AI's improved error messaging redefines the developer experience by embedding context and clarity directly into runtime diagnostics. As illustrated through QuickMart's transition, these enhancements reduce the time and effort spent on debugging SQL and system configuration issues—allowing engineering teams to focus on innovation rather than resolution. The chapter also reinforces Oracle's broader evolution toward transparency and efficiency in developer tooling.

CHAPTER 12   DEVELOPER ENHANCEMENTS AND TROUBLESHOOTING

Internal Mechanism of Enhanced Error Messages in Oracle 23AI

Oracle 23AI's improved error messaging system leverages advanced syntax parsing and AI-driven diagnostics to analyze query structures and runtime conditions. It identifies incorrect syntax, missing elements, or exceeded limits in real-time, enhancing clarity by dynamically mapping errors to their root causes. This mechanism improves debugging efficiency by providing context-aware suggestions, reducing downtime, and optimizing database reliability.

This mechanism is visually represented in the flow diagram below.

Table 12-4. Internal Flow of Enhanced Error Messaging in Oracle 23AI

Enhanced Error Messages in Oracle 23AI
|
AI-Driven Query Diagnostics
|
Advanced Syntax and Runtime Analysis
|
Real-Time Error Identification
|
Context-Aware Debugging Suggestions

Real-Time Business Use Cases for Oracle 23AI's Enhanced Error Messages

Understanding the internal mechanics of Oracle 23AI's enhanced error messaging is essential, but its true value is best realized through **practical resolution of database issues**. By providing clearer, context-aware feedback, these messages reduce troubleshooting time and help ensure critical business workflows remain uninterrupted.

Table 12-5. Real-World Applications and Benefits of Enhanced Error Messaging in Oracle 23AI

Use Case	Example Scenario	How Enhanced Error Messages Help	Business Impact
Real-Time Sales Reports	Sales dashboards must refresh instantly during peak hours.	When the process/session limit is reached, the error explicitly shows current vs. configured limits, guiding DBAs to adjust settings immediately.	Prevents dashboard downtime, ensuring continuous visibility and faster decisions.
Fraud Detection	Fraud checks run in real-time on payment transactions.	If memory or session resources are exhausted, enhanced ORA- messages pinpoint the exact resource constraint, avoiding guesswork.	Keeps fraud detection real-time, reducing financial losses.
Inventory Management	Stock levels updated continuously from POS and warehouses.	In case of deadlocks or locking errors, messages identify the blocking session/object directly.	Faster conflict resolution ensures accurate stock levels and avoids shortages.

Common Questions About Oracle 23AI Enhanced Error Messages

As developers adopt Oracle 23AI's improved error diagnostics, several common questions arise. One major inquiry is how these new messages enhance troubleshooting. The answer lies in their precision—errors now explicitly identify the issue, such as missing syntax elements or incorrect groupings, making resolution faster and more intuitive.

Security is another focus. Enhanced messages clearly highlight invalid inputs, which helps developers catch potential SQL injection risks early. This leads to more secure applications with reduced exposure to vulnerabilities.

Developers also ask how these messages help with complex SQL. In scenarios involving joins or aggregates, the clarity of error messages reduces debugging time and improves developer productivity.

Overall, Oracle 23AI's enhanced error messages reduce guesswork, shorten downtime, and elevate system reliability—making troubleshooting faster and development smoother.

Key Takeaway Oracle Database 23AI's enhanced error messaging represents a significant leap forward in developer experience and operational efficiency. By delivering clearer, context-rich diagnostics, it empowers teams to resolve issues quickly, reduce system downtime, and boost overall application reliability. As seen in QuickMart's case, these improvements translated into faster issue resolution, enhanced customer satisfaction, and better development agility.

With a stronger foundation in place for debugging and maintenance, the focus now shifts to performance at scale. The next chapter explores how Oracle 23AI accelerates high-speed data ingestion and in-memory processing, enabling real-time analytics and lightning-fast transaction throughput. These innovations are essential for modern enterprises seeking to process massive volumes of data with minimal latency and maximum efficiency.

CHAPTER 13

High-Speed Data Ingestion and In-Memory Processing

Introduction

This chapter explores critical advancements in Oracle Database 23AI designed to accelerate high-speed data ingestion and elevate in-memory processing performance. As modern applications increasingly rely on real-time analytics and low-latency processing—especially in data-heavy environments like IoT, ecommerce, and financial systems—Oracle 23AI introduces specialized features to meet these demands. The chapter focuses on three key enhancements: the improved Fast Ingest mechanism, Staging Tables for ultra-fast ETL operations, and revolutionary updates to In-Memory processing that streamline memory use and accelerate analytical queries. Real-world case studies illustrate how these innovations solve common data throughput and latency issues. Each section includes practical implementation steps, performance comparisons with earlier versions, and insights into the internal architecture powering these enhancements. Business relevance is clearly outlined, and common developer and DBA questions are answered to aid adoption. Each topic concludes with a concise summary to reinforce learning and guide future exploration.

CHAPTER 13   HIGH-SPEED DATA INGESTION AND IN-MEMORY PROCESSING

Enhanced Fast Ingest for High-Speed Data Processing in 23AI

Modern enterprises require database systems that can handle massive volumes of data with minimal latency. This is particularly critical in real-time environments like smart cities, financial trading platforms, and IoT ecosystems. Oracle Database 23AI introduces several enhancements to its Fast Ingest capabilities, streamlining high-speed data processing and offering substantial improvements over earlier versions such as Oracle 19c. These enhancements include support for secure LOB storage, advanced compression, native partitioning, and dynamic memory configuration—all without requiring manual SQL hints or database restarts.

CASE STUDY: REAL-TIME TRAFFIC MONITORING AT QUICKMART SMART MOBILITY

QuickMart, a company traditionally known for its retail innovation, recently ventured into smart mobility solutions for citywide traffic management. Their system required continuous ingestion of sensor data collected from roads, traffic lights, and smart surveillance units. The biggest challenge was to ensure high-speed data capture from thousands of sensors, while also storing snapshot images securely, segmenting records by time intervals, and avoiding the overhead of traditional transactional models.

The requirements were clear:

- Ingest millions of sensor records per hour.
- Store high-resolution snapshots securely using LOB compression and encryption.
- Automatically partition data based on hourly timestamps for efficient access.
- Minimize latency and system overhead.

Oracle 23AI provided the ideal solution by offering a revamped Fast Ingest architecture with dynamic memory allocation, native LOB support, and autonomous partitioning capabilities. In contrast to Oracle 19c, which lacked these advanced features, 23AI enabled QuickMart to build a robust and scalable solution.

Configuring Fast Ingest in Oracle 23AI

The first step in implementing Fast Ingest involved enabling memory optimization features. In Oracle 23AI, the MEMOPTIMIZE_WRITES parameter allows automatic fast-ingest optimizations without needing manual SQL hints. Memory for ingest operations can also be adjusted dynamically using the MEMOPTIMIZE_WRITE_AREA_SIZE parameter, as shown in Listing 13-1.

Listing 13-1. Enabling Memoptimized Writes and Configuring Ingest Buffer

```
-- Enable Memoptimized Writes at the system level (New in 23ai)
ALTER SYSTEM SET MEMOPTIMIZE_WRITES = ON;
-- Allocate memory for fast ingest (New in 23ai, No DB restart needed)
ALTER SYSTEM SET MEMOPTIMIZE_WRITE_AREA_SIZE = 500M;
```

This eliminates the limitations seen in Oracle 19c, where a database restart was needed after adjusting MEMOPTIMIZE_POOL_SIZE.

Creating an Optimized Partitioned Table

QuickMart then created a table to store real-time sensor data with features like SecureFile LOB storage, compression, encryption, and range-based interval partitioning. These features are supported natively in Oracle 23AI and dramatically improve both performance and manageability. The DDL is shown in Listing 13-2.

Listing 13-2. Creating a Partitioned and Secure LOB-Enabled Table for Traffic Data

```
CREATE TABLE traffic_data (
    sensor_id NUMBER NOT NULL,
    event_time TIMESTAMP DEFAULT SYSTIMESTAMP NOT NULL,
    vehicle_count NUMBER NOT NULL,
    snapshot BLOB
)
LOB (snapshot) STORE AS SECUREFILE (COMPRESS HIGH ENCRYPT)  -- SecureFile
LOBs with compression and encryption
```

```
MEMOPTIMIZE FOR WRITE   -- Enable Fast Ingest
PARTITION BY RANGE (event_time) INTERVAL(NUMTODSINTERVAL(1, 'HOUR'))
( PARTITION p0 VALUES LESS THAN (TO_DATE('2024-01-01', 'YYYY-MM-DD')) );
```

Unlike in Oracle 19c, where future partitions had to be created manually and lacked support for LOBs or compression, 23AI automates partition creation and extends Fast Ingest to a wider range of data types.

Ingesting High-Volume Sensor Data

To simulate the traffic sensor workload, QuickMart wrote a PL/SQL block to insert one million rows using Fast Ingest. While the MEMOPTIMIZE_WRITE hint is optional in 23AI when MEMOPTIMIZE_WRITES is ON, it is used here explicitly for clarity. The ingestion script is shown in Listing 13-3.

Listing 13-3. Bulk Insert of Sensor Data with Simulated BLOBs

```
DECLARE
    v_blob BLOB;
BEGIN
    FOR i IN 1..1000000 LOOP
        v_blob := HEXTORAW('DEADBEEF'); -- Simulated Image Data

        INSERT /*+ MEMOPTIMIZE_WRITE */ INTO traffic_data
        VALUES (MOD(i, 1000) + 1, SYSTIMESTAMP, DBMS_RANDOM.VALUE(1, 100),
        v_blob);

    END LOOP;
END;
/
```

These operations are buffered in memory and not immediately committed, enabling rapid ingestion with minimal I/O overhead.

Flushing Buffered Data and Monitoring Usage

Since Fast Ingest stores data in memory, row counts may not immediately reflect all inserted records. Developers can manually flush the write buffer to disk for consistency checks, as shown in Listing 13-4.

Listing 13-4. Manual Flush and Record Count Verification

```
SELECT COUNT(*) FROM traffic_data;
-- Might return less than 1,000,000 as Fast Ingest buffers data in memory.
BEGIN
    DBMS_MEMOPTIMIZE_ADMIN.WRITES_FLUSH();
END;
/
SELECT COUNT(*) FROM traffic_data;
-- Now it should return 1,000,000 after forcing write to disk.
```

Oracle 23AI improves upon 19c by providing automatic flushing mechanisms triggered by internal thresholds or buffer limits. However, manual flushing remains available for explicit control.

Observing Memory Allocation

To evaluate ingest performance and memory usage, QuickMart accessed the V$MEMOPTIMIZE_WRITE_AREA view. This view displays memory allocation, used buffer space, and the count of pending writes.

Listing 13-5. Querying Ingest Memory Usage

```
SELECT * FROM V$MEMOPTIMIZE_WRITE_AREA;
```

This level of transparency aids in tuning system performance without needing to restart services or reconfigure parameters manually.

By leveraging Oracle 23AI's enhanced Fast Ingest capabilities, QuickMart was able to build a high-performance, scalable traffic monitoring system that satisfied all operational requirements. Key improvements such as secure and compressed LOB support, dynamic memory tuning, and autonomous partitioning offered a clear advantage over previous database versions. This case demonstrates how Oracle 23AI transforms high-speed ingestion use cases into efficient, low-maintenance solutions.

CHAPTER 13   HIGH-SPEED DATA INGESTION AND IN-MEMORY PROCESSING

Internal Mechanism of Enhanced Fast Ingest in Oracle 23AI

Oracle 23AI's Fast Ingest leverages **Memoptimized Rowstore** to buffer high-speed writes in memory, bypassing traditional transactional logging for reduced latency. The **MEMOPTIMIZE_WRITE_AREA_SIZE** dynamically allocates memory for efficient ingestion, with automatic or manual flushing to persistent storage. Advanced support for **LOBs, compression, encryption, and partitioning** ensures secure and scalable handling of massive real-time data streams.

This internal process is illustrated in the flow diagram below.

Table 13-1. Internal Flow of Enhanced Fast Ingest in Oracle 23AI

Enhanced Fast Ingest in Oracle 23AI
|
Memoptimized Rowstore for High-Speed Writes
|
Bypasses Traditional Logging for Low Latency
|
Dynamic Memory Allocation for Efficient Ingestion
|
Auto/Manual Flushing to Persistent Storage
|
Scalable Support for LOBs, Compression, and Security

How Oracle 23AI Enhances Fast Ingest Compared to Oracle 19c

Prior to Oracle 23AI, organizations using Oracle 19c for high-speed data ingestion faced limitations in flexibility, performance tuning, and data handling capabilities. Fast ingest was possible, but required manual hints, lacked native support for LOBs, and didn't offer integrated security or compression options. Oracle 23AI addresses these gaps with a more powerful and flexible ingestion framework that includes support for large objects, dynamic memory control, and advanced storage features. As illustrated in Table 13-2, the Fast Ingest functionality in 23AI introduces major innovations over the 19c implementation.

Table 13-2. Comparison Between Oracle 19c and Oracle 23AI Fast Ingest Capabilities

Aspect	Oracle 19c Behavior	Oracle 23AI Behavior
Fast Ingest using Memoptimized Rowstore	Supported, but required specific configurations	Retained with expanded feature integration
LOB Support (e.g., images, JSON)	Not supported during fast ingest	Now natively supported in ingestion streams
Compression for Storage Efficiency	Not available	Integrated to reduce data footprint
Encryption (Tablespace, Column, SecureFiles)	Required external configuration	Fully supported as part of the ingest pipeline
Partitioning (Interval, Hash, Sub-partitions)	Manual setup required	Ingest supports advanced partitioning options
MEMOPTIMIZE_WRITE Hint Requirement	Must be explicitly used in SQL	Optional—can be managed via initialization parameter
Dynamic Memory Allocation (`MEMOPTIMIZE_WRITE_AREA_SIZE`)	Static configuration; required restart	Memory can be adjusted on the fly without downtime

These enhancements provide a foundation for real-time ingestion at scale, streamlining development and enabling enterprises to process high-frequency data with greater reliability and reduced latency.

Real-Time Business Use Cases for Oracle 23AI's Enhanced Fast Ingest Feature

While the internal mechanism of Fast Ingest in Oracle 23AI demonstrates its technical efficiency, its true potential becomes evident when applied to high-frequency, real-time data scenarios. From financial analytics to industrial IoT systems, this feature enables businesses to ingest and act on data faster than ever before. The Table 13-3 below summarizes practical use cases across industries where enhanced Fast Ingest delivers measurable business value.

Table 13-3. Real-Time Business Use Cases and Benefits of Enhanced Fast Ingest in Oracle 23AI

Use Case	Benefit
Real-Time Sales Dashboards	Enables immediate visibility into transactions, accelerating business decisions.
Fraud Detection Systems	Ingests and analyzes transactions in real time, reducing financial losses and improving security posture.
Healthcare Monitoring	Captures continuous patient vitals from IoT devices, enabling faster response and proactive care.
Industrial IoT Monitoring	Collects high-frequency sensor data to detect anomalies and optimize machine performance.
Stock Market Analytics	Processes real-time market feeds for rapid trading and reduced financial risk.

These examples showcase how Oracle 23AI helps businesses stay competitive in a data-driven economy by turning real-time data into real-time decisions.

Common Questions About Oracle 23AI Features for High-Volume Data Ingestion and Performance

Oracle 23AI's Fast Ingest capability has raised interest around its real-world benefits and technical improvements. One common question is how it achieves low-latency performance. The answer lies in its use of MEMOPTIMIZE_WRITES, which buffers data in memory and bypasses traditional undo/redo logging, significantly speeding up ingestion.

Security is another focus area. Oracle 23AI supports native LOB compression and encryption, allowing businesses to ingest and protect large data like JSON or images efficiently. This ensures compliance without impacting speed.

Dynamic memory management is also improved. With MEMOPTIMIZE_WRITE_AREA_SIZE, memory can now be adjusted on the fly without restarting the database—critical for scaling ingestion workloads smoothly.

Partitioning support has also been enhanced. Time-based and hash partitioning help organize incoming data efficiently, improving query performance, especially in IoT, stock trading, and system monitoring scenarios.

Together, these improvements make Oracle 23AI a powerful choice for secure, high-volume, real-time data processing.

Key Takeaway   Oracle 23AI's enhanced Fast Ingest capabilities represent a significant leap forward in high-speed data processing, especially for real-time and IoT-driven workloads. By leveraging Memoptimized Rowstore and eliminating traditional logging overhead, Fast Ingest enables rapid data capture with minimal latency. The addition of LOB support, built-in compression, encryption, and advanced partitioning provides a secure and scalable foundation for ingesting large volumes of data efficiently. Combined with dynamic memory allocation via MEMOPTIMIZE_WRITE_AREA_SIZE, these features empower businesses to streamline real-time analytics and accelerate operational insights.

While Fast Ingest offers speed and flexibility at the memory layer, Oracle 23AI also introduces a complementary feature—**Staging Tables**—designed to handle high-volume inserts with lightweight, disk-based storage. In the next section, we explore how Staging Tables serve as a buffer zone for ETL workflows and event-driven architectures, enabling seamless real-time data ingestion with minimal processing overhead.

Accelerating Real-Time Data Ingestion with Staging Tables in 23AI

Modern enterprises face a growing demand for real-time data processing, especially in high-volume environments like logistics, finance, and retail. Oracle Database 23AI introduces a powerful new construct—**Staging Tables**—that dramatically reduces data ingestion latency. Designed specifically for high-speed inserts, these tables bypass traditional undo/redo logging and disable features like compression and index maintenance, creating a lightweight, transient layer for efficient ETL pipelines and streaming applications. By eliminating unnecessary overhead during ingestion and simplifying data preparation for downstream systems, Staging Tables enable modern applications to remain responsive, scalable, and efficient.

CHAPTER 13 HIGH-SPEED DATA INGESTION AND IN-MEMORY PROCESSING

CASE STUDY: ACCELERATING SHIPMENT TRACKING AT QUICKMART LOGISTICS

QuickMart Logistics, a subsidiary of the retail giant QuickMart, manages tens of thousands of shipment updates daily. Their existing system suffered performance degradation during peak data ingestion times, leading to delayed order tracking, strained transactional systems, and increased operational overhead. To resolve this, the team adopted **Staging Tables in Oracle 23AI** to streamline data capture from IoT-enabled tracking devices before applying transformation logic and persisting relevant records into their core shipping ledger.

Creating the Shipment Staging and Final Tables

The team began by creating two tables—one for rapid ingestion and another for final storage—using the FOR STAGING clause for the ingestion layer. This is illustrated in Listing 13-6.

Listing 13-6. Creating Staging and Final Tables for Shipment Tracking

```
DROP TABLE IF EXISTS shipment_staging PURGE;
DROP TABLE IF EXISTS shipment_final PURGE;

-- Create Staging Table for Fast Ingestion
CREATE TABLE shipment_staging (
    tracking_id    NUMBER GENERATED ALWAYS AS IDENTITY,
    shipment_id    VARCHAR2(50),
    location       VARCHAR2(100),
    status         VARCHAR2(50),
    update_time    TIMESTAMP DEFAULT SYSTIMESTAMP NOT NULL
) FOR STAGING;

-- Create Final Table for Processed Data
CREATE TABLE shipment_final (
    tracking_id    NUMBER GENERATED ALWAYS AS IDENTITY,
    shipment_id    VARCHAR2(50),
    location       VARCHAR2(100),
    status         VARCHAR2(50),
    update_time    TIMESTAMP NOT NULL
);
```

High-Speed Ingestion Using the Staging Table

The logistics system then inserted bulk updates—such as location and delivery status—directly into the staging table. The simplified and optimized design allowed them to bypass logging mechanisms, ensuring minimal ingestion time even with high data volumes. Listing 13-7 demonstrates how bulk data was inserted into the staging table using a CONNECT BY clause to simulate high-frequency input.

Listing 13-7. Bulk Inserting Real-Time Tracking Data

```
-- Bulk insert real-time tracking updates
INSERT INTO shipment_staging (shipment_id, location, status)
SELECT 'SHIP' || LEVEL,
       'Location ' || MOD(LEVEL, 10),
       CASE MOD(LEVEL, 3)
           WHEN 0 THEN 'In Transit'
           WHEN 1 THEN 'Delivered'
           ELSE 'Pending'
       END
FROM dual CONNECT BY LEVEL <= 10000;

-- Verify inserted data
SELECT COUNT(*) FROM shipment_staging;
```

The operation completed almost instantaneously, confirming the optimized nature of staging inserts.

Transforming and Moving Data to the Final Table

Once the data was ingested, only relevant records—such as confirmed deliveries or in-transit updates—were moved to the final table after applying business transformation logic. This is shown in Listing 13-8.

CHAPTER 13 HIGH-SPEED DATA INGESTION AND IN-MEMORY PROCESSING

Listing 13-8. Transforming and Migrating Filtered Data

```
-- Move data after necessary transformations
INSERT INTO shipment_final (shipment_id, location, status, update_time)
SELECT shipment_id, location, status, update_time FROM shipment_staging
WHERE status != 'Pending';

-- Delete processed records from staging table
DELETE FROM shipment_staging WHERE status != 'Pending';
```

This selective migration reduced unnecessary data storage and improved reporting clarity.

Converting a Staging Table to a Regular Table

For analytical purposes, the logistics team occasionally converted staging tables into regular heap tables. This allowed them to run ad-hoc queries and join the data with historical shipment logs. Listing 13-9 shows the conversion process.

Listing 13-9. Altering Staging Table to Heap Table for Analytics

```
-- Convert staging table to a normal heap table
ALTER TABLE shipment_staging NOT FOR STAGING;
-- Verify table type
SELECT table_name, staging FROM user_tables WHERE table_name LIKE
'SHIPMENT%';
```

The output confirmed the conversion and readiness for analytical workloads.

Verifying Compression and Statistics Behavior

To demonstrate how staging tables behave differently from regular tables, the team reconverted the table back into a staging format and inspected compression and statistics settings, as shown in Listing 13-10.

Listing 13-10. Checking Compression and Statistics Enforcement

```
-- Convert heap table to a staging table
ALTER TABLE shipment_staging FOR STAGING;

-- Check compression status (should be disabled)
SELECT table_name, staging, compression FROM user_tables WHERE table_name
LIKE 'SHIPMENT%';

-- Try to gather statistics (should fail)
EXEC dbms_stats.gather_table_stats(null, 'SHIPMENT_STAGING');

--expected ORA-20005: object statistics are locked (stattype = ALL)
```

This confirmed that compression was disabled and traditional statistics gathering was blocked, relying instead on dynamic sampling for execution planning.

Lifecycle Management and Cleanup

Upon completion of processing, the staging table was dropped. Oracle 23AI ensured that it was immediately purged without moving it to the recycle bin, reducing unnecessary space usage. Listing 13-11 illustrates the final cleanup step.

Listing 13-11. Dropping Staging Table and Checking Recycle Bin

```
-- Drop Staging Table
DROP TABLE shipment_staging;

-- Check if it is in the recycle bin
SHOW RECYCLEBIN;
```

Business Benefits of Using Staging Tables

The introduction of FOR STAGING tables provided measurable operational improvements for QuickMart Logistics. Table 13-4 summarizes the key technical features and business advantages.

CHAPTER 13 HIGH-SPEED DATA INGESTION AND IN-MEMORY PROCESSING

Table 13-4. Advantages of Staging Tables in Oracle 23AI

Feature	Business Benefit
FOR STAGING Insert Model	Enables high-speed bulk ingestion
No Compression or Indexing	Reduces latency during ingest
Dynamic Sampling	Avoids costly stats gathering during high loads
Recycle Bin Bypass	Saves space during rapid ingest/cleanup cycles
Convertible Design	Easily toggled between staging and regular usage

Staging Tables in Oracle 23AI offer a streamlined approach to real-time data ingestion—especially valuable in logistics, IoT, and ETL workflows. By bypassing traditional storage overhead and optimizing insert performance, this feature empowers businesses to ingest, filter, and act on data with minimal delay and overhead.

Internal Mechanism of Staging Tables in Oracle 23AI

Staging Tables in Oracle 23AI optimize data ingestion by bypassing undo/redo logging, deferring index maintenance, and using dynamic sampling for statistics instead of full statistics gathering. This reduces transaction overhead, allowing high-speed bulk inserts while ensuring data persistence. Unlike traditional heap tables, they prioritize rapid ingestion over long-term storage, making them ideal for ETL and real-time processing.

This mechanism is visually represented in the flow diagram below.

Table 13-5. Internal Flow of Staging Table-Based Ingestion in Oracle 23AI

Staging Tables in Oracle 23AI
|
Bypass Undo/Redo Logging for Faster Ingestion
|
Defer Index Maintenance to Reduce Overhead
|
Use Dynamic Sampling Instead of Full Stats Gathering
|
Optimize Bulk Inserts for ETL and Real-Time Processing

Differences: Staging Tables vs. Fast Ingest (MEMOPTIMIZE FOR WRITE)

Oracle 23AI offers two powerful mechanisms for high-speed data ingestion: **Staging Tables** and **Fast Ingest (MEMOPTIMIZE FOR WRITE)**. The following table highlights the six most critical distinctions between them, helping businesses choose the right model for their data flow requirements.

Table 13-6. Key Differences Between Staging Tables and Fast Ingest in Oracle 23AI

Aspect	Staging Tables (FOR STAGING)	Fast Ingest (MEMOPTIMIZE FOR WRITE)
Primary Purpose	Bulk data capture before transformation	Ultra-fast inserts for real-time streaming
Persistence Model	Data is persisted immediately	Data buffered in memory, flushed later
Redo Logging	Minimal redo logging	No redo logging until flush
Data Durability	Persistent by default	Volatile until memory is flushed
Indexing Support	Indexes allowed (post-ingestion)	Indexes not supported
Ideal Use Case	ETL, real-time ingestion pipelines	IoT, telemetry, financial tick data

This comparison helps guide the selection of the appropriate ingestion strategy, depending on whether speed, durability, or post-processing is the top priority.

Real-World Use Cases of Staging Tables and Fast Ingest in Oracle 23AI

While the internal mechanisms of **Staging Tables** and **Fast Ingest** highlight their technical strengths, their real-world impact is best illustrated through business scenarios that require high-throughput data ingestion with minimal latency. The following table presents six practical use cases across diverse industries where these features drive operational efficiency and real-time responsiveness.

Table 13-7. Business Use Cases of Staging Tables and Fast Ingest in Oracle 23AI

Use Case	Business Scenario	Benefit
IoT Data Ingestion	Collect real-time sensor readings (temperature, pressure, GPS, etc.) from edge devices.	Enables ultra-fast data capture with minimal I/O and logging overhead.
Ecommerce Inventory Updates	Sync inventory data across warehouses and digital platforms in near real-time.	Improves stock accuracy, reduces overselling, and enhances customer satisfaction.
Financial Transactions Processing	Stream incoming trade or payment records into a staging layer before risk checks.	Facilitates rapid ingestion and downstream transformation for timely settlements.
Customer Behavior Tracking	Ingest clickstream and interaction logs from websites and mobile apps.	Provides immediate visibility into customer activity, enabling real-time analytics.
Telecom Network Monitoring	Capture performance metrics from cell towers and routers for anomaly detection.	Delivers low-latency insights to support proactive issue resolution.
Supply Chain and Logistics	Ingest live shipment updates from delivery fleets and logistics hubs.	Ensures accurate tracking and smoother coordination of fulfillment operations.

Together, **Staging Tables** and **Fast Ingest** offer a powerful foundation for real-time data pipelines, making Oracle 23AI a strong choice for businesses aiming to optimize responsiveness, scalability, and decision-making.

Common Questions About Oracle 23AI Staging Tables and Fast Ingest

As Oracle 23AI introduces powerful features for high-speed data ingestion, users naturally have questions about their performance, best-use scenarios, and real-world applicability. This section addresses the most frequently asked questions, providing expert insight into how **Staging Tables** and **Fast Ingest** operate and complement each other.

CHAPTER 13   HIGH-SPEED DATA INGESTION AND IN-MEMORY PROCESSING

A key question is how Oracle 23AI's **Staging Tables** accelerate data ingestion. These tables bypass traditional undo and redo logging mechanisms and defer index maintenance. They also avoid compression and rely on dynamic sampling for statistics collection rather than full stats gathering. As a result, they significantly reduce overhead during bulk inserts, making them well-suited for fast, transient ingestion operations in real-time systems.

Many users ask where Staging Tables are most beneficial. The answer lies in high-volume, real-time applications such as ETL pipelines, IoT telemetry, logistics, and financial data collection. These use cases demand rapid data capture and transformation without the performance drag of transactional overhead, making Staging Tables an optimal fit.

Another frequently discussed topic is the combined use of **Fast Ingest** and **Staging Tables**. Fast Ingest captures incoming data in-memory using **Memoptimized Rowstore**, enabling ultra-low-latency insertion. Once buffered, this data can be flushed and moved into Staging Tables for transformation and further processing. This workflow leverages the best of both worlds—speed from memory writes and flexibility from transient staging.

Lastly, it's important to recognize the operational scope of Staging Tables. While they are highly efficient for intermediate data processing, they are not intended for long-term storage or analytics. Their design excludes compression, disables the recycle bin, and limits statistics collection—traits that favor ingestion over retention.

These capabilities position **Staging Tables** and **Fast Ingest** as essential tools for modern data-driven environments, particularly where speed, scalability, and transformation throughput are paramount.

Key Takeaway   Oracle 23AI offers two complementary technologies—Fast Ingest and Staging Tables—that, when used together, deliver unmatched speed and efficiency in handling real-time and high-volume data.

Staging Tables (FOR STAGING) are purpose-built for rapid bulk ingestion with minimal transactional overhead, making them ideal for ETL workloads and intermediate data transformation. By bypassing undo/redo logging, deferring index maintenance, and relying on dynamic sampling for statistics, they enable quick data capture without sacrificing downstream processing flexibility.

Fast Ingest (MEMOPTIMIZE FOR WRITE) is designed for ultra-low-latency, high-frequency writes—ideal for scenarios such as IoT telemetry or financial tick data. It holds incoming data in memory for immediate ingestion, dramatically reducing latency before asynchronously flushing it to disk.

To maximize performance and reliability, the following **combined strategy** is recommended:

- **Capture** time-sensitive data using **Fast Ingest** for immediate buffering in memory.

- **Transfer** this data periodically into **Staging Tables** for cleansing, transformation, and validation.

- **Load** the processed data into final transactional or analytical tables for long-term storage and business use.

This layered approach allows businesses to harness real-time responsiveness while maintaining structure and governance in data processing workflows.

With real-time data efficiently captured and processed, the next logical step is to explore how Oracle 23AI enhances performance for analytical workloads. In the following section, we dive into **In-Memory enhancements**, which revolutionize how queries are executed—delivering lightning-fast insights across massive datasets.

Revolutionizing In-Memory Performance in Oracle 23AI

Oracle 23AI marks a transformative step in the evolution of in-memory computing, offering advanced capabilities that significantly enhance performance for both analytical and real-time workloads. This chapter explores how Oracle 23AI streamlines in-memory management, reduces query latency, and delivers intelligent automation—ultimately simplifying operations while boosting efficiency.

CHAPTER 13 HIGH-SPEED DATA INGESTION AND IN-MEMORY PROCESSING

> **CASE STUDY: ACCELERATING FINANCIAL ANALYTICS AT QUICKMART**
>
> QuickMart, a financial services division, faced consistent challenges in processing high-frequency trading data. Query latency, memory overhead, and the need for real-time analysis pushed the limits of their infrastructure. By upgrading to Oracle 23AI, QuickMart harnessed the full spectrum of In-Memory enhancements—achieving rapid query execution, automated memory scaling, and optimized JSON analytics.

Automatic Enablement of In-Memory Features

In earlier versions, DBAs had to manually enable key performance features like Join Groups, Bloom Filters, and vectorized arithmetic for In-Memory operations. Oracle 23AI changes this paradigm by enabling these features automatically based on workload analysis.

With a simple command as shown in Listing 13-12, Oracle dynamically applies optimizations, including advanced join techniques and vector-based operations.

Listing 13-12. Enabling In-Memory Query Optimization

```
ALTER SYSTEM SET INMEMORY_QUERY = ENABLE;
ALTER SESSION SET INMEMORY_QUERY = ENABLE;
```

This eliminates manual tuning and ensures consistent, high-speed performance.

Automatic In-Memory Column Store Sizing

Prior to Oracle 23AI, resizing the In-Memory Column Store (IMCS) required manual intervention and restarts, creating operational overhead. In contrast, Oracle 23AI integrates IMCS with Automatic Shared Memory Management (ASMM).

Memory adjusts dynamically with no downtime, as shown in Listing 13-13, and usage can be monitored via V$INMEMORY_AREA.

Listing 13-13. Monitoring In-Memory Memory Usage

```
SELECT POOL, ALLOC_BYTES, USED_BYTES FROM V$INMEMORY_AREA;
```

Multilevel Joins and Aggregations

Before Oracle 23AI, optimizing multilevel joins and aggregations required manual hints or materialized views. This was inefficient and hard to maintain.

With vectorized execution now built-in, Oracle 23AI processes joins and aggregations in-memory using SIMD techniques. Listing 13-14 shows a use case where QuickMart executes a complex aggregation query over three In-Memory tables.

Listing 13-14. Executing Multilevel Joins and Aggregations

```
CREATE TABLE date_dim (
    datekey NUMBER PRIMARY KEY,
    year NUMBER,
    month NUMBER
) INMEMORY;

CREATE TABLE part (
    partkey NUMBER PRIMARY KEY,
    brand VARCHAR2(50)
) INMEMORY;

CREATE TABLE lineorder (
    lo_orderkey NUMBER PRIMARY KEY,
    lo_orderdate NUMBER,
    lo_partkey NUMBER,
    lo_revenue NUMBER
) INMEMORY;

INSERT INTO date_dim VALUES (20230101, 2023, 1);
INSERT INTO part VALUES (101, 'BrandX');

INSERT INTO lineorder VALUES (1, 20230101, 101, 5000);
COMMIT;

SELECT d.year, p.brand, SUM(lo_revenue) AS total_revenue
FROM lineorder l
```

```
JOIN date_dim d ON l.lo_orderdate = d.datekey
JOIN part p ON l.lo_partkey = p.partkey
WHERE d.year = 2023
GROUP BY d.year, p.brand
ORDER BY total_revenue DESC;
```

This vectorized pipeline yields faster execution with no manual tuning.

In-Memory Optimized Dates

Filtering by year or month in older versions required function-based indexes or precomputed columns, which added complexity.

Oracle 23AI introduces memory-resident date optimization, allowing direct evaluation of EXTRACT functions. Listing 13-15 demonstrates date-based aggregation over In-Memory tables.

Listing 13-15. Optimized Date Filtering Using EXTRACT()

```
SELECT d.year, p.brand, SUM(lo_revenue) AS rev
FROM lineorder l, date_dim d, part p
WHERE l.lo_orderdate = d.datekey
AND l.lo_partkey = p.partkey
AND EXTRACT(YEAR FROM TO_DATE(d.datekey, 'YYYYMMDD')) = 2023
GROUP BY d.year, p.brand;
```

This approach is 3x faster, eliminating the need for extra indexes or MV structures.

Hybrid Exadata Scans

Previously, Exadata Smart Scans and In-Memory scans worked independently. Oracle 23AI introduces Hybrid Exadata Scans that merge both technologies within a single query execution.

As shown in Listing 13-16, Exadata reads disk-resident blocks while IMCS serves hot data, boosting scan performance by up to 2x.

Listing 13-16. Hybrid Scan Execution Example

```
SELECT /*+ FULL(lineorder) INMEMORY */
    lo_orderdate, lo_revenue
FROM lineorder
WHERE lo_orderdate BETWEEN 20230101 AND 20231231;
```

This automatic integration reduces I/O and optimizes throughput for large scans.

In-Memory Columnar JSON

Querying JSON fields used to require full parsing and often necessitated secondary indexes. Oracle 23AI solves this by storing JSON in a compressed, columnar format directly in IMCS.

In Listing 13-17, a JSON field is queried with no index, yet performance remains high due to columnar layout.

Listing 13-17. Querying Columnar JSON In-Memory

```
CREATE TABLE json_data (
    id NUMBER PRIMARY KEY,
    data CLOB
) INMEMORY COLUMN STORE COMPRESS FOR QUERY HIGH;

INSERT INTO json_data VALUES (1, '{"order": "123", "price": 500}');
commit;

SELECT JSON_VALUE(data, '$.order') AS order_id
FROM json_data;
```

Query response time is up to 5x faster, with lower CPU overhead and no indexing.

Native In-Memory Advisor

In older releases, identifying hot data for In-Memory was manual and error-prone. Oracle 23AI introduces a built-in advisor that analyzes access patterns and suggests what should reside in IMCS.

The advisor recommendations are available through the query in Listing 13-18.

Listing 13-18. Retrieving In-Memory Advisor Recommendations

```
SELECT * FROM DBA_INMEMORY_ADVISOR_RECOMMENDATION;
```

This streamlines decision-making, allowing DBAs to adopt optimal In-Memory strategies based on real usage.

Oracle 23AI redefines In-Memory performance through automated tuning, hybrid processing, vectorized execution, and JSON optimization. QuickMart's success story illustrates how modern businesses can unlock real-time analytics, reduce resource overhead, and scale operations efficiently.

Internal Mechanism of In-Memory Performance in Oracle 23AI

Oracle 23AI dynamically optimizes In-Memory processing by leveraging **Auto-Sizing** Column Store, Hybrid Exadata Scans, and Vectorized Joins. It intelligently manages memory allocation based on workload demands, ensuring efficient query execution with minimal latency. The Native In-Memory Advisor further automates **table and column selection**, maximizing performance with minimal DBA intervention.

The operational flow in Table 13-8 illustrates the architecture that drives Oracle 23AI's advanced in-memory performance capabilities.

Table 13-8. *Operational Flow of In-Memory Query Processing in Oracle 23AI*

Revolutionizing In-Memory Performance in Oracle 23AI
|
Auto-Sizing Column Store for Dynamic Memory Management
|
Hybrid Exadata Scans for Faster Query Execution
|
Vectorized Joins to Reduce Processing Overhead
|
Native In-Memory Advisor for Automated Optimization
|
Minimal Latency with Adaptive Resource Allocation

Real-Time Business Use Cases for Oracle 23AI In-Memory Enhancements

While understanding the internal workings of Oracle 23AI's In-Memory architecture is essential, its real power lies in practical business outcomes. This section showcases how organizations across different industries are leveraging these enhancements to gain speed, insight, and operational efficiency through real-time analytics and reduced latency.

Table 13-9. Real-World Applications and Business Benefits of In-Memory Enhancements in Oracle 23AI

Use Case	Business Scenario	Benefit
Financial Services	Analyzing high-frequency trading data for market trends and risk management.	Faster query execution enables quicker, informed decisions.
Ecommerce	Delivering dynamic product recommendations based on user interactions.	Real-time personalization improves customer engagement.
Healthcare	Accessing and processing patient vitals and diagnostic data.	Faster access enhances decision-making and treatment.
Retail	Forecasting demand and optimizing stock levels using current sales trends.	Improved inventory accuracy and reduced overstock.
Telecommunications	Monitoring network traffic and usage patterns for real-time alerting.	Lower latency leads to faster response and better uptime.

Common Questions About Oracle 23AI In-Memory Enhancements

As Oracle 23AI continues to push the boundaries of in-memory processing, several questions arise regarding the automatic tuning, hybrid scan integration, and advanced JSON capabilities it introduces. This section answers some of the most frequently asked questions, offering expert insight into how these features enhance performance, simplify administration, and empower modern data-driven applications.

One of the most common inquiries centers on how Oracle 23AI determines the optimal size of the In-Memory Column Store. The database now dynamically adjusts memory allocation based on active workload demands—such as query complexity, frequency of access, and system resource availability—without requiring a database restart. This automatic sizing is handled via integration with Automatic Shared Memory Management (ASMM), allowing for intelligent resource allocation in real time, which is especially useful in multitenant or fluctuating workload environments.

Another key question involves the performance gains from Hybrid Exadata Scans. Prior to Oracle 23AI, Smart Scans and In-Memory Scans operated independently, often requiring the DBA to choose one execution path or the other. Oracle 23AI now merges these two paths seamlessly, enabling a single query to pull from both disk-based Smart Scan and memory-resident data depending on data availability. This hybrid approach can yield performance gains of up to 2x by optimizing scan paths dynamically.

The new In-Memory Columnar JSON feature also draws attention, particularly from organizations dealing with semistructured data. This enhancement allows JSON data to be stored natively in a compressed, columnar format within the In-Memory Column Store. As a result, JSON queries no longer require full document parsing or manual indexing, leading to execution speeds up to 5x faster while reducing CPU and memory overhead. It simplifies querying large-scale JSON datasets—especially useful for analytics, event logs, and telemetry data.

Finally, many DBAs ask about the role of the Native In-Memory Advisor and whether it replaces manual tuning efforts. This built-in advisor automatically analyzes workload heat maps to recommend which tables or columns should be loaded into memory for optimal performance. By providing actionable recommendations, it eliminates much of the trial-and-error typically associated with memory tuning and allows for better performance management with minimal administrative overhead.

These enhancements make Oracle 23AI not just a more powerful in-memory engine but also a significantly more autonomous and workload-aware platform—ideally suited for the next generation of high-speed, data-intensive enterprise applications.

Key Takeaway Oracle Database 23AI marks a pivotal advancement in enterprise data management, particularly through its transformative In-Memory capabilities. By intelligently integrating automatic memory optimization, vectorized multilevel joins, hybrid Exadata scans, and native support for columnar JSON processing, Oracle 23AI redefines what is possible in real-time analytics and decision-making.

These enhancements collectively lead to query execution that is 2 to 5 times faster than previous versions, while simultaneously reducing the operational burden on DBAs. Features such as the Auto-Sizing Column Store and Native In-Memory Advisor ensure that systems dynamically adapt to changing workloads with minimal human intervention. Whether processing high-frequency trading data, personalizing ecommerce recommendations, or analyzing massive IoT streams, Oracle 23AI delivers unprecedented performance at scale.

Most notably, Oracle 23AI simplifies the management of complex analytical environments, empowering organizations to extract deeper insights with greater speed and reliability. Its ability to efficiently handle large volumes of structured and semistructured data positions it as a cornerstone for modern, data-driven enterprises.

Final Thoughts

As enterprises face increasing demands for speed, scale, and intelligence, Oracle 23AI offers a forward-looking platform designed for agility, resilience, and insight. The features explored throughout this book—from enhanced error diagnostics and fast ingest capabilities to lock-free reservations and intelligent memory management—underscore Oracle's ongoing commitment to delivering database technology that is not only high-performing but also highly adaptive.

With Oracle 23AI, organizations are better equipped than ever to transition from traditional data processing to real-time, AI-driven operations. It is not just a database upgrade—it is a strategic enabler for digital transformation, operational excellence, and competitive advantage.

This book has aimed to uncover the architecture, mechanics, and real-world applications that define Oracle 23AI's value. As the data landscape evolves, Oracle continues to stand at the forefront, empowering enterprises to unlock the full potential of their information assets—securely, efficiently, and intelligently.

Index

A

Accuracy, 206
ADB-S, *see* Autonomous Database Serverless (ADB-S)
Advanced data processing SQL/PGQ, 260–268
AI-driven analytics, 149
AI-driven anomaly detection, 248
AI/ML-Based Customer Retention Prediction, 107
    common questions, 106, 107
    CUSTOMER_RETENTION_ MODEL, 101
    DBMS_DATA_MINING package, 104
    enable model training, 102
    insert labeled historical data, 101
    insert new customer profiles, 102
    internal structure, 104
    new_customers table, 102
    predict retention outcomes, 101
    QuickMart, 100
    real-time business use cases, 105, 106
    store historical customer behavior and retention status, 100
    See also Query Elapsed Time Prediction
AI-powered applications, 152, 159
AI-powered query optimization, 121
    common questions, 128
    create and populate dataset, 122
    evaluate performance metrics, 123
    GV_$SQL_REOPTIMIZATION_HINTS view, 123
    internal structure, 125
    NO_QUERY_TRANSFORMATION, 121
    OPTIMIZER_FEATURES_ENABLE parameter, 121
    post-optimization performance evaluation, 124
    Pre-ADB-S *vs.* ADB-S databases, 126
    real-time business use cases, 127
    traditional static methods, 121
Analytic functions, 194–196
Annotation metadata, 210
Annotations feature, 211
    advantage, 214
    applications and benefits, 214
    comments, 212
    internal flow, 212
    metadata, 212
    metadata views, 211, 214
    in Oracle 23AI, 211
    real value, 213
    security perspective, 215
Annotations management, 210
Artificial intelligence, 1, 98, 151
ASM, *see* Automatic Storage Management (ASM)
Auditing capabilities, 207
Auditing features, 221
Audit policy, 217, 218
Audit Trail Results, 219

INDEX

Automated bigfile tablespace
    shrinking, 26
  analyze reclaimable space, 27
  common questions, 32
  fragmentation, 32
  internal flow, shrinking mechanism, 30
  modernize storage, 27–29
  operational and business impacts, 29
  pre-23AI approach, 30, 31
  real-time business use cases, 31, 32
Automatic optimization, 204
Automatic SQL Transpiler, 202–205
Automatic Storage Management (ASM), 66
Autonomous Database Serverless
    (ADB-S), 1, 2, 60, 99, 131
  B-tree structures, 63
  essential tasks, 1
  integrate AI/ML (*see* AI/ML-Based
    Customer Retention Prediction)
  internal workflow, 63
  practical questions, 65, 66
  vs. Pre-ADB-S, 64
  real-time business use cases, 65
Auto-Tuned Query Execution, 113,
    114, 117–120
  common questions, 119, 120
  execution strategies, 114
  initial query with performance
    issues, 115
  internal structure, 118
  practical impact, 117
  real time business use cases, 119
  review optimization
    recommendations, 116
  run auto-tuning, 116
  sample dataset creation and
    population, 114
  SQL performance, 117

B

Baseline Query, 201
BLOB and CLOB data movement, 134
BLOB Data, 134
BLOB report, 134
Blockchain tables, 141
  data integrity and tamper-
    resistance, 142
  expired rows, 146
  Metadata Columns, 143
  operations, 147
  Oracle 21c, 142
  Oracle 23AI, 146, 148, 149
  QuickMart, 142
  with retention policies, 142
  row integrity, 145
  system-generated internal
    columns, 143
Boolean columns, 169
Boolean data type, 167
Boolean logic, 168
  advantages, 176
  business use cases, 176
  data integrity, 176
  dataset, 170
  data type architecture, 173
  logical conflicts, 171
  Oracle 23AI, 173
  in Oracle Query Engine, 174
  organizations, 174
  in place, 170
  PL/SQL constructs, 168
  pre-23AI and oracle 23AI, 175
  table, 169
  unavailable employees, 171
  usage in PL/SQL, 172
Built-in similarity operators, 154

C

CASE Statement, 55
CHECKSUM analytic function, 177
    analytic function, 184
    cryptographic hashes, 184
    data changes, 183
    data consistency, 177
    internal workflow, 183
    inventory quantities, 180
    inventory table, 178
    laptop and smartphone, 181
    in Oracle 23AI, 182
    tablet and monitor, 182
Cloud Credential, 132
Cloud-native architectures, 131
Column aliases, 188, 190
Column Alias Resolution, 189
Column alias support, 190
Column-level auditing, 215, 219, 220, 222
Concurrent refreshes
    architects and DBAs, 289
    business impact, 287
    configuration, 286, 287
    CPU and memory use, 289
    creates the materialized view, 286
    data consistency, 289
    fast refresh operations, 285, 286
    feature, 283
    internal workflow, 287, 288
    definition and population of inventory and sales tables, 284, 285
    materialized view logs, 285, 286
    real-time use cases, 288, 289
    ROWID tracking and SEQUENCE ordering, 289
Conventional methods, 131
CREATE SEARCH INDEX syntax, 67, 70, 71, 73

Cumulative duration, 194
Customer Orders Table, 216, 218

D

Database Administrators (DBAs), 3
Database annotations, 207
Database auditing, 221
Data integrity
    with domain-based constraints, 269–276
Data privacy regulations, 215
Data redaction, 249
Data redaction capabilities, 247
Data security and privacy, 149
DBAs, *see* Database Administrators (DBAs)
DB_DEVELOPER_ROLE, 232
    CONNECT and RESOURCE, 234
    design, 233
    flexibility, 235
    Oracle 23AI, 234
    real-time business, 234
    SQL activity, 235
    structure, 233
    workflows, 233
DBMS_CLOUD-based integration, 139
DBMS_CLOUD package, 131, 138
    AI/ML workloads, 141
    file workflows, 140
    implementation, 132
    Oracle ADB-S, 138, 139
    Oracle object storage, 134
    real-time business, 140
    retention and analysis, 133
    SQL performance, 132
    version control and data integrity, 141

INDEX

DBMS_DATA_MINING package, 101, 104, 105, 109
DBMS_SPACE.SHRINK_TABLESPACE, 27, 30, 31
DBMS_SQLPA package, 117
DBMS_SQLTUNE package, 116, 117
Developer-focused enhancements
    database efficiency with JavaScript
        challenges, 321, 322
        internal flow, 324
        Java *vs.* JavaScript stored procedures, 325
        migrating, 322, 323
        MLE module, 319, 322
        product catalog, 320
        real-world applications and benefits, 326
        SQL Wrapper to Execute, 323
Developer switch teams, 231
Digital payments, 163
Distributed ledger technologies (DLTs), 148
DLTs, *see* Distributed ledger technologies (DLTs)
DML capabilities, 315
DML RETURNING clause, 310–314, 316
Domain-based constraints
    business logic at data layer, 269
    creating the orders table, 270
    database performance, 275
    data validation, 269
    distributed database environments, 275
    inserting and validating order data, 271
    internal flow, 272–274
    practical value of domains feature, 275
    Pre-23AI *vs.* Oracle 23AI constraint enforcement mechanisms, 273, 274
    real-time business use cases, 274, 275
    retrieving validated order data, 271, 272
    reusable domains for business rules, 269, 270
    traditional CHECK constraints *vs.* ENUM workarounds, 275

E

Employee Table, 209
"enq: TX-row lock contention", 10, 11, 13, 15
Enterprise databases, 185
ENUM data type, 270
Error messages, 328–334
Escrow Column Concurrency Control, 11

F

Fast ingest mechanism
    time-sensitive data, 352
    and staging tables, 349, 350
Fast ingest mechanism for high-speed data ingestion
    configuring, 337
    dynamic memory management, 342
    flushing buffered data and monitoring usage, 338, 339
    high-volume sensor data, 338
    internal flow, 340
    memory allocation, 339
    optimized partitioned table, 337, 338

Oracle 19c, 336
Oracle 19c *vs.* Oracle 23AI, 340, 341
and performance, 342, 343
performance and manageability, 337
real-time business use cases and
    benefits, 341, 342
in real-time environments, 336
security, 342
Firewall status, 236
Function-based Index, 246

G

GET_OBJECT procedure, 137
GV_$SQL_REOPTIMIZATION_HINTS
    view, 124

H

Hands-on implementation guidance, 151
High-speed data ingestion
    fast ingest mechanism, 336–343
    real-time data ingestion with staging
        tables, 343–352
High-throughput environments, 141

I

IMCS, *see* In-Memory Column
    Store (IMCS)
Immutability period, 149
In-Memory Column Store (IMCS),
    353, 354
In-memory performance
    advisor recommendations, 356,
        357, 359
    analytical and real-time workloads, 352
    automatic enablement, 353

Columnar JSON, 356, 359
Hybrid Exadata Scans, 355, 356, 359
IMCS, 353, 354
multilevel joins and aggregations,
    354, 355
operational flow, 357
optimal size, 359
optimized dates, 355
real-world applications and business
    benefits, 358
Intelligent data interaction, 149
Internal redaction workflow, 248
INTERVAL datatypes, 197

J, K

JavaScript stored procedures
    challenges, 321, 322
    internal flow, 324
    vs. Java, 325
    migrating, 322, 323
    MLE, 319
    in Oracle 23AI, 327
    product catalog, 320
    real-world applications and
        benefits, 326
Java Virtual Machine (JVM), 320, 321
JSON-based indexes
    in ADB-S, 60 (*see* Autonomous
        Database Serverless (ADB-S))
    on email for QuickMart CRM
        Table, 61, 62
JSON enhancements
    efficient and flexible storage, 36–38
    internal mechanism, 40
    leverage JSON_VALUE for object
        instantiation, 39, 40

INDEX

JSON enhancements (*cont.*)
    operational flow, advanced JSON processing, 40, 41
    practical questions, 43, 44
    Pre-23AI *vs.* Oracle 23AI, functional comparison, 41, 42
    querying and transformation, 36
    real-time business use cases, 42, 43
JSON functions, 309
JSON indexing, 40, 43, 63, 64, 66, 85, 86
JSON-Relational Duality Views, 74
    common questions, 81, 82
    creation, Customers and Sales Tables, 75
    definition, 76
    internal design, 79, 80
    Pre-23AI *vs.* 23AI features, 80
    querying data, 77, 78
    QuickMart Solutions, 78
    QuickMart's use, 79
    real-time business use cases, 81
    relational model, 75, 76
    sales_data_dv, 76
    schema evolution, 82
JSON Schema Validation
    common question, 97
    create FRUIT_INVENTORY Table, 91
    data integrity, 90
    inserted valid inventory entries, 92
    internal structure, 95, 96
    invalid data triggered schema validation errors, 92, 93
    querying inventory, 94
    real-time business use cases, 96, 97
    table creation statement, 91
    VALIDATE keyword, 90
    valid inventory data, 93

JSON search index
    for product specifications, 68
JSON_TEXTCONTAINS queries, 73
JSON_TRANSFORM function, 44
JSON_TRANSFORM enhancements
    backups and removing entries, 48
    conditional logic and aggregate functions, 55
    copy and delete product entries, 48
    create Products_JSON Table, 45
    in-memory processing, 57, 58
    internal mechanism, 58
    merge and filter product data, 49
    modify and add inventory elements, 46
    nested transformations and arithmetic calculations, 53
    operations, 44
    performance and scalability, 60
    practical questions, 59, 60
    real-time business use cases, 58, 59
    sort and enrich product attributes, 51
JSON_VALUE function, 36, 38–40, 42, 43, 60, 64, 85
JVM, *see* Java Virtual Machine (JVM)

L

Lifecycle management tools, 147
LISTAGG Aggregation, 264
LOBSEGMENT rename
    business impact and operational benefits, 280
    enterprise-scale workloads, 276
    features, 276, 282
    internal workflow, 280, 281
    LOB-related optimizations, 282
    partitioned LOB tables, 278–280
    real-time use cases, 281, 282

in regular table, 278
table creation and viewing the original segment, 277, 278
Lock-free reservations, 4, 8
batch processing, 13
common questions, 15
concurrent transactions, 12
effect, 13
insert sample inventory, 11
internal mechanism, 14
on numeric column, 11
in OLTP, 13
real-world applications and benefits, 14, 15
revert to traditional behavior, 12
transactional integrity, 13
validate business constraints, 12
Logical Partition Change Tracking (LPCT)
data changes and stale partitions, 295
defining, 292
features, 298
high-volume environments, 299
identifies and refreshes, 290
initial setup and table creation, 291, 292
internal flow, 296, 297
logical tracking, 299
materialized view creation, 293
optimizes analytics, 290
partition freshness tracking, 293
performing targeted partition refreshes, 295, 296
query rewrites, 295
in real-time analytics, 299
real-time business use cases, 297, 298
refresh operation, 298
scanning/refreshing, 298
Logical Partition Change Tracking (LPCT)
LPCT, *see* Logical Partition Change Tracking (LPCT)

M

MATCH Clause, 264
Materialized view refreshes concurrent refreshes, 283–290
Memoptimized Rowstore, 351
Mixed-version environments, 198
MLE, *see* Multilingual Engine (MLE)
Modern database systems, 199
Modern enterprise databases, 207
Multilingual Engine (MLE), 319, 324, 325, 327
Multi-Version Concurrency Control (MVCC), 16
MVCC, *see* Multi-Version Concurrency Control (MVCC)

N

Native JSON Data Type, 83
create tables and insert JSON data, 84
filter JSON records, 86
operational benefits, 87
optimize query performance with JSON indexing, 85, 86
querying JSON content, 85
schema-aware validation, 84
VARCHAR2 or CLOB, 83
Native JSON Storage
common questions, 89, 90
internal design, 87, 88
real-time business use cases, 88, 89
Neo4j—a native graph database, 267
Nested paths, 53

367

INDEX

O

Operational Flow, 195
Optimizing data management
    DML RETURNING, 316
    DML RETURNING clause, 311–313
    inserting orders with multirow values clause, 313, 314
    internal structure, DML and multirow insert, 314, 315
    multirow insert, 316
    real-time business use Cases, 315
    SQL enhancements, 310
Oracle 19c, 309
Oracle 23AI, 146, 151, 152, 155, 157, 159, 166, 185, 194–196, 210, 214, 245, 250
Oracle 23AI and ADB-S
    for professionals
        data scientists and AI engineers, 3
        DBAs, 3
        developers, 3
        enterprise IT and security teams, 3
        senior management and decision-makers, 3
    use cases
        customer analytics, 4
        healthcare, 4
        IoT and real-time streaming, 4
        security and compliance monitoring, 4
        transactional systems, 4
Oracle 23AI blockchain tables, 147
Oracle 23AI's optimizer, 188
Oracle 23AI's SQL Firewall, 238
Oracle 23AI's support, 163
Oracle 23c, 309
Oracle ADB-S, 139
Oracle Audit Vault, 268
Oracle Cloud Console
    access to SQL interface, 7, 8
    autonomous database option, 6
    choose 23AI and create database, 7
    configure, 6
    Create Autonomous Database option, 6, 7
    log in, 5, 6
Oracle Cloud Object Storage, 135
Oracle Database 23AI, 1, 191, 242
    advanced data processing, 260–268
    AI-powered enhancements, 2
    concurrency optimization strategies (*see* Priority transactions)
    Concurrent MV Refresh, 288
    Database Vault integration, 2
    data consistency, 15
    data integrity, 269–276
    developer-focused enhancements, 319
    in-memory performance, 352–360
    JSON enhancements (*see* JSON enhancements)
    LOBSEGMENT rename, 276–283
    LPCT, 290–299
    materialized view refreshes, 283–290
    official installation guide, 4
    optimizing data management, 310–317
    for Oracle Cloud Free Tier, 5
    partitioning, 301–310
    performance optimizations (*see* Lock-Free Reservations)
    vs. Pre-23AI, 31
    sign up option, 5
    SQL Firewall, 2
    troubleshooting with error messages, 328–331
Oracle Directory, 138

Oracle Free Tier, 4, 5
Oracle Machine Learning pipelines, 165
Oracle optimizer, 188
Oracle's approach, 191
Oracle True Cache, 17, 25, 26
Oracle workloads, 166

P

PAR, *see* Pre-authenticated request (PAR)
Partitioning strategy
    CLOB functions, 305
    conversion functions, 310
    datasets efficiently, 301
    data structure and access, 310
    datatypes and automation, 310
    inserting sales records, 303, 304
    JSON functions, 306
    list subpartitioning, 303
    LONG datatype, 301
    monitoring partitions and
        subpartitions, 304, 305
    operational workflow, 306, 307
    Pre-23AI *vs.* Oracle 23AI, 307–309
    querying total sales by year and
        region, 304
    range partitioning, 302, 303
    real-time business use cases, 308, 309
    sales table, 302
    subpartitioning, 302, 303
Pattern-matching queries, 263
PL/SQL, 322
    design, 198
    engine, 201
    function, 321, 324
    logic, 203
Policy-driven access control, 228
Policy-driven redaction, 249

Pre-authenticated request (PAR), 133
PREDICTION SQL function, 103
Priority transactions, 17
    automatic rollback, 20
    common questions, 23
    configure parameters, 18
    create inventory table, 18
    dynamically set transaction
        priorities, 24
    high-priority tasks, 17
    internal mechanism, transaction
        concurrency, 21, 22
    observe transaction behavior, 20, 21
    priority-based wait threshold, 23
    real-world applications and business
        benefits, 22
    simulate transaction conflicts, 19
    transaction priority levels, 17
Priority Transactions and Oracle True
    Cache, 25, 26
Privilege enforcement, 254
Production environments, 257
Productivity—making complex queries, 185
products_json, 45

Q

Query Elapsed Time Prediction
    collect SQL performance metrics, 108
    common questions, 112, 113
    internal structure, 111
    ML model development, 108
    predict execution time, 110
    proactive database management, 110
    realistic use cases, 111, 112
    training and validation sets, 109
    training dataset, predictive regression
        model, 109, 110

INDEX

QuickMart, 9, 10, 142, 144, 159–161, 163–166, 168, 169, 171, 175, 178–180, 186, 187, 192, 199–202, 208, 209, 211, 217, 226, 229, 232, 234, 252, 253
- Lock-Free Reservations (*see* Lock-Free Reservations)
- priority transactions, business impact, 21
- products table with numeric tracking fields, 10
- revert to traditional locking behavior, 12

QuickMart's analysts, 193
QuickMart's case study, 138
QuickMart's database, 227

R

Read-Only Access Control, 255
Read-Only User, 252
Read-Only User feature, 251
Read-Only User capability, 256
Read-Only User feature, 251, 253, 255, 257
Read-Write Behavior, 253
Real-Time Business, 197
Real-Time Business Use Cases, 241
Real-world case studies, 225
Real-world practices, 256
Retention Period, 145

S

Schema privileges
- administrators, 226, 227
- capability, 228
- consolidated role, 230
- in Oracle 23AI, 227
- real-time business, 229
- sales, 226
- security, 230
- security principles, 230
- structure, 228
- traditional role-based access, 229

Semantic Vector Search, 162
Set operators, 246
shrink_tablespace, 27–29
SIMD techniques, 354
Social network graph, 264, 265
SQL expression, 199
SQL Firewall, 224, 235, 238
- capabilities, 240
- enforcement, 239
- execution paths, 238
- injection techniques, 242
- Oracle 23AI, 239, 242
- organizations, 241

SQL Firewall Administration Privileges, 236
SQL Firewall Allow-List, 238
SQL Health Check Report, 133
SQL Property Graphs (SQL/PGQ), 258
- analytics with relational data, 260
- creation, 262, 263
- graph analytics, 268
- index-optimized graph structures, 266
- internal mechanism, 266
- Neo4j—a native graph database, 267
- operational flow, 266
- output, 264
- querying for mutual friends, 263, 264
- QuickMart, 260
- real-time use cases, 266, 267
- relational database, 267
- scalability, 267
- security, 268

INDEX

social network graph, 264, 265
user and relationship data, 260–262
SQL_RPT_DIR directory, 132
SQL Transpiler feature, 201
Staging tables
    advantages, 348
    business benefits, 347, 348
    business use cases, 349, 350
    compression and statistics behavior, 346, 347
    converting into regular tables, 346
    creating staging and final tables for shipment tracking, 344
    data ingestion, 343
    data preparation, 343
    and Fast ingest, 349–352
    high-speed ingestion, 345
    internal flow, 348
    lifecycle management and cleanup, 347
    transforming and migrating filtered data, 345, 346
System-wide consistency, 184

T

Table and Data Definition, 186
Tamper-evident data storage mechanism, 146
Text search index
    for customer reviews, 70, 71
Traffic management, 336
Transaction contention, 17
Troubleshooting
    complex SQL, 333
    creating and populating the customer orders table, 329
    debugging and maintenance, 334

error messages, 328
GROUP BY clause, 329, 330
    after Oracle 23AI, 330
    before Oracle 23AI, 330
internal flow, 332
precision—errors, 333
query/displaying, 328
real-world applications and benefits, 332, 333
resource exhaustion
    after Oracle 23AI, 331
    before Oracle 23AI, 330
    configuration values, 330
    process limit breach, 330
    promotional campaigns, 330
security, 333
SQL execution with identifier validation
    after Oracle 23AI, 331
    before Oracle 23AI, 331
    debugging and security, 331
    invalid SQL execution, 331

U

Unified Auditing, 215, 220, 221
Unified search index
    common questions, 73
    internal design, 71, 72
    real-time business use cases, 72

V

VECTOR data type, 152, 155
Vector-based search, 162
VECTOR data type
    AI/ML applications, 157
    algorithms, 155

INDEX

VECTOR data type (*cont.*)
   databases or custom, 156
   indexing, 158
   in Oracle 23AI, 155, 157
   traditional Oracle databases, 156
Vector-driven intelligence, 158
Vector-Encoded Product, 160
Vectorized Transaction Data, 164
VECTOR(n) datatype, 154
Vector operations, 152
Vector search process, 154

Virtual Private Database (VPD), 215, 268
VPD, *see* Virtual Private Database (VPD)

W

WHERE Clause, 264

X, Y, Z

XML Search Index
   for logistics data, 69

GPSR Compliance
The European Union's (EU) General Product Safety Regulation (GPSR) is a set of rules that requires consumer products to be safe and our obligations to ensure this.

If you have any concerns about our products, you can contact us on

ProductSafety@springernature.com

In case Publisher is established outside the EU, the EU authorized representative is:

Springer Nature Customer Service Center GmbH
Europaplatz 3
69115 Heidelberg, Germany

www.ingramcontent.com/pod-product-compliance
Lightning Source LLC
LaVergne TN
LVHW081346060526
838201LV00050B/1723